Is There a Home in Cyberspace?

Routledge Research in Information Technology and Society

Is There a Home in Cyberspace?
The Internet in Migrants' Everyday Life and the Emergence of Global Communities

Heike Mónika Greschke

Routledge
Taylor & Francis Group
NEW YORK   LONDON

First published 2012
by Routledge
711 Third Avenue, New York, NY 10017

Simultaneously published in the UK
by Routledge
2 Park Square, Milton Park, Abingdon, Oxfordshire OX14 4RN

First issued in paperback 2014

Routledge is an imprint of the Taylor and Francis Group, an informa company

Library of Congress Cataloging-in-Publication Data
Greschke, Heike Mónika.
 Is there a home in cyberspace? : the Internet in migrants' everyday life
and the emergence of global communities / by Heike Mónika Greschke.
   p. cm. — (Routledge research in information technology and society
; 14)
 Includes bibliographical references and index.
 1. Internet and immigrants. 2.   Immigrants—Cultural assimilation.
 3.   Internet—Social aspects. 4.   Transnationalism. I. Greschke,
Heike Mónika.   II. Title.
  JV6225.G744 2012
  302.23'1—dc23
  2011039483

ISBN: 978-0-415-89312-1 (hbk)
ISBN: 978-0-415-75459-0 (pbk)

Typeset in Sabon
by IBT Global.

For Angie

Contents

Figures

Tables

Preface

Women purportedly lack in role models who by simply being who they are encourage others to follow them on the rocky road of scientific careers. I am very lucky to have been guided through the scientific adventure documented in this book by several people who have been role models for me, yet in a more creative sense. First and foremost, I would like to thank Professors Jörg Bergmann, Bettina Heintz, Ruth Ayaß and Luis Guarnizo, who, by being who they are, have encouraged me to follow my own inquisitiveness. They have shared with me their knowledge, experience and passion for research, enabling me to bring to light an unknown phenomenon. My gratitude goes as well to the participants of the "EMCA study group" and the "World Concepts and Global Structural Patterns research training group" at Bielefeld University for creative data analysis sessions, criticism and surprising findings. I would like to give special thanks to Sarah Hitzler, Anja Jacobi, Antonia Krummheuer and Paul Mecheril for their constructive advice and also for questioning well-defined interpretations. I am indebted to the German Research Foundation. Without their financial support, neither the research nor its publication would have been possible. Finally, I owe a great personal debt of gratitude to the inhabitants of Cibervalle for receiving me wholeheartedly and making me one of them; and to my mother, for having unquestionable confidence in me.

April 2009, Heike Mónika Greschke

Preface to the English Edition

This study was originally written in German and published in 2009 with the German publisher Lucius & Lucius. For the English-language edition, some parts of the book have been revised in order to include the current state of the (methodological) debate as well as recently published Spanish literature on Paraguayan migration. I am indebted to Professor Wulf D. v. Lucius for relinquishing the English-language rights to the book. I would also like to acknowledge the financial support of the German Research Foundation for making the English edition possible. Finally, my deepest thanks go to Tink Diaz, Matthew DiFranco and Johanna Gesing. Without their great commitment and support, this English edition would not have been written.

Generic terms from the field, which are essential for the cultural household of Cibervalle, are here kept in the original, marked with a † and explained in the glossary of this book.

Part A

Migration—Media—Everyday Life

1 Introduction

> You don't realize how quickly Cibervalle turns into your everyday life. At least once a day you have to go there, check what's up, see if everyone's okay, nobody's having any worries, what hairstyle Eduardo is wearing for work today.[1]
>
> (Ana, France, Cibervalle Forum)

The idea for the present study arose from my observations during stays in Paraguay, Bolivia and Spain between 1999 and 2003. In both Paraguay and Bolivia, I found that the advantages and disadvantages of migration were a frequent subject of conversation in everyday life, as well as in the mass media. At the same time, the proliferation of commercial Internet cafés was obvious in these Latin American countries as well as in Spain: They seemed to have sprung up like mushrooms. While I was checking my mails in Internet cafés in Bolivia and Paraguay, I often noticed older people sitting next to me, sometimes accompanied by small children. They would frequently ask the Internet café staff for help with computer problems. I found this irritating at first, assuming that the Internet is a 'First World' technology primarily used by young people. Why were there so many Internet cafés in the poverty-stricken towns of Bolivia and Paraguay? And what were those people doing there?

While studying in Sevilla, eighteen months after my last stay in South America, I noticed that the local Internet cafés offered not only Internet access, but also cheap phone calls and currency transfers, especially to Latin America. In the seminars I attended at the *Departamento de Antropología Social* of the *Universidad de Sevilla*, there was talk of an increase of migration to Spain, particularly from Latin America, and subsequently of an intensification of social relations between the migrants' countries of origin and the receiving countries due to so-called 'transnational practices' of migration. I had the impression that my observations in Paraguay and Bolivia were associated with those in Spain, and examination of the usage of new media in migration contexts could be interesting. I began to research and found that there were innumerable online resources in Spanish, including websites, electronic bulletin boards and news groups, that were clearly directed at, or used by, Spanish-speaking migrants. But there was hardly any literature about this phenomenon from a social science perspective.

While searching the World Wide Web (WWW) for empirical data for the conception of my research, I chanced upon a Paraguayan website with a publicly available electronic bulletin board: www.cibervalle.com[2] offers a virtual meeting place to Paraguayans all over the world. Like me, many of the primarily Paraguayan users came upon the Internet discussion forum by chance while searching online for information about Paraguay.

> I got here accidentally. I first visited this site in order to use the search machine for the most important news on Paraguay. I then read some Tópicos. That's how I got familiar with the personalities of the users. I found out who is whose rival, who knows whom, the troubled ones, the squabblers, those complaining about their lives all the time, etc. Rafael and Anna made me dizzy, they had dozens of daughters and nieces. I couldn't understand their relationship with Blossom, who lives in Ciudad del Este, whereas they live in Europe. (Sandra, Paraguay, Cibervalle Forum)

Like Sandra, I was confused at first, but also fascinated with the goings-on in the Cibervalle Forum. Many of the first contributions that I read dealt with migration-related issues. I learned a lot about the how and where of migration, about motives and anxieties, about the different problems in the lives of migrants and about the way in which the Forum[3] users support each other. The familiarity of their communications struck me. Many of the users seemed to know each other, although they lived thousands of kilometers apart. There seemed to be no common focus; the Cibervallers discussed every topic under the sun, they quarreled and made up again and new participants kept coming in, always welcomed by the rest of the community. There were even photos of a 'peace treaty' between two participants: The commentary said that these two people had just met in person for the first time ever. It was hard to make sense of all this.

In the course of the two years during which I kept up with, and for some time participated in, the Cibervalle activities, the Forum, its users and the Cibervallers' way of life gradually became more intelligible and familiar to me. Similarly, reading and writing in the Forum slowly becomes a routine for many participants, and the daily communication with other users soon constitutes a natural part of their social relations. As Ana remarks in the quotation at the start of this chapter, Cibervalle becomes quite unobtrusively a part of everyday life. By appropriating the communication media made available through the Internet in their own creative ways, the users have transformed Cibervalle into a long-term relationship. Cibervalle allows its users to live together regardless of geographical distance and to communally shape a part of their everyday lives. But what does 'everyday life' and 'living together' mean in this case? How can an electronic bulletin board turn into a part of somebody's everyday life? And where does Ana go when she wants to see if everyone's okay? How can she see Eduardo's newest hairstyle, when they do not even live on the same continent?

Assuming that most of the readers are not familiar with a computer-mediated mode of togetherness as described in this book, I will commence with a piece of ethnographic *docu-fiction* designed to provide insights into social life in Cibervalle. The following narrative is documentary in the sense that it focuses on an event that actually happened. Also, this narrative concentrates on naturally occurring data, which was produced independently of my intervention. In this case it was a "Tópico," or a discussion thread,[4] in the Forum created by several participants from different geographical locations who jointly observed a tragic incident, which had occurred in Paraguay's capital, Asunción, in August 2004. A fire in the supermarket *Ycua Bolaños* killed nearly four hundred people. For a brief time Paraguay was the center of the world's media attention. The narrative "Tragedy in the supermarket *Ycua Bolaños*" attempts to enrich the description of the communication in the Forum with ethnographically generated data. This is done in order to illuminate the everyday life context of the individual protagonists as well as to clarify the basic features of the social formation examined in this book, including its pluri-locality and multidimensionality, the public framing of private communication and, last but not least, the specific practices of media usage. The narrative is fictional in the sense that, firstly, it defines ideal types of practices and protagonists on the basis of empirical data and, secondly, it describes a situation simultaneously from different local perspectives. The nature of this account is in a sense as peculiar as the social formation it seeks to illuminate, and as innovative as the methodological concept that it reflects. The story is told as a prelude to this book and as an invitation to the reader to enter my research field. *¡Buen Viaje!* (Have a nice journey!)

2 The Tragedy of *Ycua Bolaños*
Ethnographic Prelude

Ariel is sitting in the living room of the small house he occupies with his mother, his two sisters and one brother. His other brother, the youngest, currently lives with their aunt in Paraguay, where he has started primary school. Ariel's mother and elder sister are working together in the little sewing studio next door. They are doing commissioned work for the local textile market. By the following morning they must deliver a commission of evening dresses to one of their regular clients, an expensive boutique on Avenida Santa Fe. Ariel's mother has been sewing nonstop for almost two days. Her daughters take turns in helping her. Meanwhile, Ariel is flipping through the available Argentinean TV channels, muted so as not to disturb his sister, when he is suddenly transfixed by pictures of a burning building that somehow seems familiar to him. He turns on the sound and, from the distraught voice of the reporter, learns that the burning building is a supermarket of the *Ycua Bolaños* chain in the capital of his home country Paraguay. Absolutely horrified, Ariel discovers that crowds of people appear to be locked into the building. Between thick black clouds of smoke, which pour from all crevices of the building, he can see soot-covered arms and hands reaching through the fencing of the supermarket's main gate. From the outside, vendors (who usually offer their goods in front of the supermarket) are using sticks and stones trying to break the glass bricks on the ground floor so that the desperate people inside can leave the deadly trap. They are screaming at the top of their lungs: "Open the doors, open the doors!" Ariel wakes up his sister, grabs the telephone and dials the number of his cousin, who lives very close to the supermarket. While he waits for his cousin to answer the phone, he informs his sister about what he has just seen. As she looks at him anxiously, he says, "There's no reply." Both of them know that after church on Sundays their cousin usually takes her family for lunch in the restaurant of this supermarket. Ariel and his sister sit in shocked silence. Then he turns to his computer, logs into the instant messaging client[5] and retrieves one by one the webpages of the Cibervalle Forum as well as the online version of *ABC Color*, a Paraguayan daily newspaper. Although he has no problem entering the Forum, an error message appears instead of the webpage of *ABC Color*. He tries again to no avail, but immediately finds a Tópico with the title "Tragedy in the supermarket *Ycua Bolaños*" in the "Recent News" category of the Forum.

BOSTON (US), 1 AUGUST, 2004, LOCAL TIME: 2 P.M.

Maríana and her two flatmates are in their kitchen preparing a snack. They want to spend the afternoon in the nearby park. Maríana came two years earlier to Boston, where she has taken over her sister's job as a housekeeper. The sister had to give up the job when she became pregnant. She bought a flight ticket for Maríana and sent money for her passport and tourist visa. Now Maríana is running the household of strangers and looking after their children while leaving her own family behind in Paraguay. As she does not have a residence permit, she would risk being denied reentry if she were to leave the country. As a result, she has not seen her husband and her two children in two years. It makes Maríana sad to think of her children. Her eleven-year-old son plays football for *Club Olimpia* now. He is very talented and she can now afford to pay for his tuition with regular money transfers. At this moment, he is probably on his way home from a football match. She is waiting for him to check into the Internet café on the way, to tell her the results of the match. Maríana's brother-in-law got her a cheap secondhand computer, and as she shares the flat with two Columbian women, she can afford an Internet connection. Now she can be online whenever she wants.

And there it is!—the familiar sound made by her computer whenever one of her contacts in the Forum addresses her via instant messaging client. Maríana quickly walks over to her bedroom, expecting to say hello to her son. A small conversation window has opened on the computer screen, but it is not her son. It is her friend Anastasia from the Forum who greets her with a link to a Tópico from the Forum. Maríana types a short reply, asks how Anastasia is, and casually follows the link:

"Tragedy in the supermarket *Ycua Bolaños*."

At about 1 p.m. an unusually big fire broke out in the supermarket *Ycua Bolaños* in the Trinidad quarter of the capital. What's happening there is really unfortunate. Once more it's apparent that this country is not prepared for a tragedy of this scale.

Nick: gato_verde
E-Mail: g-ra-d—-@*mail.com
IP: 200.85.34.*
Answers: 7
Last answer: 01/08/2004

13:35 Tragedy in the supermarket: The president of the Republic, Nicanor Duarte, appeared at the location and announced that the emergency rescue plane is being prepared to fly serious casualties abroad.

11:47 The number of casualties is still not known, but at least 50 injured people are currently being evacuated to a number of different hospitals. The flames are not yet under control.

11:38 The supermarket *Ycua Bolaños* (situated between Artigas and Santísima Trinidad) is up in flames. The fire was caused by an explosion in the carpark. The firemen are fighting to extinguish the fire.

Source: http//*www.abc.com.py*

gato_verde
IP: 88.120.103.*
01/08/2004

You'd think it's more than a hundred dead . . . it's crazy what the people in Asunción have to go through . . . God help the victims' families . . .

Anastasia
IP: 88.120.103.*
01/08/2004

How terrible! What terrible news . . .

Iwashita
IP: 200.76.45.*
01/08/2004

wow. .What a tragedy. .

Mister_Darkness
IP: 76.132.54.*
01/08/2004

It's a shame . . . when the fire broke out, the doors of the supermarket were locked, so that people couldn't get out . . . then the customers smashed the glass windows . . . There were no proper emergency exits and it seems that there was no fire precaution system in the building

Anastasia
IP: 88.120.103.*
01/08/2004

THEY SAY THAT THE OWNER CLOSED THE DOORS OF THE SUPER-MARKET TO PREVENT LOOTING!! UNBELIEVABLE!! THIS BASTARD-OWNER-SON-OF-A-BITCH!!!

CARLOS_FLORIDA
IP: 68.234.126.*
01/08/2004

They closed the main door of the burning supermarket, to prevent theft, there are some 1000 people trying to get out.

gato_verde
IP: 200.85.35.*
01/08/2004

While Maríana is reading this terrible news, she is trying in vain to open the website of the daily newspaper *ABC Color*. At the same time, Anastasia, who lives in the Paraguayan border town Ciudad del Este, is using the instant messaging client to tell Maríana that the Paraguayan TV stations have stopped their regular programs to report about the ongoing disaster. Anastasia is describing the awful pictures to her friend in Boston as she is watching them on the Televisión. Just now the better-equipped firemen of the airport are arriving. Maríana thinks about her husband, who is a member of the voluntary fire brigade. She picks up her telephone and dials his mobile number. No connection. She tries again and again, but to no avail. Then she types the following question into the private conversation window that connects her to Anastasia: "Do you know if all firefighters have arrived yet? I can't reach my husband." Maríana copies part of the message and inserts it into the electronic form at the end of the Tópico, which invites commentaries and discussion about the fire: "Does anyone know whether a state of emergency has been declared? Are all firefighting units in action?"

Anastasia has quickly inquired among her local sources and now tells her friend in Boston that all fire units are in action. Maríana proceeds to send Anastasia her husband's telephone number, in the hope that she will be able to reach him. When Maríana looks up from the screen, she sees her flatmate Nelly standing by the door. She hadn't noticed her coming in and didn't hear Nelly calling out for her. The two flatmates want to go out with Maríana and marvel at her spending so much time with her computer again. But when Nelly sees that Maríana's face has turned very pale, she comes over and looks at the screen. Maríana briefly informs Nelly what has happened while continuing her online conversation with Anastasia in Paraguay. Her Paraguayan friend is just telling her that she can hear the ringing tone of Maríana's husband's mobile phone, but that he doesn't answer. Now the other flatmate approaches and the two women join Maríana at the computer. Together with Anastasia they discuss the options for how to contact Maríana's husband. Anastasia suggests that she call Eduardo in Asunción. At this time of day during the week, he can normally be approached online via the instant messaging client. Today being a Sunday, she calls him at home. He has already heard of the tragedy and is now glued to the TV with his family. Anastasia tells him about Maríana's problem and he offers to drive to the scene of the disaster to find Maríana's husband. While they impatiently wait for Eduardo's call, Maríana and Anastasia transfer their conversation to the discussion within the Cibervalle Forum. Meanwhile, more and more participants have joined the Tópico and new ones keep coming in.

> On CNN they say that there are more than 130 dead. Is that possible?? . . . :(
> **Mister_Darkness**
> **IP:** 69.143.67.*
> 01/08/2004

My God, they won't be able to handle that!
   Maríana
   IP: 69.143.67.*
   01/08/2004

Thank you, gato_verde and Anastasia, that you keep us informed with us being so far away. It's impossible at the moment to access the webpages, all networks are busy, maybe the webpages cannot be retrieved because everyone's trying to get in at the same time. What's happening there, is a real disaster. I pray for the victims and their families, they'll be inconsolable.
   Villariqueña
   IP: 215.653.206.*
   01/08/2004

Yes, Mister Darkness, that's the number that's being cited at the moment . . . and it's assumed that it is going to be even more . . . Maríana . . . the state of emergency has been declared . . . all firemen are there and all hospitals like the IPS, the specialist hospital for the treatment of injuries from burning, and the military hospital are on alert.
   Anastasia
   IP: 88.120.103.*
   01/08/2004

The owner . . . what a shame, how stupid. One more reason to be prepared from now on and have a national fire emergency plan for all businesses, schools, kindergardens.
   Maríana
   IP: 69.143.67.*
   01/08/2004

That's not stupidity, that's downright egotism! He only thought of himself or, to be more precise, of what he had to loose. He didn't consider anyone else.
   Villariqueña
   IP: 215.653.206.*
   01/08/2004

That's part of the stupidity, Villariqueña, but what I'm more interested in at the moment is what's happening with the fire. Anastasia, could you please describe it to me?
   Maríana
   IP: 69.143.67.*
   01/08/2004

Please give us more details of the fire; we don't hear anything about it here in Spain, there's no news about it and the webs are all defunct right now.
   Jota
   IP: 193.110.134.*
   01/08/2004

Maríana, I think the fire spreads in some spots, but in others the firemen got it under control. There's still black smoke clouds coming out of the building . . . and many persons have suffocated.
Anastasia
IP: 88.120.103.*
01/08/2004

Thanks for the info! . . . But what a shock that was! I've phoned Asunción to ask about my relations, God bless, all are well . . .
. . . I'm trying to get into the Internet-radiostations, but can't
. . . how sad it all is! . . . from Switzerland we send our prayers to the families of the victims :(
Raquél
IP: 62.143.56.*
01/08/2004

It's a tragedy that hurts us all, my God, and if all that wasn't enough, Nicanor pops up to pose in front of the cameras!!! That is the most disgusting!!!!
Diana
IP: 67.119.102.*
01/08/2004

Maríana, that's exactly it.
Via the mass media, medics and psychologists were asked to provide assistance. In addition, the population was called on to volunteer.
In the IPS, there were only three doctors available.
At the moment there's talk about a close check on all shopping centers and supermarkets, so that such a tragedy can't happen again and so that innocent people won't have to find themselves in such a situation.
The first pictures that were distributed via TV, show burnt bodies. Children, youths, adults, even a baby of about six months.
According to the media, a total of 97 corpses are currently laid out in state.
gato_verde
IP: 200.85.34.*
01/08/2004

Right now on Televisión Espanhola they are reporting on the situation there
. . . my God, how sad to see such pictures from my beloved country . . . :(
Raquél
IP: 62.143.56.*
01/08/2004

Ariel turns away from the screen of the computer, where he has kept up with the discussion about the continuing fire. Again he picks up the telephone and tries his cousin's number. His sister uses the opportunity to seize the keyboard. Ariel rarely takes an active part in the discussions; usually he just reads other people's contributions. But Larissa thinks that it is their duty in such a situation to demonstrate solidarity and offer condolences. What would others think of them if they didn't do this? She proceeds to quickly type a short text and sends it off without proofreading, before her brother can chase her away from the keyboard.

> There are two TV stations reporting live here in Buenos Aires, so we can get informed, but to be honest, it's horrible to be so far away and to think there could be family members affected, but I'm full of pride when I see that there are so many hospitals, private clinics and so many people helping, I hope the source of the fire will be discovered and God, please console the victims . . . from the distance we're with them in their pain.
> Larissa
> IP: 168.229.12.*
> 01/08/2004

Then she hears Ariel saying, "Thank God, I've finally reached you!" She turns round and sees the relieved expression on her brother's face: Their cousin is alive; everybody is okay! The church service had taken a little longer today, he reports after putting down the receiver. On the way to the supermarket *Ycua Bolaños*, where the family had intended to eat their lunch, they heard the terrible news on the radio. As they were already nearby and the traffic was diverted, they had only just arrived home when the telephone rang. Ariel sits down next to his sister in front of the screen and sees that Iwashita has contacted him on the instant messaging client. He takes over the keyboard again and begins a chat with his friend, who lives in a different part of Buenos Aires. Both of them have lived here for about five years, but they met only a year ago during one of the regular meetings held by the Cibervallers Group in Buenos Aires. Whereas twenty-year-old Ariel has finished school in Buenos Aires and plans to study medicine soon, Iwashita, who is five years older, had lived with her mother in Paraguay until she finished school. She then went on to study and live with her father and sisters in Buenos Aires, where degree courses in the state-run university are free of charge and of better quality than those offered in Paraguay. Nevertheless, studying is far from easy for both Ariel and Iwashita, because their families need every penny and expect them to contribute to the family income. Iwashita's mother commutes between Buenos Aires and the village in Paraguay where both she and her children were raised for parts of their childhoods. In this way, she can spend time looking after the three daughters in Buenos Aires as well as the remaining son in Paraguay. Ariel now learns from Iwashita that, luckily, none of her relatives were affected by the disastrous fire. Ariel and Iwashita then notice simultaneously that their friend Carlos has just logged into the instant messaging client. Iwashita invites Carlos to join her chat with Ariel. Carlos has only just heard on the phone about the fire in Paraguay. He immediately went to the Internet café near his sleeping place to get more information. Carlos and Ariel both originate from Misiones, a region in Paraguay near the Argentinean border. They too got to know each other via Cibervalle. Carlos is eighteen years old, one of the youngest of the group. He came to Buenos Aires on his own and has since been working as a laborer on building sites, where he usually finds a place to sleep. Ariel had invited Carlos to a Cibervallers meeting after he had introduced himself to the community. Carlos now spends most weekends at Ariel's. They are like brothers and Carlos gets on well with the rest of Ariel's family. After a short exchange, Ariel now invites both of them to come over to his place. His aunt, who arrived a few days ago to fetch the little brother, has brought fresh *yuyos†* from Paraguay. Ariel tells Iwashita and Carlos that he will make a delicious *tereré†* from the *yuyos†*. They promise to come over right away and Ariel sees both of them log out of the instant messaging client.

ASUNCIÓN (PARAGUAY), 1 AUGUST 2004, LOCAL TIME: ABOUT 2.30 P.M.

Eduardo can see from far away how the dark smoke billows through the streets surrounding the supermarket. He has spent nearly an hour trying to get to the vicinity of the fire by car. He finally gives up, leaving the car by the roadside and continuing on foot. The smoke makes him cough and his eyes are burning long before he can actually see the supermarket. Although he has already seen some pictures on TV, the actual sight is a shock: pitch-black clouds, masses of people running around in fright, volunteers with T-shirts over their noses as makeshift breathing masks frantically diving into the smoke in search of survivors, a seemingly never-ending number of charred victims being carried out of the building and the whole eerie scene enveloped in a choir of screams and wails. As Eduardo tries to make his way towards the on-site rescue command, being careful to avoid the center of the mayhem, he suddenly spots a former colleague who seems to belong to the firefighting team. Eduardo quickly grabs his arm and asks for Maríana's husband. The man is completely exhausted, but points the way towards the command center. With tears in his eyes he says, "I've never seen anything as terrible as this in my whole life." The commander does not know where Maríana's husband is. He says, "Everything is totally chaotic, we haven't got any breathing masks for our men and just look at those hosepipes." Eduardo watches the firefighters standing on the porous hoses so that as little water as possible can seep out. Suddenly a young woman approaches: "Are you the commander? Have you got a megaphone?" When the man in the uniform nods, she says, "We need blood and plasma, urgently! Can you please ask the bystanders here to go to the nearest clinic and make their contribution toward saving those who come out of the inferno alive?" The controller promises to do what he can immediately. Eduardo sets out to the nearest hospital. After making his small donation, he goes back to see the commander, who says, "The disappeared person is back! He's sitting over there, having a rest." Eduardo thanks him and runs to Maríana's husband, telling him that his wife is very worried because she can't reach him on his mobile. Completely exhausted, Maríana's husband staggers over to the commander vehicle to retrieve his mobile telephone. Eduardo is already on his way to the next cybercafé. He logs into the instant messaging client and sends the good news to Maríana and Anastasia. He then enters the Forum and adds his commentary on the fire disaster:

> I've just been to the local hospital, please, whoever is able to go there now, should do so, blood- and plasma-donations are needed urgently.
>   **Eduardo**
>   **IP:** 200.85.34.*
>   01/08/2004

> How nice to read you! How was it? And how are you?
>   **Maríana**
>   **IP:** 69.143.67.*
>   01/08/2004

> I'm well, but it wears you out completely to see what's going on there. I swear, you can't count the desperate people coming there asking about their relatives . . . it's a totally eerie scene.
>   **Eduardo**
>   **IP:** 200.85.34.*
>   01/08/2004

> I can imagine, my husband's just been telling me that he's completely knack-ered, I've just talked to him, he's okay so far, but it has really thrown him mentally.
>   **Maríana**
>   **IP:** 69.143.67.*
>   01/08/2004

"I'm going home now to my family, they're probably worried already. See you tomorrow." Eduardo writes this text into the little window in which he conducts the private conversation with Anastasia and Maríana. Then he logs out from the instant messaging client, closes the Forum's webpage and walks over to the cash till of the Internet café. The young woman at the till looks distraught. Eduardo says, "It's been a horrible day, hasn't it?" She looks at him and says, "My uncle is in hospital with really bad burns. He works in the supermarket bakery. I want to go see him, but people keep coming here to phone their relatives abroad to tell them they're still alive. So I can't go." Eduardo gives her a warm smile before he pays and walks home. The air is still ripe with soot. He thinks of his work tomorrow and of his family. He shares a small house in a quiet part of Asunción with his wife, their five-year-old daughter and his younger brother. Eduardo's mother died of cancer three years ago, his father has retired to the countryside about fifty kilometers from Asunción. Eduardo is an IT specialist working for city hall. It is a secure job and for Paraguayan standards relatively well paid. Free Internet access is an added bonus. At work he is online almost nonstop, which means he logs into the instant messaging client as soon as he gets to work. Quite often he comes in early in order to check what's been going on in the Forum since he checked out from work the day before. He keeps the page open throughout his workday, so that he can throw at least an occasional quick glance at the current discussion topics. However, he doesn't usually have time to actively participate until his lunch break. When there are quarrels, it is often Eduardo who mediates between the involved parties. He does not like childish fights tarnishing the image of Cibervalle. For Eduardo, Cibervalle offers the chance to exchange opinions and experiences, to learn from each other and to show solidarity when somebody is in need. He knows that Cibervalle is an important place, especially for his compatriots abroad, for soothing their homesickness and cultivating social relations amongst one another. Eduardo tries hard to make this place as interesting and pleasant as possible. Via Cibervalle he has met many interesting people and found friends all over the world, and his relationships are not one-sided. He knows he could count on them if he were in need himself. There have been many instances of solidarity among Cibervallers. The annual fundraising campaign that he organizes with some other Forum participants every Christmas is one example. This year they will collect food, medicine, toys and school supplies for a children's home in Asunción. The home is run by a lone woman who does not receive any financial support from the government. She simply provides her house and takes in children who do not want to live on the streets anymore and have nowhere else to go. Eduardo hopes to have enough time tomorrow to participate via the Forum in the coordination of help for the victims of *Ycua Bolaños*. He locks his car, considering this initiative; as he looks up he sees his little daughter, Marisól, open the front door of their house and come running towards him.

Maríana takes leave of her flatmates, who want to go to the park after all. She has decided to stay home at the computer to carry on talking to her Cibervalle friends about the awful fire in their hometown. She's not sure whether acquaintances or relatives of hers are affected directly, and now the first list of names of the dead and injured are being announced. She clicks the refresh button of her browser constantly to update the webpage. As yet, none of the names that appear on the screen is familiar to Maríana. Now she reads that the owner of the supermarket, who is accused of having ordered to close the doors, has fled the scene. Maríana feels her anger rising. She literally hammers her next commentary into the keyboard:

THERE IS A REASON BEHIND THE FACT THAT THEY CAN'T FIND THIS BA . . . ARD
Maríana
IP: 69.143.67.*
01/08/2004

Sorry, but being so far away makes you feel so powerless.
Maríana
IP: 69.143.67.*
01/08/2004

Slowly the day fades away. The fire is under control; the owner of the super-market has finally been tracked down. The number of the dead and injured rises continually, many not identified as yet. Again and again, people pop up in the Forum who cannot contact their relatives on the phone, hoping to try to locate them with the help of other participants or find out whether their relatives are among the victims. There are some first deliveries of medicine as well as offers of rescue flights from the neighboring countries, to take the badly injured to hospitals in Argentina and Brazil. Financial aid is also being offered by governments and firms of neighboring countries. Together with an instant messaging friend, Maríana is debating the possibility of fundraising, especially among Paraguayans resident in the US. Anastasia would open an account, while Maríana would mobilize the people in her vicinity. Maríana places their idea on the bulletin board for discussion and starts composing an e-mail, which she intends to send to all her contacts in the US. The phone rings. It is Maríana's sister, coming home from a family outing, wanting to invite Maríana for dinner. Maríana accepts. The unsuspecting sister asks Maríana about her day and Maríana answers: "I had a terrible day, but will tell you all about it later, okay?" She has a quick look at the current discussion in Cibervalle, where there is speculation about the cause of the fire; one person even supposes a terrorist attack. Another participant, apparently one of the active helpers, is compiling a list of medical items desperately needed by the hospitals. Maríana closes the page, sends off the e-mail she has just written, says farewell to Anastasia, changes her status from "online" to "I'm at Aunt Ana's" and types "home about 10 p.m., call you later, wish you a good night, kiss"—a text that will appear as an answer should her husband or children contact her again today.

3 The Making of Globality in Migrants' Mediatized Everyday Lives

How is global togetherness possible? How does the availability of the Internet alter migrants' everyday lives and senses of belonging? This book attempts to illuminate how Internet technologies influence everyday life patterns in transnational milieus. Based on an empirical case study, the present study exemplifies that complex combinations of global media use and face-to-face encounters emerge in response to the specific needs of transnational populations and bring about new global forms of togetherness. In the foreground lies the question of which intrinsic logic is developed through globalization processes on a microstructural level, and conversely, how globality is achieved by the structural idiosyncrasies of computer-mediated communication.

Some of the most instructive studies in the history of qualitative social research, which still influence present methodologies, have a focus on media usage in migration contexts. These studies already indicate that migration implies media socialization and that media have been appropriated in migration cultures for substituting physical presence. Robert E. Park, who in the beginning of the twentieth century examined ethnic press publications in large US cities, observed:

> Our great cities, as we discover upon close examination, are mosaics of little language colonies, cultural enclaves, each maintaining its separate communal existence within a wider circle of the city's cosmopolitan life. Each one of these little communities is certain to have some sort of cooperative or mutual aid society, very likely a church, a school, possibly a theater, *but almost invariably a press.* (Park [1922] 1970, 6; italics mine)

Park counted altogether 463 newspapers in twenty-eight languages. Paradoxical to the large number of foreign-language papers is the observation that most of their recipients could not read at all before they migrated, let alone read newspapers. Park concluded that the ethnic print media grew to be so important because they facilitated the social organization of migrants and their adaptation to the new living situation.

One reason why immigrant peoples read more in America than they do at home is because there is more novelty and more news. News is a kind of urgent information that men use in making adjustments to a new environment, in changing old habits, and in forming new opinions. (Ibid., 9)

Furthermore, Park found that living in migration enforces patriotism as well as the need to foster one's mother tongue, traditions and the relations to one's context of origin. "Loneliness and an unfamiliar environment turn the wanderer's thoughts and affections back upon his native land. The strangeness of the new surroundings emphasizes his kinship with those he has left" (ibid., 49). According to Park, it is no coincidence that nationalistic movements frequently come into being abroad or are supported by persons in exile, by refugees or migrants. In this perspective, the immigrant press of the 1920s served both as a mouthpiece of the nationalistic movements and as a medium of participation in the political processes in the home country. The results of Park's analysis are astonishingly similar to those of current migration research. Thus, Glick-Schiller and Fouron (2001) have coined the term "long distance nationalism," denoting political activities across national borders with which contemporary transmigrants practice their belonging to the national community of their country of origin and at the same time reconstruct the ethnic and national group in the country of destination.

The study *The Polish Peasant in Europe and America* by Thomas and Znaniecki ([1918–20] 1958), published only a few years before Park's *The Immigrant Press and Its Control* cited earlier, focused primarily on the practices of long-distance communication, through which migrants kept up their relationships with their families despite geographical distance. This comprehensive study is based mainly on the correspondence between Polish migrants in Chicago and their relatives in Poland. The communication between the young emigrant generation and their parents' generation was taken by the authors as a suitable source of the (today one would say 'translocal' or 'transnational') mundane lifeworlds of Polish migrant families. Similar to Park, Thomas and Znaniecki ascertained that as migrants, the Polish peasants were—in comparison to earlier—incessantly reading and writing letters, even though reading and writing was difficult for most of them. Furthermore, the authors identified structural patterns in these letters, which shed some light on their social function. According to these authors, the letters serve to maintain solidarity among family members despite the separation: "Every letter, in other words, whatever else it may be, is a bowing letter, a manifestation of solidarity" ([1918–20] 1958, 304). The authors' typification of the different kinds of letters is interesting, primarily because it provides some indications of the practices of substituting and synthesizing (physical) presence. For example, the ceremonial letter is taken to be a substitute for the physical presence of the absent relative, who would normally be present during family festivities. The literary letter, on the other hand, substitutes not merely the mutual music-making or recitation of poems at festivities or informal meetings: These letters differ from the rest, because they are read aloud at suitable occasions, which in a sense synthesizes the presence of the geographically distant part of the family.

The history of migration, in other words, has been strongly shaped by the history of media (including technological development and cultural appropriation). However, migration researchers have rarely used these established paths to follow the footsteps either of their predecessors or of their research subjects. Rather than being attentive to their subjects' media skills, they have been primarily concerned with 'ethnic' media. In other words, the main focus is still on the technology's potential for promoting political activism and long-distance nationalism while negotiating ethnic identity and—from the receiving country's perspective—its potentials and constraints for cultural and social integration. At present, the Internet seems to have taken over the role that the ethnic print media used to play in the social organization of migrant groups at any one location. Similar to the immigrant press in the 1920s, today so-called migrant portals (Androutso-poulos 2005) combine information about the country of origin with information about the social situation of the ethnic group in their respective country of residence. Moreover, they present the opportunity of networking and exchange between the users. Because of its potential globality and the plentitude of information that it has to offer, the Internet represents what is often the only opportunity for many migrants to regularly receive current information about their region of origin. According to Appadurai (1998), it is not merely satellite and cable Televisión, but primarily the Internet, in combination with the increase in human mobility such as migration, escape and tourism, that promote the process of "deterritorialization"—or more precisely globalization of (imagined) community-building. Whereas Glick-Schiller's and Fouron's "long distance nationalism" (2001) relates to those practices that are situated in two concrete national contexts—the one in which one is actually living and the other context to which one belongs—Appadurai's concept of "ethnoscapes," i.e., the landscapes of collective identities, emphasizes primarily the problem of localizing and clearly demarcating cultural production:

> As groups migrate, regroup in new locations, reconstruct their histo-ries, and reconfigure their ethnic projects, the ethno in ethnography takes on a slippery, non-localized quality, to which the descriptive practices of anthropology will have to respond. The landscape of group identity—the ethnoscapes—around the world are no longer familiar anthropological objects, insofar as groups are no longer tightly territo-rialized, spatially bounded, historically unselfconscious, or culturally homogeneous. (1998, 48)

Of interest in Appadurai's concept "ethnoscapes" are, on the one hand, the growing importance of imagination, and, on the other hand, the striving for globality, both of which the author assumes to be central elements of present day collective identity constructions. Similar to Anderson (1985), who interprets the national community as a collective imagination effort supported by the print media, Appadurai sees the global electronic media playing a key role in the construction of collective identities and images of the world. According to Appadurai, in these times of satellite TV, Internet and globally operating media conglomerates, many people do not live in imagined communities anymore but in imaginary worlds. In this process, a multitude of world images arise, which are created concurrently with media production and consumption alongside the participants' own multi-faceted mobility practices. Appadurai himself refers to "the multiple worlds that are constituted by the historically situated imaginations of persons and groups spread around the globe" (1998, 33). However, *natio-ethno-cultural belonging*[6] seems to be a category that is rather more growing in importance than getting lost in global noise.

Karim (2003b) examines Appadurai's scenario by means of different case studies and confirms that the media practices of "diasporas" lead to a partitioning of worldviews into a multitude of cultural maps existing in parallel. Under the heading "virtual diaspora," a number of case studies have currently studied the ethnicization of cyberspace. In these studies, the Internet is conceived as an instrument that reunites into an imagined community the members of a nation/ethnic group that have been dispersed by migration. To cite just three examples, Schmidt and Teubener (2007) scrutinize the specifically Russian practices of Internet usage, whereas Adams Parham (2004) and Uimonen (2003) examine the effectiveness of political online activism by taking a look at its actual political influence in respectively Haiti and Malaysia.

In regions that are affected by mass emigration the Internet seems to be especially suited to reintegrate social relations that have been severed by geographical distance. E-mail and online chat communication enable parents to participate in their children's everyday lives, to be called on for advice in important decisions and thereby to practice their parental role despite geographic distance. Where telephone contact is temporarily limited due to costs, the regular chat conversation is more suited to bring about a feeling of togetherness (Miller and Slater 2000). In other words, the Internet supports the maintenance of primary relationships, which had formerly been practiced in one location based on copresence and are now being continued translocally with the aid of communication technology.

4 www.cibervalle.com
A Global Lifeworld 'à lo Paraguayo'

The publicly accessible discussion forum Cibervalle presents a virtual meeting point for Paraguayans in nearly all parts of the world. Due to its instable economic situation, Paraguay has been affected by a continuing flow of migration, especially towards Argentina, the US, Spain and Japan. The Forum offers users living abroad the opportunity to stay connected to their imagined home country or to reapproach it. Via the discussions in the Forum, one can receive current information about one's region of origin and converse with fellow compatriots in one's own language about topics that spring from a shared set of experiences. For many users, migration means a (temporary) loss of social relationships, familiar places and habits and, last but not least, a conversion into precarious living conditions. As migration is in many cases undocumented, one has limited access to citizens' rights and is susceptible to exploitation and violence. In this situation, characterized by transition, isolation and risks, the Forum—frequently called "the window to Paraguay"—offers its users cultural continuity, social community and mutual solidarity. For the users resident in Paraguay, the Forum does indeed have the function of a window to the world, presenting them with views of different ways of living and with the opportunity to extend their knowledge and their horizons, as well as the opportunity to prepare themselves for possible migrational ventures.

In addition to providing a look through the virtual window to or from Paraguay, the electronic network also offers users the opportunity to locate fellow compatriots who live nearby and to get to know them in person. However, the physically grounded contacts enabled by the Forum do not at all substitute the virtual relationships. Rather, it appears to be constitutive for this social form that local events are connected to the virtual level. In other words, in users' respective places of living, regular meetings are held, which are initially announced via the Forum and subsequently shared with the global community with the aid of photos and newly dramatized as a collective narration. In this manner, the anonymous socio-electronic network has transformed itself over the years of its existence into a global community, which—though based on natio-ethno-cultural belonging—detaches this belonging from the territorial place of residence.

GLOBAL MODES OF LIVING TOGETHER

In the empirical case that is the basis of the present study, the combination of Internet practices that are typical for migration has led to the emergence of a mutual supportive community on a global scale. The most surprising aspect of Cibervalle is not just that most of its members did not know each other personally before they met in the Forum. Rather, it is astonishing that the users from nearly all parts of the world access this electronic network not merely to receive current information about their country of origin or to organize their migration projects or to discuss political, cultural and social concerns, but also that they first and foremost want to share concerns about everyday life. Unlike Miller and Slater's (2000) study, in this case the concern is not just the maintenance of already existing physically grounded relationships. Rather, there is another dimension to this electronic medium, which entails that mutually supportive communities and modes of togetherness can be developed on the basis of anonymity and geographical distance.

Cibervalle differs from the migrant portals examined by Jannis Androutsopoulos (2005) as well as from the Internet platforms of the "virtual diasporas" mostly established by migrants themselves, which primarily focus on political and ethnic topics. In fact, the Forum was initially nothing other than a functioning part of the interactive communication environment of a commercial Paraguayan web portal. The operating company set it up online and left it to its own devices. More or less accidentally, the as yet lifeless Forum was then discovered and occupied by the first (Paraguayan) Internet travelers. Today the Forum houses a multitude of themes and communicative practices, which are more reminiscent of everyday conversations than of topic-centered exchanges of arguments. In Cibervalle, people laugh together, tell each other of the film they watched the previous night, exchange recipes, invent games that help kill time, quarrel and make up again and have a good cry and get some comfort from the others. In other words, Cibervalle is a social formation that allows its members to live together regardless of geographical distance. But how is it possible that a community arises from an anonymous communication network of participants who are first of all complete strangers to each other and who, moreover, live scattered lives across the globe? A community, furthermore, that is based on mutual solidarity and support, exhibits a high degree of emotionality and shares everyday life? Which social and technological conditions are at the basis of the emergence of such a form of community, which is apparently not dependent on either local or family ties, but which would not be adequately described in Anderson's (1985) sense as an imagined community—even though belonging to (and imagination of) a shared national geographical context appears to play a fundamental role?

The results of the present study illustrate that one dimension of globality, which emerges in the context of everyday Internet usage in migration contexts, can be described as a development of *global forms of living together*. The mutual natio-ethno-cultural belonging, information and solidarity are the essential modes of social integration by which Cibervalle reproduces itself in its different dimensions and through which it is maintained. The communicative architecture of global togetherness in Cibervalle is based on the complex interplay of mediated and copresent forms of communication, as well as on physical and virtual mobility. In a process of mutual interaction between practices of appropriation and technology, forms of presence and togetherness are generated that are not necessarily tied to the body. Nevertheless, physical presence certainly does not become obsolete in this process. Rather, the close interconnection of mediated and copresent, physical and virtual encounters as practiced in Cibervalle increasingly blurs the boundaries between presence and absence, interaction and communication, as well as public and private spaces of everyday life.

PERFORMING PARAGUAYAN EVERYDAY LIFE WITHIN A GLOBAL FRAME OF MUTUAL OBSERVATION

Because of its technological network-structure, the Internet is intrinsically designed for globality. Concerning the publicly accessible Cibervalle Forum, there is the added characteristic that the awareness of the public is reflexively built into Cibervalle's communications. In a sense, the role of the public functions as a reflexive consciousness of the participants, which structures their activities. The Forum can be accessed anywhere in the world and its activities can be observed anonymously. This means that the public in Cibervalle is structurally designed for a worldwide public. However, despite this global accessibility, the real scope of the Forum is limited. To be able to comprehend the communications, one needs to have the necessary linguistic skills. For a start, one has to find the Forum in the endless depths of the WWW. To do so, one has to either be informed about its existence or find it accidentally while surfing online. Due to the logic of interconnection of the WWW, the probability of reaching the Forum is greatest when one is searching for information about Paraguay. But Paraguay belongs to those regions of the world that—apart from the World Cup—play no role on a global level. Paraguay is neither a global player in the political and economic sense, nor does it have a noteworthy tourism industry or cultural production, which might globally transmit a cultural image. In fact, Paraguay hardly ever features at all in the global mass media. So the question is, who might search for Paraguay online and thus chance upon the Forum? Only if and when they change their own marginal position, Paraguayans are confronted with the construction of a world in which they do not play a significant role. This happens in the case of migration, but also during virtual journeys, when they encounter inhabitants of geographically distant regions in international chats and discussion forums.

Finally, an extraordinary event can throw a location—and the actors who feel they belong to it—into the spotlight of global interest for a short time. Through such an exceptional situation, the marginality of this location in normal circumstances is reflected.

Thus, a further focal point of this study is concerned with a sense of globality that may enable reflexive self-perception within a global horizon of mutual observation. As the analysis shows, it is helpful to scrutinize the concept of the public in order to assess this dimension of globality and its ramifications for the participants' activities. By means of the addresses in the Forum communications, the imagined Cibervalle public can be differentiated into unknown spectators and known spectators, as well as potentially interested members. Finally, the analysis of the activities in Cibervalle in connection with the fire in the supermarket *Ycua Bolaños*, which for a short while drew Paraguay into the focus of worldwide mass media attention, highlights as a central theme the relationship between potentially and situationally realized globality. The main focus here is on the question of how the Cibervallers reacted to the sudden global interest in Paraguay, as well as to the image that was produced by the mass media in connection with the supermarket fire. By means of this example, it can be demonstrated that whereas an Internet-based public is potentially global, it exhibits multiple globality references. In Cibervalle, the globality references oscillate between the internal public of the active members on the one end of the scale and the imagined world public on the other end. Globality in the sense of the facilitation of reflexive self-perception is therefore a flexible entity that moves between, firstly, potentiality and imagination and, secondly, situative realization and communicative affirmation. In any case, the public framing of communication affects the self-perception and behavior of the participants. The everyday nature of the activities, in particular the practice of meeting in the Cibervallers' physically grounded localities and the meetings' mediatized re-creation in a global public communication space, increases their reflexive self-perception. At the same time, their everyday life is increasingly turned into a potentially global frame of mutual observation. In other words, Cibervalle's inhabitants become 'global players,' while sharing private issues and everyday life concerns with each other.

5 Methodological Challenges and Book Structure

The increasing awareness of globalization is mirrored in the social sciences not merely in a large number of empirical and theoretical studies on globalization phenomena, but also in a reflexive (re)consideration of the discipline's own concepts. Faced with increasing mobility worldwide, economic expansion and the emergence of supranational order structures, not only the nation-state but also the social sciences must legitimize themselves as well as their basic concept of 'society.' Bauman (2000) sees the main task of the social sciences in the production of concepts that serve to construct a certain social reality and that are fortified by a collective perception of objective reality. The methodical and conceptional problems arising from the close ties between the conceptional repertoire of the social sciences and the societal model of the nation-state continue to be discussed under the heading of "methodological nationalism." Wimmer and Glick-Schiller (2002) relate this concept, which was introduced by Anthony D. Smith in 1979 (quoted in Bommes 2002), primarily to the practice of social scientific migration research. On the basis of a number of empirical case studies, in which the scientific field of transnational migration research emerges, they criticize the basic theoretical assumptions and the analytical procedure of classical migration research grounded in the assimilation paradigm. The concept of society behind the assimilation theory is, Wimmer and Glick-Schiller argue, stamped by nation-state ideologies insofar as it starts from the assumption that there is one homogenous cultural system, which is then in a second step equated with an analytical reference of society. According to these authors, sociological migration research based on the assimilation paradigm is therefore not able to keep an analytical distance to nation-state discourses, loyalties and presumptions. Instead of making these the objects of their research, assimilationist migration researchers adopt the perspective of the nation-state (politics) and presuppose that its order mechanisms present a self-evident frame for the explanation of migration phenomena.

If the social sciences' main task is the production of concepts that contribute to the objectification of a certain blueprint of social reality, then the following question is crucial for the present study: How can one produce adequate concepts for describing a reality that differs from that reality on which the conceptual body of the social sciences is based? How does one learn to sharpen one's perception of social phenomena and how can one adequately express the uniqueness of these phenomena by means of social scientific description? The fact that Park as well as Thomas and Znaniecki were able to describe phenomena that had generally been overlooked by migration research and were only recently rediscovered by transnationalism researchers illustrates not least the special value of the methodical procedure and data types used by the Chicago School. The set of questions asked by both studies were in fact not designed to detect transnational practices in migration. Rather, Park as well as Thomas and Znaniecki were primarily interested in examining the social milieus of large US-American cities. In the face of social and ethnic heterogeneity and the social change that occurred as a result of industrialization and urbanization, these authors were mainly concerned with questions of integration. That they nevertheless succeeded in looking over and beyond the national analytical context towards the more significant phenomena has its basis in primarily methodological reasons:

> What is so special about the material of the Chicago School is (. . .) its restraint in using material elicited from experiments or interviews and in turn their preference for 'undesigned records' as Park calls that material which arose free from the influence of a research design. (Ayaß 2006, 51; *own translation*)

REFLEXIVE METHODOLOGICAL APPROACH TO A TECHNO-SOCIAL REALITY

The present study ties in with the conceptional and methodological work of these two classics of sociological research. It does so in an attempt to link two research areas, which have hitherto developed independently. There, the present study has been inspired conceptionally by empirical contributions of transnational migration research as well as social scientific Internet research. The second link to the classics of the Chicago School lies in the usage of data generated by the field itself, with which the present researcher "may get an intimate glimpse into the smaller world of the immigrant" (Park [1922] 1970, 113; quoted in Ayaß 2006, 53).

The special character of the social formation Cibervalle, which stretches from a virtual space to a multitude of physically grounded social spaces and that in its scope is potentially global—despite a clear geographical reference of belonging—turns out to be a challenge for delimiting the research field as well as for developing suitable research methods. The research design therefore emerges from a reflexive examination of the research subject and is embedded in a broader discussion of different approaches to ethnography as well as ethnomethodological procedures of communication analysis.

The proposed reflexive research procedure, however, contributes not only to the understanding of social realities in the light of globalization, but also to an advancement of sociological methods and concepts for researching social phenomena in global landscapes.

This study interconnects both ethnomethodological and ethnographic aspects of 'becoming member' as well as the gathering of undesigned records with reconstructive procedures of data generation. Moreover, the study focuses on the reciprocal effects between technological development and its domestication by the participants, in order to examine the specific techno-social practices with which global forms of living together are made possible. Reflexivity therefore plays a decisive role in the methodological discussion of this research: Firstly, with respect to the relation between researcher and field; secondly, with regard to the reciprocal effects between the methods deployed, i.e., the research instruments and the constitution of the field; and, thirdly, in view of the relationship between participants and media or—to put it more abstractly—between sociality and technology.

The empirical material on which the case study is based consists of different data formats. That part of the data that may be described as digital recordings of the computer-mediated social reality consists of communication forms for which so far no adequate analytical tools have been developed. A deeper methodological examination concerning the handling of these data will therefore precede the communication analysis, Part D, of this study.

OVERVIEW OF THE BOOK'S STRUCTURE

The problem of methodological nationalism as mentioned earlier—a nationalism that restricts the conceptual body of the social sciences to the societal model of the nation-state—becomes apparent in ethnography especially in the relation between researcher and researched persons, the differentiation between the other and the self and in ethnography's central concepts of culture and field. In Part B of this book, the crisis of ethnography in connection with (post)colonial globalization processes will be discussed. The requirements for ethnographical practice and methodology, which seek to fulfill modes of globality that emerge in connection with migration and the everyday use of the Internet, are critically examined primarily with respect to the concept of 'field.' The particularities and methodological challenges of the present research field are subsequently discussed. Part C, which deals with ethnographic topics, begins with the description and analysis of an exemplary migration biography. For the analysis, an attempt is made to constructively interconnect the systems' theoretical suggestion of a global analytical frame with the empirically guided methodological procedure of transnational migration research. The conceptual reflection of the social scientific concept of space in Part C, derived from the methodologically

inspired field discussion in Part B, introduces the ethnographic description of the social landscapes of Cibervalle. As its geographical reference,
Paraguay is examined regarding the relationship between migration and
the constitution of social spaces. In a second step, the techno-social space
Cibervalle is then introduced from the different perspectives of its users.

A discussion of ethnomethodological procedures of analysis and their
applicability to the analysis of Internet-based communication begins Part
D. Whereas the ethnographic part of the study is focused on the subjective
meaning of Cibervalle from the participants' points of view, Part D explores
the structural conditions of the techno-social organization of Cibervalle.
Here the technology is introduced as a participant alongside the human
participants. After a reflexive-methodological approach to the specific
communicational form and the evaluation procedures that are adequate
for this form, the communicative architecture of Cibervalle is described.
More precisely, the Forum communication is examined with regards to
its structural characteristics, which in turn will then be scrutinized with
regard to their social embedding. Changes in the Forum, which were implemented over the years, are then analyzed in order to understand the reciprocal effects between technological development and practices of media
appropriation and to distill specific modes of the construction of globality.
Subsequently, ethnographically generated data are used to closely examine
the participants' everyday communicative practices, on which the global
forms of togetherness in Cibervalle are based. In the concluding chapter of
the communication analysis part of this study, the focus is on the second
dimension of the construction of globality: The structural condition of the
public and of the potential scope of communication in the Forum is more
closely examined with regards to its importance for the way in which the
participants act.

Part B

Hopping-On—Hopping-Off

The Art of Positioning Ethnography in Global Landscapes

The present research deals with an 'alien people' that inhabits a common virtual space in the WWW, while being physically located in different socio-geographical contexts. Nonetheless, as so-called 'transmigrants,' most of the members do not remain 'located' anywhere at all. They are profoundly mobile, traveling virtually and physically between different sites of being, sites of wanting-to-know and sites of belonging[1]—to name just a few. Ethnographic research on mediated cultures of mobility poses a set of problems that require thorough reflection as well as a search for creative solutions: We must delimit and enter fields that transcend the notions of classical ethnography in the literal sense, we find multimedia data types for which there are hardly any tested methods available and we aim to describe realities for which the social sciences are literally at a loss for words. As the everyday lives of migrants become increasingly more mobile and (computer-)mediated, the procedures and assumptions that have long been taken for granted in ethnography turn out to be less suitable.

This part discusses the theoretical and methodological problems that an inquiry into 'placeless' phenomena encounters. The meanings of some key concepts of classical ethnography are critically examined, such as field, field entrance, positioning fieldwork and (non)participant observation. The chapter begins with a review of the crisis of ethnographical representation, relating the changes in ethnographic discourse and practice to globalization processes. Since George Marcus in 1995 initiated the global turn in ethnography, a vast amount of literature on the meaning and practicality of multi-siting has emerged. This debate will be addressed firstly by indicating and clarifying some conceptual misperceptions and secondly, by contributing a set of multi-siting methods, which have been developed along with the research on Cibervalle. I will offer an example of how ethnographers can use reflexivity as a resource, first to develop 'uniquely adequate' methods and concepts (Garfinkel and Wieder 1992) and second to analyze the interactions between advancing technologies and the cultural practices of appropriation. With reference to recent debates on multi-sited and global ethnography on the one hand and virtual ethnography on the other, I explore ethnography's capacity for understanding the new cultural practices and techno-social realities that have emerged along with the digital media usage in contemporary migration contexts.

6 Ethnographers on Their Way to World Society

The ethnographer's mission, following the Malinowskian tradition of studying an alien people, may be explained to newcomers as follows: Approach the alien people's home; establish yourself there for a while; engage with the locals; participate in their everyday life; learn their language, practices and rituals; and try to assume little by little their cultural patterns of interpretation. Along the way, write down in great detail whatever you see and hear, and ask questions whenever you do not understand what you perceive. After a while, you will start to arrange your notes and prioritize your observations and impressions, in order to relate them to theoretical concepts and to generate new theoretical outcomes. The ethnographer fulfills his mission if he relates observations with theoretical concepts in a verisimilar way and manages to 'translate' the foreign culture into a text that is intelligible for the scientific community at home.

Ethnography seeks to describe alien cultures from within. It provides concepts and methods for exploring implicit cultural knowledge as well as for the modes and rules of producing and sharing social reality within a social group. Social anthropologists had long been looking for those 'aliens' mostly on remote islands, which were as clearly bounded as distant from their own 'civilization.' Consequently, ethnographic modes of constructing fields and generating data had also been developed along with a preference for clearly demarcated, territorially bounded 'fields' and social groups that are manageable in size. Due to its research practice, social anthropology has created a sense of culture in terms of static and homogeneous entities that are fixed in time and place (Appadurai 1996; Abu-Lughod 1991). Classic ethnographic practice, in other words, tends to equate concepts of field and culture with geographically distant and territorially bounded units of investigations.

The 'old-school' ethnographer distinguishes him- or herself from both the scientific community one is part of and the foreign culture one represents, due to the fact that one 'was there'—and returned. The ethnographer's account achieves authenticity through fieldwork. His or her authority relies on the fact that neither the subjects of investigation nor the scientific community are able to scrutinize this account. Against the background of the liberation movements in the global South—whose inhabitants so far had predominantly been perceived as 'silent objects' of anthropological studies—"the tension of proximity–distance between ethnographers and natives" (Guber 2001, 36; *own translation*) had to be reconsidered. At the same time, the publication of Malinowski's diaries[2] provoked a crisis that damaged the perceived authority of ethnographers in general and the reliability of their representations. In the course of this crisis, the traditional scientific mode of representation was called into question: 'Ethnographic realism' was criticized because it aimed at objectively portraying social reality, thereby hiding the ethnographer's social role in the field, as well as the dependency of his interpretations of cultural patterns based on his own—mostly Western—cultural background. Highly influenced by the discussion about gender in ethnography (MacCormack and Strathern 1980), *reflexivity* has become a central term in ethnographic practice and methodology (Guber 2001; Bergmann 2006; Macdonald 2007). Since then, the role of the ethnographer has been taken into account more seriously, particularly with regard to his position and social relations within the field, both of which extremely influence his points of view and interpretations. Against the background of reflexivity, the practice of writing ethnographies (Clifford and Marcus 1986; Berg and Fuchs 1993) also appears in a different light. The growing awareness of the complex "relationship between the ethnographers' selves, the selves of 'others' and the text they both engage in" (Atkinson et al. [2001] 2007, 3) finally helps to supersede the concept of ethnography as a factual description of social reality.

A closer look at this debate reveals that not only the ethnographic practice of constructing realities, but also its subsequent deconstruction relate to advancing globalization processes: In the course of European colonization of the 'new world,' ethnography turns out to be a basic tool for appropriating the world in Western cultural terms. Changing dynamics of global communication and mobility, however, brought about a significant difference between the colonial and the postcolonial shape of globalization. During the last five hundred years, and especially since the inventions of electric telegraphy and the steam engine, mobility and communication networks have increased steadily and onto a global scale. Throughout this progression, direction and control of the transport and communication technologies came from Europe, in particular the transnational media conglomerates, which emerged in the nineteenth century and backed up the colonial system as they:

> divided the world among themselves by operating a news cartel, which involved exclusive presence in the respective spheres of colonial influence. Transnational telegraph, telephone and transport links to colonies were constructed to serve the colonial metropolises. [. . .] Media content in the form of news and entertainment materials flowed largely from North to South, further reinforcing Northern world views. (Karim 2003a, 7)

During the course of decolonization the dynamics of globalization have changed insofar as people in the colonized regions of the world have gained access to global transport and communication technologies as well as to (scientific) discourses. These same people, now having a voice of their own, visibly and audibly refuse to comply with Eurocentric constructions of reality.

Thus, it is the postcolonial character of globalization that leads to questioning presuppositions of ethnographic practices and methodology. This is especially apparent in the discussion of the field category: In the 1980s the general assumption was that it was relatively unproblematic for an ethnographer or community researcher to define and demarcate a field, because "he can identify it with a locality or a territory" (Weidmann 1975, 10; *own translation*). Since the 1990s, however, the temporal and local fixation— "the incarceration of non-Western people in time and space" (Abu-Lughod 1991, 146)—as well as the concept of culture inherent in this practice have been increasingly under attack. Burawoy states that anthropologists "have awakened to a world in which outsider and insider, anthropologist and native, colonizer and colonist, center and periphery are no longer neat and water-tight categories" (Burawoy et al. 2000, 340). Thus, not only has the anthropological field become an endangered species, but the long-accustomed practices of demarcation and positioning, which define the relationship between researchers and their subjects as a dualism of 'us here' versus 'those others out there,' have also become questionable.

Abu-Lughod sees anthropology's primordial nature in connection with this practice of distinction and its identity-building function, and she even questions anthropology's concept of culture itself. "Culture is important to anthropology because the anthropological distinction between self and other rests on it. Culture is the essential tool for making other" (1991, 143). Berg and Fuchs emphasize the reflexive character of ethnographic representation, which always contains not only the conception of other, but also of self (1993, 11). Abu-Lughod further observes that the practice of anthropological fieldwork tends to construct cultural formations as coherent and bounded unities: "Organic metaphors of wholeness and the methodology of holism that characterizes anthropology both favor coherence, which in turn contributes to the perception of communities as bounded and discrete" (1991, 146). Thus, she questions the anthropological concept of culture in general and stresses that in view of global interconnections the assertion of isolated and bounded cultural formations is absurd (1991, 149).

Wimmer and Glick-Schiller connect the fusion of culture and territory and the resulting fieldwork practice to the successful assertion of the nation-state as the predominant societal model. According to these authors, nation/state-building processes have decisively influenced social scientific theory and practice. The development of concepts and methods was based on the assumption "that the nation/state/society is the natural social and political form of the modern world" (2002, 302). The conception of culture, ethnic community or society as a bounded entity, a holistic whole, which is hallmarked by specific cultural practices and customs, as well as by the conceptual equation of society with a territorial nation-state, is, according to these authors, the consequence of a social scientific practice that takes the nation-state for granted as a quasi-natural mode of social organization without really reflecting this basic assumption while developing concepts and theories. Gille and O Riain describe the effect of this methodological nationalism on the concept of field in ethnography: "Ethnography tends to accept these categories—either, as in sociology, generalizing to the national society or, as in anthropology, taking the local as the site of culture, which is often analyzed in terms of its relationship to the world of nations" (2002, 273).

So if there are no more insular peoples to explore, and if globalization causes everything social to be somehow globally connected, is ethnography still a suitable social scientific methodology? And how does globalization impinge on both the concept of field and the practice of ethnographic field research? According to Amann and Hirschauer (1997), the intrinsic nature of ethnography, namely, its "affinity to the curious" (*own translation*), has a potential for researching complex societies. As a consequence of migration and urbanization, the differentiation of lifestyles and the specialization of work spheres as well as functional systems, experiences of feeling 'other' are part of everyday life in modern society. The 'other' is hence not geographically distant, nor have the structures of the modern self been sufficiently explored. On the contrary, modern society offers a multitude of fields in which strange phenomena can be discovered and familiar ones are found to be strange, provided ethnography sensitizes itself for the unknown in the seemingly familiar.

Amann and Hirschauer's interpretation of ethnography has a strong affinity to the ethnomethodological research mentality. By using ethnography's interest in things unfamiliar or unknown and its ability to be amazed with cultural phenomena research subjects take for granted, an ethnomethodologically inspired ethnographer attains "even common events and fields to be turned into sociological phenomena" (1997, 9; *own translation*).

With their programmatic suggestion to engage in "othering the self" (1997, 13; *own translation*) these authors make an important contribution towards overcoming dualistic and asymmetric conceptual constructions that are rooted in anthropology's colonial history. Still, the field concept question remains unanswered. Amann and Hirschauer demonstrate ethnography's potential to study cultural formations and social structures in modern society, but they conceive their fields in terms of local units. By using the concept of the "knowledge-constituting fiction of discovery" (1997, 9n3; *own translation*), they implicitly point to present-day global interconnectedness, as a result of which hardly any more discoveries in the sense of cultural first contacts are possible on earth today. But they omit the question of how ethnography can approach the influence of global interconnections on the production of locally situated cultural formations. To be more precise, this question does not even enter their considerations. Nearly all of the ethnographic case studies in their edition focus on establishments and institutions (swimming pools, schools, administrations), that are clearly localized and bounded.[3] Amman and Hirschauer's contribution to the positioning of ethnography in modern society represents not so much a radical modernization, but more a return to ethnographic traditions, developed in the context of the Chicago School, which have been relegated off-site since the onset of structural functionalism. But there can be no doubt that the shape of modern society is closely connected to globalization processes. Functional differentiation, migration and urbanization and the differentiation of lifestyles cannot be sufficiently understood if they are not seen in a global context.

Elsewhere, the conceptual and methodological consequences of complex global interactions, in which contemporary life and cultural production are embedded, have been discussed with keywords like "multi-sited ethnography" (Marcus 1995; Hannerz 2003; Falzon 2009) and "global ethnography" (Burawoy et al. 2000; Gille and O Riain 2002). These discussions will be examined in the following chapter with regard to their applicability for the present study. During the course of this appraisal, the relationship between locality and field, as well as between local and global dimensions of field, will be clarified. Following that, the problems arising from the specific characteristics of the present research focus will be explicated in order to, finally, present the methodological approach, field construction and concrete methods of *multi-siting*, which were developed and deployed for the present study.

7 Multi-sited Ethnography
A Methodology for the Mediatized Global Society?

Classical ethnography not only constructs its research object as a locally bounded and culturally homogenous unity, but also contextualizes and interprets this unity in a macrosociological framework like that of the capitalist world system. In contrast to this, Marcus (1995) subsumes those procedures under the heading of *multi-sited ethnography*, in which research objects are constructed multidimensionally, thereby providing for their respective unique dynamics.

> Ethnography moves from its conventional single-site location, contextualized by macro-constructions of a larger social order, such as the capitalist world system, to multiple sites of observation and participation that cross-cut dichotomies such as the 'local' and the 'global,' the 'life world' and the 'system.' (Marcus 1995, 95)

The concept of *multi-sited ethnography* takes into consideration that cultural formations are not territorially fixed and do not develop in isolation from each other, but rather they are expressions of complex networks and global mobility. Multi-sited ethnography examines the shifting of cultural meanings, objects and identities on the move, and in so doing becomes itself a mobile methodology that follows people, things, symbols, narratives, biographies and/or conflicts; thus constructing its research object in the movement between the different *sites*.

Subsequent discussions of Marcus's approach often reduce *site* to a synonym of (physical) location. Also, the quality of ethnographic research under the conditions of globalization is based one-sidedly on 'having-been-there.' Tied to this reductionist reading of multi-siting is the opinion that the ethnographer can only sufficiently grasp her research object if she actually visits all the locations related to the cultural formation at hand. Hannerz (2003), for example, talks about 'multisite' instead of 'multi-sited' ethnography while pointing to the limited feasibility of ethnographic research that attempts to consider all localities related to the research subject. This type of ethnography, according to Hannerz, is bound to turn into an 'art of the possible.' With his focus set on the central role of global communication media, Wittel (2000) emphasizes that the ethnographic practice of participant observation over a long period of time and in a bounded local context neglects not only movements, but also electronically mediated communication and connectivity. In a globalized world such a practice will, according to the author, end up achieving the opposite of what it set out to accomplish, because essential parts of the context of its research subjects are excluded from the researcher's vision. Instead of locally bounded fields, modern ethnography should describe networks. In particular, the social processes and dynamics 'in-between' (the relationships between people, things, actions and meanings) should be scrutinized because they permanently re-create culture. According to Wittel, blurring the field concept has consequences for the time management of the ethnographer, as she will now have to divide her time between several locations.

Both Hannerz and Wittel only go so far as to identify the problems that arise from attaching ethnographic practice to certain places, but they do not present adequate solutions to these problems: They fail to resolutely abandon the territorial concept of field and the methodology of holism. Marcus's concept of *multi-sited ethnography* points in another direction, as it contains a conceptual extension of the notion of field in anthropology. For Marcus, multi-siting is not distinguishable by having been everywhere or having observed one's research object from all involved local perspectives. Rather, *multi-siting* entails focusing on the complex interconnections (networks), and thus the embedded multidimensionality through which a cultural formation can be understood. In other words, *multi-sited ethnography* breaks with a social scientific tradition, which both searched for the local in territorially bounded lifeworlds and localized the global on the macro level of the world system. Instead, Marcus suggests that the local–global dichotomy should be abandoned and the global be defined as the emergent dimension of a discussion of the relations/connections between the sites of a *multi-sited ethnography*. This perspective resists the idea of the global as a macro-structural context in which the local is manifested and interpreted on the micro level.

Marcus's conception of the relation between global and local dimensions of the social comes very close to Robertson's concept of *glocalization* (1995), which he proposes as an alternative to the usual dualistic confrontation of local versus global. Deduced from the Japanese, *glocalization* means the adaptation of global principles or worldviews to local conditions, i.e., the specific expressions of very general phenomena. As Robertson suggests, the global and the local should not be conceived as antithetic but rather conjunctive concepts. Hence, the local is an aspect of globalization and Robertson defines it as a 'linking of localities.' The development of a global consciousness enables the abstraction of the local and thereby a reflexive awareness of it. The local is thus newly produced within a comparative global horizon, wherein many localities are linked.

Numerous questions have so far arisen from the attempt to newly position ethnography in a world that conceives itself reflexively. In other words, this is a world aware of *glocal* links, embedded in which are localities, lifeworlds, cultural formations, social practices, etc., a world that assumes that these links will be intensified even more, due to increasing mobility (Urry 2000) and "mediatization" (Livingstone 2009; Krotz 2009) of social life. These questions have posed a challenge for the conception of the present study, resulting in an experimental approach to methodological premises. How can research fields be sensibly defined and demarcated in view of global dynamics determining present-day social life and cultural formations? How can the ethnographer identify relevant *sites* and relate them to each other? As Gille and O Riain have pointed out, Marcus does not offer much help and provides very few concrete suggestions as to how these questions could be answered (2002, 286). Candea complains that problems related to field construction in multi-sited projects are mostly omitted. "Multi-sited ethnography's weakness lies in its lack of attention to processes of bounding, selection and choice—processes, which any ethnographer has to undergo to reduce the initial indeterminacy of field experience into a meaningful account" (2009, 27). To answer these same questions, empirical studies that take on the challenge to reform ethnography in a radical way are needed—despite the danger of getting lost in the global field of flows and networks, multiple meanings and discontinuities, hybrids and 'impure.'

In my research on Cibervalle, the difficulties of developing an ethnographic project were manifested in particular social and technological challenges. I faced a nomadic field, in which the actors were moving constantly between different local sites, be it physically, imaginatively or virtually (Urry 2000). The computer-mediated sites of the field were not distant in geographic terms, although the users' access locations were scattered across the globe, including even the ethnographer's neighborhood.[4] Pluri-locality, mobility and unboundedness, or to put it differently, the 'transnational irony' of contemporary fieldwork (Appadurai 1996, 57) turned out to be main features of the field. But how is it possible to move within such a complex and obviously borderless field without getting lost? How to define appropriate field sites and boundaries in virtual contexts? The following chapter starts with the presentation of several ethnographic approaches to the Internet, which have been developed within the framework of Internet research. Subsequently, these approaches will be discussed in relation to the preceding questions.

8   Developments in Internet Research (and) Cultures

To begin with, there is no one single field of Internet research. Rather, in the course of the massive worldwide spread of the Internet, social scientific interest in its use and significance has steadily increased and developed independently in different disciplines. By looking at the development of central methodological and epistemological questions, one can gauge the history of the spread and implementation of new Internet technologies. Since the commissioning of ARPANET, a decentralized network originally built per order of the US Air Force for enabling military communication during wartime breakdowns of established channels, the worldwide computer network for electronic communication and information exchange has not merely changed the working and communication practices of the members of scientific and military institutions. The Internet, which emerged from ARPANET and initially connected only scientific institutions with each other, was by the early 1990s facilitating commercial and private use via the WWW. This in turn led to the rapid global spread of Internet access and set a (still ongoing) process in motion, by which an ever-increasing number of people worldwide rely on the Internet as an instrument for the facilitation of everyday life.

Several social scientific disciplines discovered the Internet as an ethnographic field in the 1990s. Initially, the main focus was on the exploration of 'cyberspace.' Numerous case studies examined new cultural formations, types of communities, communicative forms, patterns of identity-building, etc., in cyberspace. Scientific perspectives and methods changed according to the extent by which the Internet established itself as an everyday life and mass medium. As a result, users' appropriation practices of the new technologies and the integration of these technologies into their everyday life came to the fore. Finally, the adoption of new terms and concepts from Internet jargon, for example, 'social software' (Stegbauer and Jäckel 2008) or 'Web 2.0' (Reichert 2008), points to an increasing awareness of the "interactivity" (Rammert 2000; Krotz 2007) of Internet-based media in social scientific discourse. Most importantly, it has been acknowledged that not only production and reception of media *texts*, but also technological development and practical appropriation of media *formats* are inextricably interlinked.

EVERYDAY LIFE IN THE INTERNET—
VIRTUAL ETHNOGRAPHY

It would seem that the social scientist whose field exists via the Internet would not have to worry about gaining field access. Without ever leaving her desk, she must only start her web browser, and then she is suddenly off exploring strange worlds 'out there.' Numerous public discussion forums, e-mailing lists, personal homepages, weblogs,[5] MUDs,[6] chats, etc., open up views of the beautiful new world of cyberspace. As an ethnographer, she can—without ever having to reflect her own influence on the field—use the safe position of *lurker* (i.e., the anonymous reader) to observe online communities doing a great number of things: discussing political topics or Television series, exchanging recipes, presenting their family life or impressions of their last holiday, creating fantastic virtual identities or offering consolation and support to each other in self-help groups, to name only a few.

In fact, the first decade of social scientific Internet research was guided by the idea that cyberspace opens up a new level of reality that unfolds its own dynamics regardless of the specific living contexts of the individual participants. This new level of reality would eventually develop into an experimental field for multiple identity blueprints as well as for different forms of community and communication (Jones 1995; Turkle 1995). Using the argument "that on-line communications can be analyzed in their own terms for the form of meaning, the shared values and the specific contextual ways of being which emerge in on-line environments" (Hine 1998), online ethnography confines itself to the exploration of cyberspace as an independent cultural and social space. As a rule, the problem of constructing an ethnographic field is solved by choosing individual e-mailing lists, chats or discussion forums. Field research can be restricted to anonymous observation and textual analysis of public open communication platforms, or the ethnographer can become a temporary member of a research field, whereby she adopts an insider's perspective. In addition, she deepens her knowledge by interacting with other Internet participants and by learning the practices of the field herself.

INTERNET IN EVERYDAY LIFE—ETHNOGRAPHY
OF 'REAL' LIFE CONTEXTS AND PRACTICES

Contrary to predictions made in the first decade of Internet research, the Internet can hardly be said to have led to an emergence of virtual worlds that bring about identities and ways of living that are independent of users' actual living situations, biographies or bodies. Rather, the shaping of cyberspace as well as its interpretation is inevitably tied to the physical lifeworld of the individual, similar to the way in which virtual activities impinge on individuals' everyday life. Observing that "people do not exist as ethereal creatures," Boase et al. (2002, 1) point to the physical-contextual relations and framings of social activities on and with the Internet. The location of Internet access influences not only users' behavior, but in addition, "the place where people use the Internet also affects who will be online and with what sort of facilities" (ibid.).

Thus, the second decade of Internet research mirrors the process of the technology's integration in everyday life: "Where the first age of the internet was a period of exploration, hope and uncertainty, the second age of the internet has been one of routinization, diffusion and development" (Wellman and Hogan 2004, 61). So the second decade of Internet research is not so much determined by hopes, fictions and utopias. Rather, from the position of users, the question is asked how the Internet is integrated into their everyday life (Bakardjieva and Fraser 2001; Wellman and Haythornthwaite 2002). Kendall (1999) therefore pleads for the method of participant observation in Internet research, including everything happening in this virtual space as well as the situation in front of the computer—in other words, the social context of user groups. Klemm and Graner focus on the communicative appropriation of the new technologies and concentrate on talk in front of the monitor, because talking about the technological artifacts provides an important source for "researching the linguistic-communicative construction of the medium computer from the perspective of everyday life as well as users or user groups themselves" (2000, 159; *own translation*).

THE MEANING OF THE INTERNET FOR
TRANSNATIONAL POPULATIONS

This lifeworld-oriented approach, which reflects the social scientific conception of the Internet as a medium of everyday life, has up to now been concerned primarily with user groups situated in the Western (cultural and geographical) Hemisphere. Even though transnational migration research increasingly acknowledges the importance of the Internet, it rarely perceives Internet users—in contrast to 'sedentary' populations situated in the Western Hemisphere—as active participants of everyday life. Most transnational migration research is focused on politically and ethnically relevant themes. Whenever the Internet for 'sedentary' populations is conceived as a medium of everyday life, transnational studies methodologically omit users' lifeworld contexts. Cyberspace is conceived primarily as a space for negotiating ethnic or national identity (Adams 2004), or as a platform for the exertion of political influence in the user's country of origin (Uimonen 2003) on which *virtual diasporas* are formed (Karim 2003b).

In this approach, cyberspace is conceived as an ethnically structured level of reality, which again is implied to be independent from users' real life. By presenting 'migrants' primarily as political agents whose identities are determined by their ethnicity, this approach also projects a distorted picture of people with migration experience in relation to 'sedentary' populations. However, it can be presumed that most people's everyday lives, regardless of whether they have migration experience or not, are determined much less by political activism than by mundane matters and interpersonal relations. In transnational populations, certainly, these relations reach across long distances. Therefore, the social consequences of the daily use of communication technologies in migration contexts is of great relevance for the social sciences, even though they have so far received very little attention.

FROM TRINIDAD TO THE INTERNET

One of the few exceptions is Miller and Slater's study, *The Internet—An Ethnographic Approach*. They approach the significance of the Internet and cyberspace from a Trinidadian perspective, insisting that 'virtuality' should not be taken as a property of sociality. In response to the common practice in Internet research that—by limiting fieldwork mostly to the virtual sites—tends to mystify 'virtual reality,' these authors suggest the reverse path: "If you want to get to the Internet, don't start from there" (2000, 5). They observe that Internet-based social relations are in certain situations interpreted by the protagonists themselves as an added reality level, which is distinct from their physically based lifeworld. The authors chose to examine this observation rather than take it uncritically as the basic assumption of their research. The empirical example of Trinidad allows them to study both the manifold practices of Internet usage in a specific location as well as the way in which it is embedded in people's everyday lives. They also look at the repercussions on Trinidad's societal situation.

Miller and Slater themselves are critical of their own concept of locality, noting that it is—in (good old) anthropological tradition—limited to an island. They want to understand how Internet technologies are used and integrated in a specific local context (2000, 1). At the same time, they admit that the significance of the local reaches far beyond the island itself, "because Trinidad stretches diasporically over much of the world" (ibid.). The medial shaping of transnational relations in Trinidadians' everyday life is actually a central aspect of their study, albeit primarily from the perspective of those remaining on the island. Concerning the authors' recommendation not to start in the Internet if one wants to get there, the question remains what implications would have arisen in this case from approaching the field via the Internet. It is possible that Miller and Slater would have reached the conclusion that the Trinidadian Internet is shaped far more from outside the island. This deduction might even have led them to the inclusion of more localities in the fieldwork and to an examination of the integration of the Internet into the everyday lives of Internet users in migration.

THE QUESTION OF NONPARTICIPANT OBSERVATION IN ETHNOGRAPHIC INTERNET RESEARCH

In contrast to what Miller and Slater suggest, I indeed started my research within the Internet. I approached Cibervalle as a lurker. That is to say, I entered the public online discussion forum and followed the activities, thereby hiding myself in front of the screen. Some literature on virtual ethnography calls this practice nonparticipant observation, in contrast to participant observation, which is the case if the researcher actively takes part in the communications. The distinction between these two modes of observation strikes me as less plausible than the decision for only one of these practices of engagement with the field. Ethnographic research aims at studying social situations and cultures in their own terms and complexities. Because lurking is a 'native' practice of the field, the lurking researcher gains access to those dimensions of computer-mediated social life that are not just open to, but specifically *addressed* to *lurkers*; active and competent participants of public virtual spaces act in the knowledge that they always can be observed anonymously. The very fact that there is a term for this role indicates that the *lurker* has a firm place in the social structure of public online formations. According to Boyd, the invisible audience is one of the "four key architectural properties of mediated sociality to keep in mind"[7] (2009, 30) while studying digital cultures. This raises the question of whether one should talk about nonparticipant observation at all.

Whatever it is called, if one adopts lurking as a research practice, one should be aware that one takes only one possible position within a complex system of communications. Ethnographers who only adopt the role of the lurker may easily get access and a great deal of—even 'naturally occurring'—data (Silverman 2007) at a low cost. What they see and what they are able to understand, however, remain as limited as nineteenth-century armchair ethnography. Mann and Stewart emphasize the epistemological limitations of lurking, pointing to the 'hidden areas' of Internet-based communication: "It is only researchers who both 'find' these secret places, and who then negotiate access, who begin to grasp the boundaries of the community" (2000, 90). Beaulieu accordingly argues that "like in more conventional fieldwork, knowledge comes from engagement and interaction, always both purposive and incidental" (2004, 150). The more important part of the term 'participant observation,' then, is the 'participant,' i.e., the ethnographer herself, who aims to become a member of the studied group and lives among these people for a considerable period of time, participating and thereby learning the cultural practices and the social order of the group.

This discussion indicates that the Internet should not be simplified, neither in spatial terms nor as a virtual reality separated from physically grounded contexts. As Markham (1998) argues, from the actors' point of view the Internet may be perceived and practiced in spatial terms, but it can also be considered a tool or a way of being. Hine (2009) maintains that one of the challenges of ethnographic research on the Internet is to explore cultural constructions in a field without prematurely assuming its boundaries. Defining the boundaries of the research project thus becomes an ongoing task during the whole research process. It requires taking a set of decisions during fieldwork, regarding entrance or starting points, the traces to follow and when to stop fieldwork. *Multi-siting* in ethnographic Internet research thus becomes crucial in terms of moving around sites, relating sites of production and use, online and offline, and following traces across social networks and different media.

Ethnography, in conclusion, offers several pathways for approaching computer-mediated social spaces as well as for understanding users' cultural practices and systems of meaning. However, these pathways are available only if the ethnographer gets involved in the 'uniqueness' of the phenomena he wants to examine, and, secondly, if she adapts her methodological and conceptual paths to the peculiarities of the field. In the attempt to meet this challenge, ethnography can open itself to inspiration by a number of ethnomethodological premises and principles.

EXCURSION: ETHNOMETHODOLOGICAL REMARKS ON ETHNOGRAPHY

The 'Unique Adequacy Requirement'

Under the premise that you get to know a research object only insofar as the methods used (are able to) tell you about it, ethnomethodology—through its founder Harold Garfinkel—formulates the radical methodological imperative of the 'unique adequacy requirement' (Garfinkel and Wieder 1992). In order to grasp the specifics of a research object, the methods and terms used to approach this object have to be individually adapted to it. Instead of prematurely fixing a method, which is then used like a static form to cloak the research object, the methodological costume should be tailor-made to fit the individual figure of this object (see also Bergmann 1993). Similarly, the preceding authors request ethnographers to refrain from preconceived theoretical terminology: Here, too, they demand that the researcher should use his concepts in a restrained, heuristic way. If he is prepared to allow phenomena to remain as unique as they are, "while describing an observed occurrence, he should not use predetermined concepts, but rather develop his concepts for that description from within the observation of that occurrence itself" (Bergmann 2006, 19; *own translation*). However, it would be naïve to think that one could simply eliminate one's prior theoretical and methodological knowledge, or drop it like a coat at the entrance to the research field. It would be equally wrong to presume that ethnomethodologically oriented social scientists could do without any theory- and method-building. Quite the contrary: A broad and intensive method training is as important for the genesis of an adequate methodological corpus as a repertoire of sociological and commonsense knowledge is for identifying and sensibly interpreting social phenomena in the first place. But how to solve the paradox that, on the one hand, social phenomena can only be approached from one's own communicative 'household,' whereas, on the other hand, the singularity of individual phenomena remains invisible behind the researcher's terminology? Or, to put it differently, how may one discover the new while describing something without using well-worn terms or concepts?

'Becoming a Member'—Central Moments in the Research Process

One option for the ethnographer to gain access to the interpretation patterns and practices of the participants is the temporary membership of the researcher in the field. For ethnography, the prospect of learning the practices of the field presents a chance to compensate for the dilemma that other people's subjective knowledge is not directly accessible. The researcher adopts an inside perspective and tries to "become as familiar as possible with the lifeworld that he examines . . . he attempts to reconstruct that world in a sense through the eyes of an ideal type of any member's concept of normality" (Honer 2003, 198; *own translation*). Ethnography thus aims at reconstructing the actors' subjective patterns of meaning and advises the researcher to learn the practices of the field to achieve this goal.

A closer look at actual research practice shows that most often reconstructing procedures of data generation and analysis are used. That is to say, common social scientific practices are not different from everyday practices insofar as they appropriate social reality by reconstructing past events in a way that make them become coherent and meaningful for the researcher. This is done either in interaction with the subjects by means of narrative or biographical interviews or by the researcher himself memorizing and writing up his own observations. However, in order to understand a biography or an event by way of reconstruction, the researcher initially has nothing to rely on except for his own familiar patterns of interpretation, which in turn are based on commonsense and scientific knowledge (Schütz [1953] 1967). In other words, even if the researcher delves deep into the field and tries to take up an inner perspective while attempting to grasp the social reality of his field, he inevitably ends up deploying his own cultural systems of meaning, even though they might have been partially altered through interaction with the field. The deployed methods and terminology, the questions asked, the selection and description of what is considered to be relevant or, last but not least, the meaningful reconstruction of events in which the researcher took part during the research process are all conducive to the construction of his research object: "Thus, the scientist himself contributes decisively to the data he is looking at, so that he always ends up meeting himself in and among his data" (Bergmann 2006, 22–23; *own translation*).

However, from an ethnomethodological perspective, 'becoming a member' is directed less at the reconstruction of subjective meaning than at the reconstruction of a social order characteristic of particular 'social situations' or 'gatherings' (Goffman 1964). With reference to Schütz's idea, that the social world is structured and organized in a meaningful way, ethnomethodology suggests focusing on how social order is formed in the first place, in order to gain access to the singular structures of the research object. In doing so, ethnomethodology distances itself from the structural functionalist approach of Parsons, who explains social order as the internalization of a cultural value system that exists independently from individual members of a society (cf. Heritage 1984; Bergmann 1988). Ethnomethodology does not take social order as given. On the contrary, it transfers its focus from the macro to the micro level of situations in which competent members of a particular sociocultural group interactively produce social order. Cultural values and norms in the sense of a shared intersubjective interpretation practice cannot be sufficiently mediated through socialization. Rather, what is needed for the interpretation of cultural values and norms in different situations is the cultural competence of the participants. They decide interactively how each situation is to be comprehended and which conduct is appropriate. In other words, the meaning of a social situation is not defined until it is interactively performed. In this process, the participants use so-called 'ethno-methods' to produce and maintain a shared sense of social order.

Therefore, the major epistemological concern of ethnomethodology is to examine "how the world is described, explained and made visible in everyday activities as a meaningfully structured and orderly world, which is expectable but at the same time often imponderable in its course of events" (Bergmann 1988, 21; *own translation*). This methodology therefore focuses on the interactive production of social reality and aims to identify the shared patterns of mutually constructing the meaningful orderliness of social situations. In doing so, ethnomethodology takes advantage of the following premise of social interaction:

> Mutual intelligibility is only made possible in and through the enactment of recognizably recurrent local orders of shared enacted practice. [. . .] If the individuals are to achieve mutual intelligibility in their endeavors they must produce practices that others recognize the meaning of. (Rawls 2002, 25)

So, if it is indeed a precondition for a social interaction to succeed, that the procedures used by the participants to define a social situation are mutually observable and recognizable, then they are observable and recognizable for the researcher as well. The methodological principles 'unique adequacy requirement' and 'becoming a member' are closely tied together, because learning the ethno-methods is an essential requirement for the researcher to be able to recognize and describe the social order in the terms of the field. At the same time, 'becoming a member' has an added resource, which is utilized by ethnomethodology: Whenever outsiders enter the field, its social order is disturbed, because they do not yet know the rules and practices necessary for maintaining the order. In such a case, the ethno-methods, which are self-evident for competent members, are explicated for the new member, so that the social order is restored. The same applies to the treatment of troublemakers, i.e., members who ignore the implicit rules and thereby threaten the social order. This in turn gives the established members cause for unfolding and clarifying the rules. Thus, entering the field (Lindner 1981; Wolff 2003) and the process of 'becoming a member' can be treated as important sources for data on the social order of the field. These results can be validated in additional naturally occurring breaching situations, in which the treatment of new members as well as troublemakers can also be studied.

9 A Tailor-Made Research Design for Cibervalle

When Marcus coined the widely quoted term *multi-sited ethnography* (1995), he surely was not thinking of Internet research in the first place. Studies on computer-mediated cultures and social life, however, are hardly comprehensible without *multi-siting* strategies. This holds particularly true for the case study of Cibervalle, which deals not only with global communication technologies, but also with transnational practices of migration. The research design discussed in the next section combines premises from both *multi-sited ethnography* and ethnomethodology. It connects ethnomethodological with ethnographic aspects of 'becoming a member' for two reasons: Firstly, to gain access to the unique structures of meaning and orderliness of the studied field and, secondly, to understand the meaning of the techno-social relations from the perspective of the members as embedded in their lifeworld context. In the following I focus on the methodological challenges that arose while trying to develop an ethnographic project. I do this by examining a cultural formation that has been constantly moving within a global landscape of seemingly infinite interconnections and overlapping contexts. As a matter of fact, both researchers and users have to find ways of accessing and moving within such a confusing landscape. I therefore depart from the perspective of a user and follow the steps and practices by which she has explored Cibervalle. By doing so, I illuminate the different dimensions and places of Cibervalle as well as how they are interrelated. Furthermore, following a user's pathway, I suggest a way of developing a uniquely adequate research design consisting of methods and choices that are geared to and reflect the idiosyncrasies of the studied culture. With reference to the questions raised earlier regarding the particularities of this field of research, I furthermore introduce a procedure freely adapted from Miller and Slater's (2000) suggestion: If you want to get to the Internet start from there but don't stop there.

LOGGING INTO THE FIELD: WHERE TO START
AND WHICH SUBJECTS TO FOLLOW?

> One day I was sitting in front of the computer being bored and thinking internet, internet, my boyfriend says there is everything for anyone, ndeeee†† imagine that! and me, what I am going to do? Very well then google: Paraguay, the first thing to appear was cibervalle.com. I entered, registered myself and read the commentaries, occasionally I wrote something [opinaba†] and one day I decided to open up a thread on my own . . . I got to know some [members] from Argentina, I went to an *encuentro* [Spanish for "meeting"] and so I had my first meeting with Paraguayans in Argentina. (Iwashita, Buenos Aires, Cibervalle Forum)

This statement was cited from the online-forum Cibervalle. A user who lives in Buenos Aires—she calls herself Iwashita for the purpose of my research report—explains how she came across Cibervalle. Iwashita's statement does not only exemplify a typical way of becoming a member of the Cibervalle community, it also alludes to the different dimensions of which this socio-electronic formation consists. Most of the users incorporate themselves into the socio-electronic network before they have any personal relations within the group. Like Iwashita they may come across the website by chance, while trying to look around the infinite depths of cyberspace, or while looking for particular information about Paraguay. Normally, *newbies* first follow the discussions conducted by others as *lurkers*, that is to say, invisible to the active members. They do this in order to become familiar with the topics and the implicit rules of participation before they register and present themselves to the community as active participants. The members of the community then welcome the new participants and invite them to the next meeting, which is usually organized in the respective localities of residence, like Buenos Aires, Asunción or New York. However, the local subgroups, which have been evolving over time, by no means supersede the virtual relationships. The members' activities on the local sites are rather reconstructed collectively on the globally accessible online-forum in order to share the event with the geographically distant counterparts. By these means, a global community has evolved over time, consisting of different local sites that are interrelated with a jointly created computer-mediated site of social life. Table 9.1 provides an overview of the different sites, their linkages and the problems of defining boundaries that arose due to the hybridization of public with private and virtual with physical grounded sites.

Potentially global in its geographical extent, this social formation is constituted by means of interrelating virtual-global dimensions with physically grounded parts of the actors' lifeworlds. More precisely, Cibervalle becomes a shared social space that spans between physically grounded localities in some Paraguayan cities, Buenos Aires, New York and other

Table 9.1   The Manifold Research Fields of Cibervalle

sites as techno-social conduits	the sites' positions and linkages within Cibervalle	constraints and devices of defining boundaries
online-discussion forum text- and image based, many-to-many-communication, asynchronous/synchronous, lurker, active participant	virtual site, the community's center stage	open to the public, potentially global in extent, real range can neither be controlled nor assumed
instant messaging client text-, image-, voice-, video-based, private talk between two or more buddies, synchronous/virtual presence (through status display) active user/present buddy	virtual sites, the community's back stages, deeply interrelated with the activities on the online-discussion forum and the respective physical grounded sites	potentially global in geographical terms, real range controllable and limited to technological constraints and social networks (buddy lists), which divides the global network into local (mostly time-zone dependent) subgroups
public local meetings (are previously announced and afterwards documented on the online discussion forum): face-to-face-communication/local meetings in *public* places (due to the subsequent documentation on the online discussion forum, even if the local event occurs in private)	physically grounded sites in the respective places of residence in Paraguayan cities, Buenos Aires, France, New York, Japan, etc.	basically open to the public, real range not controllable, but mostly limited in geographical terms to the users places of residence, new members are always expected
private local meetings (are announced only within the respective local subgroups via instant messenger, sms or phone): face-to-face-communication/local meetings in public, semi-public or private places	physically grounded sites in the respective places of residence in Paraguayan cities, Buenos Aires, France, New York, Japan, etc.	extent limited/ controllable to local subgroups/social networks in the respective places of residence, differ from the public and the private virtual sites

places all over the world. In addition, the community's social life relies on cross-media architecture, joining the WWW-based public site with more privately mediated forms of communication such as instant messaging and the use of (mobile) phones for copresence-based encounters.

OCCASION-GUIDED CONSTRUCTION OF THE FIELD

The construction of Cibervalle as a place to meet friends for the purpose of joining events and sharing everyday life is a practical achievement first and foremost of the *user*. The ethnographer's decisions in the process of field construction should therefore rely on the users' "first order constructions" (Schütz [1953] 1967) and reflect their networks, selections and choices. Due to the interrelation of private and public sites, the boundaries of this social formation, however, are by no means static or easy to define even for users themselves. Boyd suggests: "When we look to understand people's practices online, we must understand the context within which the individuals think they are operating. This imagined context provides one mechanism for bounding our research" (2009, 31). Following from my research experiences in Cibervalle, I propose a mode of bounding and sketching the field that I call 'occasion-guided.' This implies a search for a momentous occasion and a systematic way of observing all activities related to this incident.

The occasion on which the field construction of the present study is based is the supermarket fire already described in the *docu-fiction* "Tragedy in *Ycua Bolaños*." This accident occurred in Paraguay's capital, causing the death of nearly four hundred people. The local tragedy was transformed into a global issue when the world's media turned a spotlight onto Paraguay, and on the participants of Cibervalle. However, it was not only the number of victims that attracted the attention of the world towards a usually disregarded place on the globe, but also the news value inherent in the supermarket owner's decision to close the doors of the building in order to stop customers from leaving without paying for their goods. The tragedy of *Ycua Bolaños* caused one of the very rare (but in every moment possible) situations in which the public virtual site of Cibervalle became the focus of a globally distributed audience, consisting of individuals who came to know about the incident and searched the Internet for more information. The tragedy of *Ycua Bolaños*, in other words, demarcated the outermost extent of Cibervalle and enabled me to assume the outer limits of the field. Consequently, I decided to archive the log files of all activities that were taking place on the online discussion forum in the course of this event. For one week the *Ycua Bolaños* tragedy dominated the activities in Cibervalle, before the issue disappeared almost as suddenly as it had appeared. I thus constructed a field, by sketching a preliminary frame in which relevant dimensions and relationships, roles, practices and localities could be identified by way of analyzing a corpus of naturally occurring data (Silverman 2007, 201ff.) that had not been provoked by the researcher (e.g., data obtained by using research interviews) but existed independently of her intervention. The advantages of this approach are, firstly, that the temporal, local and social relevancies are determined by the field itself, which would otherwise have had to be defined arbitrarily by the researcher. Secondly, the archived log files could be analyzed as 'documents' of social life in Cibervalle's public virtual site. As a result of this first analytical step, I obtained a provisional 'map' of the field with relevant dimensions and places, social roles and positions, as well as practices and modalities of communication. This map then guided me on my way through the field, and led me not only to some of the users' places of residence in Paraguay, Buenos Aires, California and Germany, but also to the hidden virtual places of Cibervalle.

FIELD ACCESS BY STAGES

The process of 'becoming a member' can, as mentioned earlier, be an important data source, as the entrance to the field causes 'irritations' to which the field responds by explicating the social order. In the context of the Cibervalle research, the pluri-locality and multidimensionality of the field consistently led to access into new interaction fields, each of which maintained its own social order and all of which were interconnected via the global level of the online discussion forum. Becoming a member in such a complex field entailed that, during my research, I passed through different social positions and localities of the field so as to approach the social reality of the field from different perspectives. Like most of the users, I first adopted the position of the anonymous reader (lurker) of a public discussion forum, familiarizing myself with the topics and communicative practices, before I revealed myself to the group and registered as an active new member. As an active member I then became familiar with another dimension of the social context, the communicative practices that differ from those of the public level. As a next step, I set out into the local levels of the field. In other words, I met some of the local subgroups, which entailed not only new introductions to additional local peculiarities of the field, but also the chance to learn the linking practices of the local with the global computer-mediated dimensions of the field. Controlled self-observation and the systematic comparison of the 'entrance data' were important elements of *multi-siting*. They were helpful in accessing the different field dimensions and could be related to one another.

POSITIONAL CHANGES: FROM LURKER TO MEMBER

There was a certain risk in the decision to introduce myself as an active member of Cibervalle after a period of anonymous observation. It had to be carefully considered. Up to that point, my field access was limited, but open to anyone, so that I did not as yet have to ponder either my role in the field or my acceptance by it. On the other hand, I had already invested time and work in the research, which, I feared, might be threatened by a failure to enter the field or by a rejection by its members. Even after I was able to contact the administrator of the Cibervalle Forum without any problems (she turned out to be a supportive gatekeeper), it took me quite some time to finally make this decision. My hesitation was due to the question of how I should introduce myself and how much of my true motives I should reveal from the start, without 'frightening' the field.

According to Lindner (1981), the fear of entering the field is a manifestation of the researcher's meta-perspective, whereby he imagines the impression the field will have of him. This fear, Lindner maintains, points to the mutual observation, and thereby to the symmetry, of the relationship between the scientist and his subjects. As a result, he criticizes the instrumental usurpation of a social role in the field, which had been recommended in the literature, as a willful representation of symmetry in a situation that is thought and handled as essentially asymmetric. The instrumentalization of the social role, as well as of the interaction with the field, in order to gain access and information, "refers to the logic of empirical social science to conceive of the social role as a mere functional requisite of the scientific role" (ibid., 56; *own translation*). This 'not-till-then-logic,' according to Lindner, prevents researchers from getting involved with the situational context they seek to understand. Instead, he recommends that the primary assessments of the researcher should be kept as data, because they reflect social and cultural experiences of the studied group.

Table 9.2 Welcoming Tópico "Mafalda"

Hola soy nueva	*Hello, I'm new*
Hola gente buena de cibervalle. Hace rato que suelo leer sus charlas y ahora me gustaria participar. Soy Alemana con parientes paraguayos. Me dedico a las ciencias sociales, en particular me interesa el tema de migraciones. La verdad he aprendido mucho de todos ustedes, ya que en este foro los paraguayos viviendo en todo el mundo intercambian sus experiencias e ideas. Veo que gracias al internet la distancia ya no impide sentirse unidos. Espero compartir la buena onda† que son!	Hello, dear Cibervalle folks, I've been reading your discussions for quite some time now and would like to take part. I am German with relatives in Paraguay. I am studying social sciences, particularly interested in migration studies. To be honest, I've learnt quite a lot from you already because here in the Forum Paraguayans, who live scattered all over the globe, share their experiences and ideas. I realize that thanks to the Internet, distance cannot prevent people from feeling united. I hope I can share the buena onda† with you!
Nick: mafalda	**Nick: mafalda**
E-mail: m-_f-ld-_—@*mail.com	E-mail: m-_f-ld-_—@*mail.com
IP: 129.70.100.*	**IP:** 129.70.100.*
Respuestas: 70	Answers: 70
Última respuesta: 14/09/2004	Last answer: 14/09/2004

I told the administrator of the Forum about my considerations and asked her advice. She told me to simply present myself as a new member and then open up Tópicos, in which I could ask all questions relevant for my research without revealing myself as a scientist. Her argument was that many members asked questions in the Tópicos without conducting a study. Moreover, the Forum was open to the public and I could theoretically do what I liked with whatever I read. The gatekeeper thus turned out to be a helpful 'coresearcher.'[8] With her knowledge of the field's social order, she assisted me in the process of finding a role and position familiar to the field, while simultaneously following my research interests. I chose to present myself in a way that was common in the Forum: I opened my first Tópico with a cordial greeting to the whole community, outed myself as a lurker and clarified my connection with Paraguay. Finally, I mentioned my social scientific interest in the Forum discussions without directly referring to the fact that the Forum was part of my research field (see Table 9.2).

My first Tópico soon filled up with numerous answers. I was greeted effusively and introduced to Cibervalle's social order by the older members. As a member I tried to do everything as the other members did. I opened up my own Tópicos, read those of other members and contributed to ongoing discussions. I used the same instant messaging client as the others and talked to individual Cibervallers about this and that and primarily about the current goings-on in the Cibervalle Forum. I announced my visit to Buenos Aires and Paraguay, took part in local meetings to which I was invited and commented on photos of these meetings that were subsequently posted in the Forum.

My written contributions, as well as the communication of my participation in the local meetings, supplied information about me to members with whom I had not interacted. My lively participation in the local meetings of different groups in Paraguay and Argentina drastically and within a very short period increased the degree of my 'fame' in the global forum. This in turn increased my trustworthiness and thereby facilitated my access to individual users, even if they did not know me personally. At a bus station in Paraguay a strange man approached me and asked: "Are you Mafalda?" This man, who lived in Texas, was on his way to visit the remaining members of his family in Paraguay. He had recognized me from photographs in Cibervalle of local meetings that I had attended. He regularly followed the activities in the Forum, but rarely participated actively and never attended local meetings, so there were no photos of him from which I could have recognized his face. He was a complete stranger to me, yet he knew quite a few things about me.

Lindner recommends the reciprocity of the observing situation in the field as the starting point for reflecting social relations. He concludes postulating mutual and equal communication as the (ethical) norm in field research. However, the observing situation proves to be much more complex in a field such as the present one than in a physically grounded field, wherein the observation situation is determined by the copresence of researcher and protagonist. In a publicly accessible, computer-mediated communication space, reciprocity does not necessarily mean mutual observation. Rather, the reciprocity of an observing situation applies to the mutuality of one-sided observation situations. In other words, the researcher can observe her field without being noticed by the participants, in a like manner as they can observe her without being noticed by her.

FOLLOW THE PEOPLE

As with many other contemporary ethnographers who have read Marcus's considerations on *multi-siting*, I moved around a lot, following the people to explore their translocal landscapes. The fact that I met some people multiple times in different places in and outside of Paraguay, one of them even in a place near my hometown in Germany, also reflects the high degree of mobility of the participants. That is not to say that I only followed the people in the literal sense during their travels between sites of being and sites of belonging. I also traipsed behind them through everyday life, and they in turn taught me how to become a member of Cibervalle. Hence, the decisions I made during the research process were not only pragmatic

Table 9.3 Tópico "Definir lo Virtual"

les cuento algo que me parece muy curioso y que explica el por qué se me escaparon los ultimos posteos en mis tópicos y los dejé un poco abandonados. Lo que pasa es que cuando viajé a Paraguay casí ya no tenia acceso a la internet y por lo tanto no tenía forma de participar mucho en cibervalle. Es decir, estando fisicamente en el centro de la comunidad cibervallera me sentí al mismo tiempo desconectada, fuera de la misma. Veo que lo mismo pasa a muchos integrantes: Cuando van a Paraguay para pasar las vacaciones con sus familias desaparecen del foro y no vuelven antes de haberse alejado del contexto fisico que forma la base comun de la comunidad. Curioso, no?	I'll tell you something that seems peculiar to me and, at the same time explains why I missed the last posts in my Tópicos. While I traveled to Paraguay, I had almost no access to the Internet and so I had little opportunity to participate in Cibervalle. That is to say, when I was physically in the center of the Cibervalle community, I felt disconnected and outside of it. I have been observing the same thing happening to other members: When they spend holidays with their families in Paraguay, they disappear from the forum and won't come back before leaving the community's physical center stage. Isn't this curious?
mafalda	mafalda
Cantidad de posteos: 240	Number of posts: 240
IP: 200.69.45.*	IP: 200.69.45.*
24/02/2005	24/02/2005

decisions, but they also reflected main orientations and practices of the field: I first approached the public site of the field as a *lurker*. After some time, I presented myself as a new member and was welcomed by the other members. I participated actively in the online discussions. I maintained an instant messaging client for private conversations. I announced my travels to Buenos Aires and Paraguay on the online-forum and accepted invitations to local meetings. I commuted between Buenos Aires and several physical places in Paraguay. To my surprise, I nearly lost contact with the virtual sites of Cibervalle when I was geographically at its center, and I shared these impressions with the global community (see Table 9.3).

FOLLOW THE TECHNOLOGY

The social reality examined in this study is shaped not only by the human participants, but also by the media in use. The integration of the Internet in participants' everyday lives is a dynamic process of mutual adaptation of the technology and social practices. However, the appropriation of new technologies is always conducted on the basis of the available cultural meaning systems, and the technologies are, if possible, integrated into the familiar social practices of the participants (cf. Prasad 1997). Furthermore, the embedding of the Internet into everyday practices leads to a differentiation into a multitude of technologies, which are themselves connected to older media formats and practices (Klemm and Graner 2000). Thus, a kind of hybridization of technological artifacts and social practices can be assumed, which leads to further differentiations of communication forms. In order to gain insight into the specific forms of technology domestications (ibid.) and the resulting techno-social practices, I reconstructed the technological changes made on the main communication formats 'online discussion forum' and 'instant messaging client' and analyzed them in relation to the social practices of usage. Format changes on the Cibervalle Forum and the continuous improvement of the IM client used in Cibervalle are regarded as solutions to communicative problems, which in turn point towards these underlying problems.

In conclusion, the methodological concept of this study is based on methods of *multi-siting* and self-observation during the process of 'becoming a member.' They were developed specifically for this study. A distinctive feature of the field, namely, its pluri-locality, requires that both the participants in the field as well as the researcher are ready to be very mobile: During my six months field trip I slept in thirteen different places, traveled thousands of kilometers and made the acquaintance of more than one hundred people. More than half of them gave me relatively close insights into their lives, shared their personal history with me and allowed me to accompany them during their daily routines. As a new member of Cibervalle I was invited to the local meetings, and despite my being a stranger, the Cibervallers in Buenos Aires, Paraguay and California offered me their kind help and hospitality. Cibervalle's characteristic cultural feature, the cordiality and openness with which strangers are welcomed to the community, not only made my field research period much easier; it also opened up optimal field access as well as profound insights into biographies and ways of living.

Another unique characteristic of those dimensions of the field that are based on computer-mediated communication lies in the ability to itself generate data. Apart from the data such as observation records and memos that the researcher generated by means of reconstructive methods, the present research is based primarily on a number of 'undesigned data.' These are mainly log files of the Tópico from the Cibervalle Forum and of IM conversations and sound recordings of conversations with members, but also secondary data, like newspaper articles, reports and studies on the general situation of Paraguay, as well as studies on the situation of Paraguayan migrants in Argentina.

SAD NEWS ABOUT MAFALDA—A MUTUALLY SUPPORTIVE COMMUNITY NEEDS EMERGENCY CASES

Towards the end of my field trip, about three weeks before I had to travel back to Germany, an important part of my data collection was stolen in Buenos Aires: log files of IM conversations and of Tópicos from the local meetings I took part in, together with my passport, credit card and cash. My attempts to get at least the data back were unsuccessful. I told one of the members of the Buenos Aires group about this, whereupon he opened a Tópico in the Forum, announcing the "sad news about Mafalda." The Tópico soon filled up with answers by members from all over the world, expressing their compassion and offering help. With this markedly unfortunate event for my research, I presented the Cibervalle community an emergency case, by which they could again reproduce themselves as a mutually supportive community. It was only then that I realized how important emergencies are for the maintenance of the Cibervalle community. Surprisingly, there was a positive effect on my research: I made contact with members I did not yet know or had known only briefly. They opened up to me and gave me insights into their private as well as everyday lives. Thus, the data loss brought a gain of additional data and some deeper insights.

MIGRATION WITHIN CYBERSPACE—WHEN THE FIELD DROPS OUT BEFORE THE RESEARCHER DOES

My field research did not end with my return to Germany. Firstly, because, while being in Paraguay, I made the acquaintance of Cibervalle members who live quite near to my town in Germany. Secondly, the computer-mediated part of the field was in a sense always near. I only had to open the relevant site in the WWW or log into the IM client to immediately do some additional field research from my desk. The accessibility of my field was very helpful for data analysis, for example, when language comprehension problems arose due to my poor knowledge of Jopará†. Also, it was always possible to clear up uncertainties with regard to the analytical results by means of focused additional field research. Thus, it was not only possible to consolidate the structural patterns of communication in the Cibervalle Forum by probing additional log files of similar Tópicos, but I could also intensify my access to the perspectives of the participants in IM conversations. On the other hand, easy access to the field can lead to an endless extension of the research period with the danger of generating a mass of data that becomes too large to cope with. It became clear that if I wanted to gain the necessary analytical distance from my field, I had to take a timely leave from my role as member and devote myself solely to analyzing the data.

In due course, coincidence came to my rescue. At the same time as I began to get bored in my field, because the same themes, practices, conflicts, etc., came up over and over again, so that nothing new was left to observe, the format of the Forum was thoroughly transformed. The Forum could not be used at all for a few days, and all users had to register anew. Many lost their nicknames due to technical problems in this registration process. The fact that the administration had not announced these changes led to so much discontent among Cibervallers that quite a large group migrated to a new forum. I took the opportunity to end my own membership in Cibervalle. I did this reluctantly, as the internal differentiation process appeared extremely interesting and worthy of observation—but this may be the starting point for a subsequent research project.

Part C

Social Landscapes of Cibervalle

Given global linkages, it became apparent in the previous part that, methodologically, ethnography should—instead of being fixated on physical locations—reflect the actors' current mobility- and media-related practices. The preceding discussion of the field concept served to explicate the tight link between the conception of space and the societal model of the nation-state. Recently, globalization and globalization research have led to a general revision of the concept of space in the social sciences, a concept changed from an absolute, container-like entity to a relational one. "This interpretation is less concerned with the concrete physicality of space but rather with the potential for order accomplishment which accrues from the reference to space" (Ahrens 2001, 200; *own translation*). In other words, instead of taking physical space for granted, the relational approach emphasizes the 'constructedness' of space as well as its dependence on particular contexts. Spatial thinking thus turns into an opportunity to organize the world.

It is hard for ethnography to do without descriptions of locations or, more precisely, descriptions of context, because the protagonists' practices are invariably situated and can only be sensibly interpreted within their particular context. Therefore, the following pages will present an ethnographic sketch of Cibervalle's social landscapes as well as the social practices that shape these landscapes. The central questions are, how are such spaces constructed, dissolved, delimited or interconnected with each other by, firstly, migration and, secondly, media usage in migration? The presentation and analysis of a Paraguayan migration biography opens this part. However, the ethnographic description of Paraguay that follows does not resemble the usual applied geographical information. Rather, Cibervalle's shared geographic reference will be examined in terms of how nation-state building has been influenced by global interdependence and boundary demarcation processes. Subsequently, the ethnographic focus turns to the mutually shared social space of Cibervalle. In this connection, the different lifeworlds of Cibervalle's inhabitants will be explored in order to approach the different meanings of Cibervalle from the perspective of the participants. This part of the study will describe the social formation of Cibervalle in its individual dimensions and, finally, examine the essential modes of its reproduction.

10 Paraguay
A (Hi)Story of Migration

PAULA AND JIMENA[1]

Paula was born in a small town in Paraguay. She has eight siblings, and has never met her father. Paula's mother was not able to look after all of her children, so Paula grew up in the same town, but with the family of an uncle. When Paula was fourteen, her aunt and the other children immigrated to the US. The aunt wanted to take Paula with her as well, but Paula's mother refused. Paula's uncle also found it hard to let all of his children go. But he eventually agreed, because he thought their future prospects were better in the US. After finishing high school, Paula moved to the capital Asunción and started her university studies while sharing a flat with other students. One day, with only her aunt's telephone number in her suitcase, Paula left for Buenos Aires. She soon found a job looking after the household and children of a working couple. Eventually, Paula got to know her husband-to-be, who had also emigrated from Paraguay. The couple lived in Buenos Aires for ten years, during which time Paula gave birth to four children while continuing to work throughout as a domestic helper. In the course of the Argentinean economic crisis Paula and her family moved back to her hometown in Paraguay. Soon after, Paula attempted to immigrate to Spain. She borrowed money and tried to enter with a tourist visa. However, she was held at the airport and sent back to Paraguay.

When I met Paula, she worked with the same family in Buenos Aires that had employed her before and now provided a room for her. Three times a week Paula telephoned with her children, who were then being looked after by her mother in Paraguay. When Paula had finally paid back all the debts from her failed attempt to enter Spain, she returned to Paraguay to live with her children. When I visited her after her return, Paula had just opened a stall with her sister Jimena on the local textile market. Both of them sold *ropa Americana* (Spanish for 'American clothes'), deriving from European and/or US-American used clothing collections. As the importation of 'ropa Americana' is illegal in Paraguay, Paula and Jimena regularly traveled to wholesalers in Bolivia and Brazil to buy new merchandise. Meanwhile, Paula's husband had begun to invest some of Paula's proceeds in agriculture: He was growing sesame on a small plot thirty kilometers outside of town, planning to sell his crops in Brazil, where he hoped to get a price ten times higher than the local price. Because they could finance the seed themselves, Paula and her husband would not be tied to a seed merchant, so they could decide who they would sell to. They were also planning to build a small house so that the family would no longer have to live in Paula's mother's house, which was already much too small for them. Paula was, however, having qualms about the isolated position of this plot. She said there was no doctor nearby and the children would have to travel some distance to school. There was no tap water, no electricity as yet and her mobile phone only received a signal if she climbed a nearby hill.

During my visit, Paula and Jimena told me that they wanted to dare another attempt at entering Spain. This time they planned to draw on the help of an informal agency that would not only finance their travel costs in advance, but would also take care of all of the organization as well as assist the two women in procuring the necessary papers. Jimena was setting her hopes on Spain because she wanted to finance the vocational training of her twelve-year-old daughter. As she had only this one child, she also felt responsible for her nieces and nephews (in fact, she was already helping them financially). Jimena told me that her business on the local textile market was tedious, tiring and far from being profitable enough. She longed for a little shop of her own, but said she would never earn enough money on the market for such a big investment. "You can work as hard as you possibly can," she said "it's always just enough to keep you going, but there's never enough left to invest in the future." Jimena had collected some information about the living and working conditions in Spain and had heard that as a private nanny she would earn about five hundred euro; however, accommodation would be three hundred euro. All in all, there would not be much money left over for other essentials, not for her in Spain or for the family back home. To this theme, Jimena told me about two female friends who had gone to Spain nine months ago and still had not earned a penny for themselves. In fact, they were still paying their debts to the agency. On the other hand, she said that many people from Asunción had gone to Spain and had built a house after quite a short time: "They work or they prostitute themselves and thereby achieve some progress for themselves and their families."

Roughly one year after my field period, I met Paula online via the instant messaging client. She told me that Jimena was already working in Spain and that she had found a job for her as a maid for a Spanish family with *cama adentro* (Spanish for 'bed inside,' i.e., a place to work and live). So Paula had once again left her children in the care of her mother and traveled to Madrid. But she said she had been treated badly there. She had to work fourteen hours per day and was on call around the clock. She never had a day off and had earned very little. A few months later she found a job with another family in the same small town near Madrid where Jimena lived. Paula moved in with her sister and was earning more, and the *patrones* (Spanish for 'bosses' or 'heads of household') were treating her relatively well. Both sisters use an Internet café to communicate regularly with their family members. They arrange to meet for video calls† at certain times. Paula said that there are Internet cafés— both in Paula's hometown as well as in their present place of residence—that have computers with a video function, so she could easily communicate, especially with her small children, who at the time had not yet learned how to read or write. Jimena and Paula were then planning for Jimena's twelve-year-old daughter to come to Spain as well.

Transnational migration research (cf. Basch, Glick-Schiller and Szanton Blanc 1994; Smith and Guarnizo 1998; Vertovec 1999) draws a complex and contradictory picture of migration, which is quite similar to the case

I described in the preceding. According to this approach, transnational migration relations and practices create social structures that transcend physical boundaries in the family sphere as well as in economic, political, health and symbolic respects. The social structure, the transnational social space (Pries 1998) or the transnational social field (Glick-Schiller 2003) within which 'transmigrants' (Basch, Glick-Schiller and Szanton Blanc 1994) organize their lives, stretch at least from the migrating person's present place of residence to his or her place of belonging (the place to which this person feels permanently attached). This kind of migration, this mobile way of life, in which the protagonists constantly orient themselves in and between at least two reference systems (which are framed as nation-states), produces paradox dynamics in respect to their socio-structural positioning (cf. Georg 2000). Whereas migration often entails a loss of status for the migrating person in the country of destination, it can improve the regard for her or his family in the place of origin if, for example, he or she contributes financially to support the local community (cf. Smith 1998).

Paula and Jimena are members of a kinship network, in which migration has structured the social organization and shaped the family members' way of relating to each other for several generations. The aunt that Paula grew up with had migrated to the US to improve the prospects of her sons, but also to support her family in Paraguay. Paula's cousins maintain close relations with their families as well as the local community from which they originated. They often spend their holidays there and contribute financially to the development of the community. Whenever she is in Buenos Aires, Paula also supports her relatives back in Paraguay. Thus, her lifeworld is structured transnationally and transculturally. She lives simultaneously not only in two countries, but also in two very different milieus—the rural and the metropolitan. Transnational practices are part of her family's everyday life—they primarily serve economic gains: Paula sells her labor power first in Buenos Aires, then later in Spain, simply because she can earn more there. Her husband grows sesame for sale in Brazil, where the price is higher. As a nanny in Spain, Paula can easily link up with her work and living experiences in Buenos Aires. For Paula and Jimena, the fruits of their constant effort materialize in the regular money transfers to their family in Paraguay, securing everyone's livelihood and providing adequate health care and better schooling for the children.

The sisters had planned their journey to Spain on the basis of detailed information. Thus, they had realistic expectations of life in faraway Europe. They had drawn their information both from the mass media that regularly report on the situation of Paraguayans in Spain and from neighbors, friends and relatives who themselves had emigrated to Spain. The Paraguayan mass media and the state administration tend to emphasize the risks inherent in undocumented migration. Both institutions warn people not to unconditionally believe the success stories, which appear to materialize in a neighboring family's new house or car. Instead, these reports highlight the precarious living conditions of Paraguayans in Spain and the risks inherent to the financial dependence on an agency. Young women are warned in particular about the possibility of compulsory prostitution.

> There is no work here, so the people have no choice but to leave the country. But many are conned and the women end up in prostitution. [. . .] The cost of living is very high there, so they haven't enough income—in the end they find they are in the same situation as they were here. (Employee, town hall registry office, Asunción, field diary, face-to-face conversation)

This statement by an employee of the Asunción registry office in charge of issuing passports reflects an opinion of current migration practices often found in public discourse in the media. This interpretation does not, however, agree with the view of the people I met during my field research. Neither Paula nor her sister has been deterred by failed entry attempts, nor have many other women from Paraguay been put off migration by the danger that they might end up as prostitutes in Spain.

In the kitchen of the Cibervaller Esther her household helper María tells me, "I want to go to Spain and work there. We are poor, my father is sick and there's no work here" (María, Ciudad del Este, field diary, face-to-face conversation). One of her friends has just gone there a month ago. María says she is doing well, working four days a week, earning two hundred euros. She knows a woman who told her that she had been working in a brothel in Spain: "I don't know if this is true but anyway, she came back here and built a very pretty villa" (ibid.). When I ask María how she is going to finance the journey to Spain, she says, "If you have relatives there, they send the money so you can go" (ibid.). She is aware of the risks, and she knows someone who was sent back at the airport. She says she is a little bit afraid of ending up in prostitution, but she is going to try anyway, because there is no other prospect for her and her family.

The coverage in the mass media as well as the mediated communication between relatives both here and there contribute to Paraguayans' detailed knowledge about living conditions in migration. On the basis of this knowledge, they are able to gauge the risks and chances in the receiving country. They know that despite their valid visas, they risk being sent back home or being caught as 'illegals' and deported to Paraguay after their limited residence permits have expired. In addition, they know that if migrants cannot find a place to sleep in the household or on the building site where they work in Madrid or other Spanish tourist centers, they might share an apartment with up to sixteen people. In addition, it is neither a secret nor necessarily discussed as a moral problem in Paraguay that the migrating men have to work mostly as seasonal laborers in agriculture or do dangerous jobs in the building trade for very little money, whereas the majority of women are engaged as sex workers or household helpers. What really counts and what is really important for the moral integrity of migrants is the responsibility taken towards the family members back in Paraguay, which is manifested in the regularity and full amount of the *remesas* (Spanish for 'remittances,' as the regular money transfers from migrants are called).

IMMIGRATION, EMIGRATION OR TRANSMIGRATION? A MATTER OF PERSPECTIVE

The complexity of migration biographies is apparent in the stories of Paula and Jimena. It is primarily a question of the perspective and methodology of a piece of research, whether or not protagonists' own meaning horizons come into focus, and whether or not their manifold lifeworld aspects as well as their transgenerational and transnational linkages are discerned. Transnational migration research has made a major contribution towards questioning the analytical frame of classical migration research. Glick-Schiller (2003) emphasizes the central importance of ethnography in this connection. She argues that ethnography's intrinsic value lies in its heuristic use of theoretical concepts and its very own ability to get involved in the perspective of the protagonists, to be guided by their actual conduct and, finally, to revise its theoretical presuppositions according to experiences made in the field.

Now, systems theory has a concept of society that provides an adequate frame for the analysis of migration phenomena. Luhmann defines society as "the most encompassing social system of all acts which are mutually reachable through communication" (1997, 11, quoted in Wobbe 2000; *own translation*). Due to the increase of global communication and transnational linkages, there are no longer several societies that coexist next to each other and in isolation from each other. Rather, systems theory assumes that there is one single global social system that encompasses all communications. All social processes take place within one 'world society.' Stichweh discusses migration processes in relation to the concept of world society and he arrives at surprising results. According to the author, migration is a typical cause for social exclusion, "because due to their relatively short period of residence in a new place, migrants cannot achieve the plural embeddedness in different contexts that would enable them to make up for instances of exclusion" (2005, 9; *own translation*). Apart from the disputable position that exclusion and social discrimination of migrants would intrinsically lessen with the passing of time, the question remains as to what kind of analytical context is implied by this approach. The author appears to tailor the question of the inclusion and exclusion mechanisms of migration wholly to the place of migrants' residence. This is exactly the assimilation paradigm of classical migration research. In light of the preceding delineation of Paula's and Jimena's biographies, and also considering how Stichweh conceives society as world society, a limited perspective such as this one reveals the shortcomings of research that is exclusively guided by theory.

The benefits of migration practices, which take place in risky circumstances such as Paula and Jimena faced, and the way in which these practices make sense to them, cannot be comprehended from the perspective of migration research, which is positioned in the nation-state context of the receiving countries and bound to the assimilation paradigm. By the same token, such migration practices cannot be understood from the perspective of the lifeworld experiences of Paraguayan journalists, administrators or social scientists, who generally belong to the (upper-)middle class. From such a perspective one tends to see exploited people who have lost their status and security, who are subjected to harassment and the arbitrary whims of an unregulated system where they work for a pittance and who retreat into ethnically structured networks instead of integrating themselves in the national context of their new place of residence.

From the perspective of the protagonists themselves, the same situation looks quite different. Their living and working situation has already been precarious and socioeconomically insecure before they migrated (cf. Lutz 2003). Quite possibly, they have been doing the same kind of work, but for no or considerably less money. Even if their personal situation initially deteriorates due to migration, they can contribute to the improvement of their families' current situation by securing their livelihood. In addition, they can invest in their own future by saving money. Thus, they will be in a position to realize a business plan on their return or to finance the education of their children or siblings, and thus open up future perspectives for them. In other words, the reasoning of migration that makes sense for the protagonists becomes apparent not so much by each migrant's actual individual living situation, but by his or her usefulness for the improvement either of the current situation of the family or of each migrant's own future prospects in his or her country of origin. These are hardly ever decisions based on individual wishes or plans. Rather, the decision to migrate is mostly a collective one, and it is also arranged collectively. The motive is to lessen the economic risks of the family or the household.[2] That is to say, life in migration makes sense for the protagonists either because it is part of a collectively lived present or in view of the individual and collective future in the country of belonging/origin, or possibly for both reasons.

If we now view the results of ethnographic research in a global analytical frame, migration can be understood as a chance to achieve inclusion, which is motivated by both sides of global inequalities: On the one hand, it is an attempt to avoid regional exclusion, manifested in rising social risks, like violence, poverty and habitat destruction.[3] On the other hand, the protagonists turn the global prosperity gap into an advantage by selling their labor power in a place where the prosperity level is significantly higher than in their family's place of residence. They thereby improve the chances for their families to gain access to education, health care and other social resources, all of which in turn facilitate inclusion.

NATIONAL, TRANSNATIONAL OR SOCIAL?
MIGRANTS DOING GEOGRAPHY

The contribution of transnational migration research is therefore well founded in the empirical procedure of adapting the analytical frame to the protagonists' perspective. Thus, this approach is able to discover phenomena to which classical migration research—apart from the exceptions mentioned in Part A—has so far turned a blind eye. Its strength lies "primarily in its empirical ability to irritate and to leave well-trodden paths in the social sciences" (Bommes 2002, 92; *own translation*). However, the continuing conceptual discussion within transnationalism research[4] reveals how difficult it is for the social sciences to progress from the revelation of the inadequacy of their terminology to the development of alternative basic concepts. The adjective *transnational* yet again places the nation-state in the epicenter. The prominence of the notion of space in transnationalism research leads Bommes to conclude that this approach lacks an alternative concept of society. But in the term *transnational space*, which subsumes all kinds of phenomena of permanent transboundary structuring, "the meaning of space becomes metaphorical." According to Bommes, "it supersedes the rejected concept of society without being able to replace it theoretically" (2002, 95; *own translation*).

As in the methodological discussion of the field concept in ethnography, we again encounter the problem of the concept of space. As we have seen, the society concept tinged with the nation-state is based on the equation of social space and space in the sense of expanse or physical area. In this model, space is conceived as a kind of container and society is situated within state-regulated boundaries. Transnationalism's assumption, however, is that social space detaches itself from physically grounded space in the course of globalization processes (Bommes 2002). Looking at the decoupling hypothesis from the perspective of world society theory, exactly the same methodological nationalism that transnationalism research had intended to overcome bleeds through. The idea of decoupling actually implies the assumption that the disengagement of social structures from national states originally resulted from globalization and notably transnational migration as well. Globalization is then understood as a process of transgressing boundaries, so the argumentation in a sense "runs 'inside out,' i.e., local relations [or national ones; *note H.G.*] are taken as the baseline" (Greve and Heintz 2005, 110; *own translation*). So, the assumption is that an increasing number of migration movements worldwide and the progressive development of global transport and communication technologies as much as economic expansion had originally caused the successive detachment of social processes from territorial boundaries as well as nation-state sovereignty. In addition, it is then implied that the world before globalization consisted of nation-states that regulated their internal social processes independently. World society approaches, however, and especially systems theory, argue in exactly the opposite direction. According to Greve and Heintz, "the emergence of a global system of social organization does not result from nation-states, but, on the contrary, these are conceived as the product of world society" (2005, 108; *own translation*). The functional differentiation of the world political system into territorially demarcated nation-states is accordingly a *secondary* differentiation.

Paraguay presents a good case for disproving the decoupling thesis of transnationalism research. Also, this country demonstrates that the process of nation-state building in South America cannot be adequately explained in terms of functional differentiation. From the Spanish and Portuguese colonization to the aborted attempt at decolonization during the foundation of the nation-state and the subsequent war of the *Triple Allianza*, the history of Paraguay up to the present day can be described as a complex process of global linkages, translocal and transnational relations as well as internal socio-spatial separation. Even if it is constructed as a deviation from the nation-state logic, migration is of utmost importance for both the formation and the maintenance of the nation-state of Paraguay, as we shall see in the following section. A short presentation of Paraguay's history will clarify why neither a homogenous national culture nor a state authority able to guarantee equal rights to all citizens developed after the first national regime, following the Declaration of Independence in 1811. The geographical space named Paraguay is compartmentalized into territories that are controlled, farmed, administered and/or populated by different groups or individuals. This short excursion into the history of Paraguay commences at the time of the European *Conquista* of the South American continent. The discussion of the connection between migration and the constitution of social spaces and their embeddedness in a historical approach here serve to capture and classify Paraguay's social reality, without resorting to the Eurocentric conception of a social order based on the ideal type of the nation-state.

THE FORMATION OF A GEOPOLITICAL SPACE IN WORLD SOCIETY NAMED PARAGUAY

Asunción, Paraguay's present capital, situated in the region of *La Plata*, was founded in 1537. It was the first and most important settlement of Spanish conquistadors, and it was considered to be the "center of the conquest and the cradle of the civilization of the Plata" (González de Bosio 2000, 183; *own translation*). The relationship between the European usurpers and the original inhabitants of the Asunción area, the *Guaraní*, was structured by means of the *Encomienda*,[5] which allowed the Spanish settlers to commit the natives to forced labor.

Towards the end of the sixteenth century, the Jesuits, on commission of the Spanish royalty, began with the Christianization of the *Guaraní*.

So-called *reducciones* were founded, settlements where members of the Jesuit order lived together with members of the autochthonous people. Contrary to the settlers, the Jesuits had no chief economic interest in the *Guaraní*. Rather, they were set on only one aim: converting the local population over to the Christian faith. The settlements were based on agriculture, the yield of which not only made their inhabitants self-sufficient, but also enabled them to trade their agricultural products. In particular, the cultivation of and trade with *Yerba Mate* and the introduction of a Christian social system based on agrarian collectivism and communal property enabled them to gain a certain measure of wealth and independence from the Spanish crown. Between 1610 and 1767 this social system, which due to its emancipation from the colonial power was called the *Jesuit State*, grew to a total of thirty settlements. These protected more than one hundred thousand *Guaraní* from attacks by European settlers.[6]

Life with the Jesuits nonetheless drastically changed the lifestyles and religious beliefs of the *Guaraní*. They were supposed to be converted to Christianity, but without having to adopt the Spanish language or European customs. The Jesuit *padres* initially adapted themselves to the local reality and blended the *Guaraní*'s former educational and other customs with Christian values and practices. Evangelization was carried out entirely in the local language.[7] Even today most sermons in rural churches are held in *Guaraní*. According to Lustig (1995), the development of *Guaraní* into a written language in the Jesuit *reducciones* played a particularly important role in the survival of this indigenous language during colonization. Today it still survives as a colloquial language in everyday life. Its preservation was written into the constitution in 1992. In 2010 the Paraguayan Congress finally approved the 'Law of Languages,' which obliges public institutions to use *Guaraní* as the second official language next to Spanish, as stated in the constitution.

The province of Paraguay played a key role in the demarcation of the "military boundary between the two colonial powers of the Iberian Peninsula" (González de Bosio 2000, 190; *own translation*) due to its geographic position between the regions claimed by the rivals Portugal and Spain, with what later became Brazil on the one side and Argentina on the other. According to the author, this geopolitical position became rather fateful for Paraguay during the course of the Hispano-American independence of the Spanish crown, as the newly founded nation-states continued to stake their territorial claims with military means. Paraguay was thus drawn into two fatal wars.

After the Declaration of Independence in 1811, the first Paraguayan political leadership under the dictatorial rule of *José Gaspar Rodríguez de Francias* followed a radical path of decolonization between 1813 and 1840. In order to free the country from colonial dependence and to destroy the power of the European elite, former colonialists as well as rulers aligned with the Church were deposed and their assets were confiscated.

Poor indigenous people profited from these sanctions insofar as they were given access to sufficient tracts of land and livestock for self-sufficiency. Mandatory demographic measures were instituted to prevent migration. Another measure encouraged the mixing of native populations with those of Spanish origin. International trade relations were prohibited, except the state-controlled trade of a few commodities with neighboring countries. At the same time, private agricultural production, which had hitherto been monoculture, was diversified and put under state control. Furthermore, shipbuilding and textile production were encouraged. Due to these radical state socialist measures of redistribution and political centralization, Paraguay experienced an enormous boom within three years. After the death of *Francias*, this economic upturn was accelerated by his two successors: They opened the borders and further strengthened trade relations, especially with neighboring countries. Thus, Paraguay became one of the most economically successful and powerful states in Latin America (cf. Hanratty and Meditz [1988] 2005).

The so-called *Triple Allianza War* (1865–70) between Argentina, Brazil and Uruguay[8] brought the prosperity phase of the young Paraguayan state to a sudden end. The reasons behind the war and the question of who was to blame are still a matter of much controversy. Interpretations vary according to the local and/or ideological perspective of the respective interpreter.[9] A look at Paraguay's geopolitical position and function in relation to the European territorial and representational appropriation of the world during the colonization process reveals that the *Triple Allianza War* was a seminal historical event that exerted considerable influence on further global developments. Paraguay was yet again turned into the arena for negotiating the territorial claims of the former Spanish and Portuguese colonies. The destruction of the Paraguayan development model and the alignment of the political and economic structures to those of the postcolonial neighboring countries were clearly advantageous for Europe and the elites of Brazil and Argentina for the following reason: They were operating within a global economic system in the making. In the course of the 'Discovery of America,' this system had expanded far beyond European borders and was now continuing to open up sources of raw materials as well as markets. Vitally important for this system was the maintenance of the economic dependence and political subordination of the former colonies.

It is indisputable that Paraguay not only lost between 60 and 80 percent[10] of its inhabitants and had to cede half of its territory to Argentina and Brazil, but that it was also faced with the complete (and lasting) destruction of its socially balanced development model, which was based on the principle of self-sufficiency. As the winners of the war, the neighboring states Argentina and Brazil exerted their powerful influence on the politics of reconstruction of the Paraguayan state. This powerful influence is reflected in the structure of party politics up to the present day. The major political party, which reigned over postwar Paraguay without interruption until 1904 and is still the most important single party[11]—the *Asociacíon Nacional Republicana-Partido Colorado (Colorados)*—arose from a group of political activists who had been supported by the Brazilian occupiers. Argentina built a political counterpart with members of a group of former exiles. Paraguay's most important opposition party arose from this group—the *Partido Liberal Radical Autentico (Liberales)* (cf. Hanratty and Meditz [1988] 2005).

On the basis of the thesis that the *Triple Allianza War* was aimed at destroying Paraguay's development model, the first political measures by the *Colorados* government aimed at economic reconstruction can be understood as a kind of neo-colonization. The free sale of government land can thus not be interpreted as a mere attempt at filling the state's empty treasury. Rather, in combination with other political instruments, this intervention led to the reinstatement of the same ownership structure prevalent in colonial times. After the war, the surviving inhabitants did not have the financial resources to acquire the land they had hitherto cultivated for their own needs. Instead, the land prices, which were low by European standards, were exorbitant for the local population. In addition, the total lack of any official obligations or constraints were highly attractive for foreign investors (cf. Hanratty and Meditz [1988] 2005). At the same time, the foundation of a national immigration authority initiated a demographic policy that aimed at immigration primarily from Europe (cf. Fischer, Palau and Pérez 1997). Whereas the immigration authority was intent on having European settlers, a large number of inhabitants were driven from the land they had cultivated. This land was now privately owned and used primarily for export purposes, most notably cattle farming.

Following from colonial conditions, this late nineteenth-century policy that promoted not only the sell-off of land, but also immigration exclusively from Europe paved the way for a social structure of inequality that continues to the present day: a small number of landowners and a mass of landless farmers.

> "These inequalities are reflected in the model of land ownership distribution in a country wherein nearly 50 percent of the population live in rural areas. Sixty-six percent of the land ownership [. . .] is concentrated in the hands of 10 percent of the population, whereas only 30 percent own a mere 7 percent of the land. Landless farmers constitute 30 percent of the population" (Luna Nueva 2005, 42; *own translation*).

But this state-subsidized immigration policy did not have the desired success, "as many immigrants left the country again" (Fischer, Palau and Pérez 1997, 5; *own translation*). They used the cheap journey from Europe to the *La Plata* region, facilitated by the Paraguayan state, in order to travel on to the neighboring states of Argentina, Brazil and Uruguay. The same immigration policy led, moreover, to the emigration of the native popula-tion. Robbed of their form of subsistence by the privatization of public arable land, they migrated to the nearby Argentinean regions *Misiones* and *Formosa*. But what is the social reality of Paraguay like today? The next section will take a look at some figures and 'facts' concerning the present-day geographic, economic and social condition of Paraguay.

PARAGUAY IN NUMBERS AND STUDIES

The landlocked country of Paraguay is geographically situated in the cen-ter of South America, bordering on Bolivia, Brazil and Argentina. With its 406,752 square kilometers, Paraguay is smaller than California and, with its roughly 6,017,000 inhabitants, one of the least densely populated Latin American countries. The river of the same name divides the country into two dissimilar parts. The geographically smaller region *Paranáeña*, situ-ated east of the river, includes the two largest cities Asunción and Cuidad del Este and is home to almost 98 percent of the population. In contrast, the inhospitable region of *Gran Chaco* constitutes 61 percent of Paraguay's territory, but is home to less than 3 percent of the total population.[12]

Paraguay is officially bilingual. The indigenous language *Guaraní*, which is the official language and is taught as a compulsory subject in schools, is spoken by 90 percent of the population (González de Bosio 2000, 181ff.). The national economy is based primarily on agroindustry, especially the export of soybeans, cotton, beef and leather. Together with its large neigh-bors, Brazil and Argentina, respectively, Paraguay runs two binational hydroelectric power plants, which produce seventy billion kilowatt-hours per year.[13] The informal sector provides most employment. It is the only source of income for almost half of the male inhabitants and for more than two-thirds of the female inhabitants of Paraguay (Zarza 1996). This includes not only microbusinesses, street vendors and private home employ-ees, but also illegal drug producers and dealers, traders of other illegal goods as well as different services in the shadow economy.

These are the kind of standardized statements that can be found in pub-lications like the Fischer World Almanac (2011) or the CIA World Factbook (2008) (see Figures 10.1 and 10.2). Yet if one travels through Paraguay, one comes across places where nearly everyone speaks Portuguese or Low Ger-man (Plattdeutsch). It is hard even for Spanish-speaking visitors to under-stand the way this language is spoken in Paraguay. Most Paraguayans in fact learn Spanish and *Guaraní* at school, but in everyday life they use the colloquial *Jopará* (*Guaraní* for 'mixture'). The term denotes a linguistic hybrid that developed from the amalgamation of *Guaraní* and Spanish (cf. Lustig 1995). In some places in the *Alto Paraná*, a district near the border to Brazil, people speak Portuguese and pay their bills in Brazilian currency.

Figure 10.1 Paraguay as a geographical construction. Source: CIA (2008).

Thus, it seems that the empirically observable reality of Paraguay differs quite strongly from its standardized description as a nation-state.

This first impression is supported by a closer look at the demographic forecasts by the Paraguayan Office for Statistics. They assume a net migration rate of -0.08 percent and simultaneously predict an annual population growth of 2.3 percent. But the last census in 2002 resulted in an official count of 5,163,198 people, 11 percent less than the expected count of 5,774,756 (cf. DGEEC 2002). Despite these figures, which were surprising for the authorities, the predictions have not been revised. So the Fischer World Almanac—based on the figures issued by the Paraguayan Office of Statistics—maintains that in the year 2004 6,017,000

Paraguay

Surface Area	(World ranking: 58): 406752 km^2
Population	(World ranking: 102): 6,238,000
Capital	Asunción
Official language	Spanish, Guaraní
Gross national income (2004 p.c.)	1140 $
Currency	1 Guaraní (G) = 100 Centimos
Political leadership	Head of state and government: Oscar Nicanor Duarte Frutos; Vice-President: Luis Alberto Castiglioni; Foreign Minister: Rubén Ramirez Lezcano
National holiday	15. May (Independence Day)
Administrative structure	17 Departamentos and the capital
Political system	constituion of 1992 – presidential republic since 1967 – Parlament (Congreso Nacional) – assembly building (Cámara de Diputados) with 80 delegates; senate (Senado) with 45 members; election every 5 years – direct election of head of state every five years (no re-election) – cumpolsory voting from age 18

Figure 10.2   Paraguay as a statistical construction. Source: Fischer World Almanac (2011).

people lived in Paraguay (Berié and Kobert 2006). Yet by reading the daily papers, watching Televisión and talking to people in supermarkets, on the street or in buses, one begins to doubt the empirical validity of these statistical figures.

In the logic of standardized nation-state systems, migration is treated as an exception to the rule, or rather as a problem in need of control and regulation. It is therefore not surprising that the nation-state's bureaucracies try very hard to defend their national societal model against the resistant practices of their citizens. In Paraguay, as in Argentina, the *ius soli* (Latin for 'law of the soil/land') is in operation; in other words, citizenship is dependent on place of birth, even if the person concerned actually lives in two countries. Moreover, because the law is constitutionally bound to the place of residence, Paraguayan citizens who emigrate practically lose their right of participation. Thus, demographic statistics like these produce empirical results that are highly questionable, because they stoically ignore the multitude of migration practices that run counter to the nation-state's sense of order. In Argentina there is also controversial discussion both about the reliability of statistical measurement instruments and the explanatory power (value) of statistical data on migration phenomena.[14] Thus, the official authorities for statistics do not appear to be reliable sources for an adequate description of the social reality of Paraguay.

LIVING BOUNDARIES—MIGRATION AND
THE CONSTITUTION OF SOCIAL SPACES

In order to understand Paraguay's actual situation in the context of its historical development from a global perspective, the concept of *frontera viva* (living boundary), might be helpful. The Argentinean historian Hebe Clementi introduced this term as a key category for the analysis of the colonial history of the American continent. Using this concept of the *living boundary*, Clementi focuses on the history of colonization as a process of expansion and boundary extension emanating from Europe. From this perspective, the author concentrates her analysis, firstly, on the different levels of the process of frontier demarcation and frontier crossing, as they are found to be embedded in the unequal power relations of Europe and the American continent. As a second step, she examines internal frontier demarcations that were shaped by the conflicting interests of the colonial powers, but which in the nation-state building phase were at least formally declared as preliminary negotiations. Clementi intended with her new concept of *living boundary* to illustrate the complex interactive character as well as the progressive nature of the construction of social spaces in America. She conceives of *living boundary* as a "graphical denomination which semantically contains the changing mobility of life itself and which allows us to examine American history in its temporal and spatial dimensions" (1987, 14; *own translation*).

Clementi's concept is closely tied to migration processes, wherein the social environment, in other words, the cultural, social and economic conditions of migrant populations in their countries of origin, as well as in the countries of destination, are correlated with each other. In this approach, a boundary or frontier is not necessarily demarcated in terms of a nation-state. And even if it is thus defined, the potential of the demographic, cultural, economic and ideological pressure and influence of a powerful nation can lead to frontier demarcations, which are divergent from and run counter to the boundaries drawn between nation-states.

When the traditional criteria of defense become obsolete in the face of foes that are less evident, though still powerful, the recognized boundary loses its real meaning insofar as it is surmounted and invalidated by uncontrolled factors (Clementi 1987, 26; *own translation*).

Inspired by Clementi's concept of *living boundary*, the following section discusses the relations between migration and the construction of social space by reverting to some examples from around and about the geographical space called Paraguay.

INTERNAL FRONTIERS—MENNONITE
COMMUNITIES IN THE CHACO

The national immigration policy of the Paraguayan government began to take effect with the arrival of the first Mennonites, who settled in the

Chaco at the end of the 1920s, and with the foundation of the first Japanese colonies that developed as part of a binational economic treaty between the two countries from 1936 onwards. The first Mennonites, who settled in the sparsely populated region of the Chaco and focused primarily on agriculture, negotiated special conditions and privileges with the Paraguayan government that enabled them to achieve a largely autonomous social organization quite different from national principles. In the so-called *Privilegium* the Mennonites were granted the right to freely practice their religion, be acquitted from national military service and run their schools on the basis of their own religion and the Low German language. Also, they were allowed to establish their own communitarian economic and social security systems (cf. Hack 1960; Johnstone 1994). In their case study of the town Filadelfia, which today is still the center of the colony *Fernheim* (German for 'home far from home'), Dittmer and Fullriede describe the effects an autonomous social organization can have on the social interaction in a region up to the present day:

> Authority and political decision making lie exclusively in the hands of the Mennonites. The colony's leadership is subject to national laws, but the Mennonites' own administration is accepted and tolerated by the Paraguayan state. The 'official administrative language' of this town is German. This prevents the remaining population from gaining access to higher education, positions and information. The Indígenas of the *misión* [a quarter of town where the non-Mennonite workers live; *note H.G.*] are in many ways dependent on the Mennonites' directives and permissions. The latter try to limit population influx to Filadelfia. Officially only relatives are allowed to move there, but this is not easily implemented. (1996, 144; *own translation, italics in the original*)

The ethnographic description of the interaction between Mennonites and indigenous groups in Filadelfia as well as the problems cited by the inhabitants of this town are strongly reminiscent of the migration 'problem' and its regulation in the nation-state (cf. Bommes 2004). However, in contrast to the nation-state, here the 'migrants' claim the right to enforce who is allowed to move into the territory, which they demarcated themselves, and who may participate in this community's own services. The Mennonite communities command a de facto self-government structure.[15] Through their independent education system, the Mennonites can transfer their ethnic and religious principles to future generations. In addition, the health and social security of their members is secured through their own social insurance system and corresponding institutions. But these structures and services are available only for bona fide community members. In order to be accepted as a full member of the community, ethnic rather than religious affiliation is considered to be of decisive importance.[16]

Members of indigenous groups living in the region at the time the Mennonites first settled there were needed as laborers. Nonetheless, they were more or less excluded from equal participation in the educational and health systems, as much as from shaping the social life of the colonies. This structural discrimination of all non-Mennonites is currently being 'self-critically' discussed in the colonies. The Annual Book 2003 of the "Association for the History and Culture of the Mennonites in Paraguay" includes the following statement:

> From a historical perspective it is clear that we came to the Indians before the Indians came to us. The Indians and the Latin Paraguayans were and are the indigenous people here, whereas we and the German Brazilians are the strangers who are now doing more to feel at home here. Whereas originally there were just a few Mennonite villages gradually putting up fences and cultivating their land, now there are huge expanses of land fenced in and cleared by Mennonites for cattle farming. Thereby, the natural landscape that the Indians and Latin Paraguayans could formerly use freely for hunting and gathering now is becoming increasingly limited. In addition, due to the intensive economic cultivation of the pastures, which up to now at best have been used extensively, these spaces become more expensive to purchase. As more land is bought by the Mennonites, land speculation will only increase, and it will be the poor Latin Paraguayans and Indians who will suffer from this. (Warkentin 2003; *own translation*)

The Mennonite colonies have gradually become economically important in Paraguay, attracting labor from outside of the region. Apart from the members of indigenous groups in the Chaco, there are the so-called 'Latin Paraguayans'[17] and 'German Brazilians.' In the face of the continuing population growth, Warkentin continues:

> Especially during the last few years, this growth has led to the need for new economic and social models in order to tackle the challenge. The questions of the right to have a place to live, health facilities for the sick, schooling and political participation are only a few of those urgent questions to which we have to find answers adequate for all concerned. (ibid.; *own translation*)

Even if the foundation and the kind of life led in the Mennonite colonies symbolize a kind of retreat from the secular world and express the wish for social distance from a societal form that is not reconcilable with their social and religious principles, the economic success as well as the institutional structure of these colonies are to some extent influenced by trans*national* relations to Germany. According to members of a Mennonite colony near my hometown, the Mennonite education system in Paraguay is supported by German aid sums, and even the economic activities of Mennonite settlers are aided by the German Chamber of Commerce. Migrating to Germany is unproblematic for Mennonites who can prove direct German ancestry. Thus, trans*local* and trans*diaconic* relations between families and communities can be maintained.[18]

SHIFTING BOUNDARIES—BRAZILIAN ENCLAVES FOR THE WORLD MARKET

Under the political leadership of the dictator Alfredo Strössner—a member of the *Colorados*, i.e., the party that had been founded in the postwar era under pressure of the Brazilian occupying power—infrastructural conditions were created that were conducive to the intensification of economic relations between Paraguay and Brazil. Immigration from Brazil increased in the 1960s and 1970s due to the following factors: firstly, the foundation of the town Cuidad del Este in the triangle near Paraguay's borders with Brazil and Argentina; secondly, the extension of road transport and other infrastructural measures; and, thirdly, the construction of the hydropower station *Itaipú* (cf. Fischer, Palau and Pérez 1997).

Grimson (2002) interprets the erection of the enormous binational power plant as a clever geopolitical move designed to strengthen Brazil's influence on Paraguay. A short time afterwards, the Paraguayan and Argentinean governments agreed to build yet another hydropower plant. This was called *Yacyretá* and it was, according to Lins Ribeiro, the "geopolitical answer to the growing Brazilian influence" (quoted in Grimson 2002, 93; *own translation*). Grimson adds that "the power station was, though economically absurd, of central importance for the regional competition with Brazil" (ibid.; *own translation*). Thus Paraguay again became a pawn in the geopolitical bargaining game of the hegemonic powers Brazil and Argentina. Both the contracts made for the use of the hydroelectric power (cf. Molinier 2004) as well as the parallel 'Brazilianization' of the frontier region of *Alto Paraná* (cf. Fogel 2005) point to this interpretation. While the power plant *Itaipú* was being built, the Paraguayan government at the same time met the demand for expansion of the Brazilian agroindustry with the commercialization of the border region *Alto Paraná*. As a result, Brazilian landowners were allowed to buy 1.6 million hectares (3.9 million acres) of Paraguayan agricultural land in this border region. Meanwhile, according to Salim (2006), the construction of the world's biggest hydroelectric plant, *Itaipú*, prompted thousands of Brazilian small farmers to migrate to Paraguay, where they in most cases could only secure contracted work for up to two years. When their contracts expired, they lost not merely their source of income but also their right of residence in Paraguay. But back in Brazil, they had also lost a place to which they could return. Neither the Brazilian nor the Paraguayan governments were apparently prepared to enable the workers to return and reintegrate themselves into Brazilian society: "These workers are neither Paraguayans, as they cannot integrate themselves in Paraguayan society, nor are they Brazilians, because they lost their rights there" (Salim 2006; *own translation*). According to Salim, the term *Brasiguayos* describes the situation of these people who lead their lives in a kind of transnational no-man's-land.

Fogel (2005), however, describes the practices of the transnational agroindustry with the same neologism.[19] These practices override national judicial and political regulations while overturning de facto the geopolitical conditions by merely buying up the agricultural land in the border region. Fogel claims that large-scale monoculture farming of soybeans in Paraguay has prevailed during the last ten years, to the extent that soybeans have now become the number one export product. In 2004, 1.9 million hectares (4.7 million acres) have been planted with this crop, which amounts to far more than half of the land used for agriculture in Paraguay. This corresponds to 2 percent of the world's total land cultivated with soybeans. The small country Paraguay has become the fourth largest soybean exporter worldwide (Fogel 2005, 2). The author emphasizes that this development is decisively influenced by Brazil, because "the capital, the technology and the producers" all come from there (ibid., 4; *own translation*). Riquelme (2004) perceives the political configuration of the regional integration project MERCOSUR as a sign of increasing asymmetry in the relation between the two neighboring states:

> While the leading countries of MERCOSUR, especially Brazil, continue to form their international relations in the spheres of migration policy and frontier protection on the basis of the classical model of the nation-state, by joining MERCOSUR Paraguay has lost some of its national sovereignty or, rather, exchanged this in return for the mere rhetoric of international cooperation, which is clearly conducted in a framework of increasing asymmetrical dependence. (33; *own translation*)

According to this author, Paraguay has unilaterally cancelled a bilateral agreement that forbade the sale of plots within a 150-kilometer-wide border region to buyers from the neighboring country. This agreement had originally been designed to prevent such a de facto shift of the nation-state's frontiers.

The continuing appropriation of Paraguayan territory by Brazilian landowners, which is politically legitimated by the MERCOSUR framework of regional integration, prolongs a frontier conflict that is older than the two nation-states of Brazil and Paraguay themselves. Yet at the same time, this conflict reaches far beyond relations between these two countries. The

"Brazilianization of the border" (Fogel 2005, 8; *own translation*) and the control of Paraguayan agricultural production by Brazilian and transnational interests transform these regions into enclaves of the export-oriented agroindustry. Increasingly, large parts of the anthroposphere are turned into soybean, cotton or wheat fields for the world market—always according to the crop the market happens to demand at the time. The expanding transnational agroindustry, set less on sustainability than on profitability, destroys the livelihood and basic income of small subsistence farmers. The negative effects of this agrarian model with its extensive land use and intensive application of *agroquímicos*[20] are plain to see: Instead of providing jobs, this kind of agriculture not only displaces the rural population, but it also causes considerable harm to the environment, not to mention people's health (cf. Palau et al. 2007). The concentration of landownership and income in the hands of very few individuals is continuously enhanced and expedited (Fariña 2004, 275), and the influence of powerful transnational companies on local agriculture "makes the producers dependent on the multinationals, who decide what is produced in which way for whom" (Fogel 2005, 8; *own translation*).

Apart from the *Brasiguayos*, Japanese immigrants also hold a share in the production of soybeans in Paraguay. In 1936 the first Japanese colony, *La Colmena*, was founded in Paraguay. The private enterprise *Colonization Brasiliera A.G.* bought eleven thousand hectares (twenty-seven thousand acres) of arable land and secured permission from the Paraguayan government for up to one hundred Japanese families to settle on this territory. Until 1941, when the first wave of immigration was interrupted by the Second World War, some 790 persons took up residence in the colony. After the war, the number of Japanese willing to settle in Paraguay grew, meaning that the company *Colonization Brasiliera A.G.* began buying up land in order to start new colonies. Again, it is striking how these colonies are also concentrated along the frontier to Brazil, the largest one covering eighty-seven thousand hectares (215,000 acres) in *Alto Paraná*. Today, some seven thousand people of Japanese origin live in Paraguay, distributed over several colonies, where they are engaged mainly in agriculture, and mainly the cultivation of soybeans. Even though the number of persons in relation to the total population is relatively small, the economic power concentrated in these colonies should not be underestimated. According to the self-portrayal of the Japanese embassy, the Japanese colonies contribute not just to the expansion of soybean cultivation: Their output represents 6 percent of Paraguay's total soy production, but also 19 percent of wheat.[21]

As mentioned earlier, the rural population finds itself forced to migrate in accordance with the extent to which the transnational export-oriented agroindustry destroys living space. The commuting migration between Paraguay and Argentina as described in the following section is closely related to these agricultural practices.

BORDER TRAFFIC—COMMUTING BETWEEN PARAGUAY AND ARGENTINA

Due to its geographical proximity and comparatively good earning potentials, Argentina attracts the largest part of the Paraguayans who are willing to migrate (Cerruti and Parrado 2007). According to Fischer, Palau and Pérez (1997), migratory movements in the direction of Argentina started at the end of the *Triple Allianza War*, as a result of which Paraguay lost a considerable part of its territory. The border between Argentina and Paraguay was newly demarcated to run along the river *Paraná*.[22] On the Argentinean side of the river the town *Posadas* was founded and soon developed into a commercial center, attracting traders from all parts of the world. In contrast, *Villa Encarnación*, as the settlement on the Paraguayan side of the river was called at this time, remained poor and insignificant. *Paseras Paraguayas*, the female mobile traders from Paraguay, crossed the river every day to sell their agricultural products and foods. Grimson (2002) emphasizes the precarious situation of the trading *paseras*:

> From this time up to the present day, the *paseras* supply the Posadeños [inhabitants of Posadas; *note H.G.*] with a multitude of foodstuffs. They do this in spite of the fact that their presence in this town has been a source of conflicts, as it was simultaneously construed as illegal and troublesome. (2002, 85; *own translation*)

Quite a few factors indicate that the case of the Paraguayan migrants mostly fits the category "commuting migration" (cf. Morokvasic 1994). This is not perceived as such by the administration, as these persons immigrate with a tourist visa that they renew over and over again during their regular stays in Paraguay. This practice of commuting migration between Paraguay and Argentina may have started with the *Paseras Paraguayas*. Whereas the two countries developed unequally, the commuting migration between them expanded geographically and concentrated communicatively in the course of continuing developments of the transport and communication technologies in both countries.[23] Nearly all members of the Argentinean group of Cibervallers with whom I became acquainted during my field research practiced commuting migration and embedded their family life in a transnational context, such as the following example.

IWASHITA

At the time of my field research, Iwashita had lived in Buenos Aires for six years. The first four of these years she had spent with her father and two sisters. Subsequently, she moved into the flat of her Argentinean partner. Iwashita grew up in a small town in Paraguay where most of her mother's family lived. She stayed there until she finished school. Her grandmother and two of her aunts resided on the same plot. The family commuted many years between Buenos Aires and the small town in Paraguay. Iwashita's father, son of a Polish immigrant father and a Paraguayan *Guaraní* mother, had himself grown up in Buenos Aires and had then lived for a time in Paraguay, where he got to know Iwashita's mother. He had then moved back to Buenos Aires to secure the family income. At the time of my research, he worked as a caretaker and janitor in a small factory and shared a house on the factory grounds with Iwashita's two sisters. This had been in bad shape, almost inhabitable, but the factory's management allowed him to renovate it and live there with his family. When Iwashita had finished school she moved there with her mother and brother. For a while, the whole family lived together in this house in Buenos Aires. The mother with her three daughters and a neighbor ran a small sewing business producing clothes for the local market. When the neighbor stopped working, they had to close down. Iwashita's mother and brother then moved back to Paraguay and Iwashita's mother started commuting back and forth from the family household in Paraguay to the one in Buenos Aires. By bus it takes her eighteen hours. Usually, she starts in the afternoon and arrives the next morning. She stays an average of three months in each place.

Today, transnational family forms are characteristic in many places in Paraguay and Argentina, whereas the capital Buenos Aires is clearly one of the centers of attraction for migrants from Paraguay (cf. Fischer, Palau and Pérez 1997). Whereas the 2001 census counted a mere 323,000 Paraguayan migrants, the Argentinean government estimates their number at roughly one million, only half of whom have a legal residence permit (Palau Viladesau 2004, 164). The Cibervallers living in Buenos Aires act on the assumption that there are twice as many Paraguayans and their offspring in Argentina, pointing to figures published by the Argentinean daily newspaper *El Clarín*. The significant presence of Paraguayans in Argentina is clearly visible on the streets of Buenos Aires: A multitude of Paraguayan associations concerned with the social needs of their countrymen and women; music clubs specializing in Paraguayan *Polka* or *Cachaca*; Paraguayan bakeries and food stores that sell all the ingredients needed for Paraguayan dishes; street vendors with the obligatory basket on their heads, in which they transport *Chipa* wrapped in white cloth; and in fact whole quarters where almost all inhabitants are Paraguayans. In numerous conversations with Cibervallers in Buenos Aires, people repeatedly voiced the opinion that there is no big difference between life in Paraguay and in Buenos Aires: "It's as if Buenos Aires is a province of Paraguay." During an online instant messaging conversation, one participant told me about an article in *El Clarín* that had reported on a Paraguayan football match that was regularly held in *Villa Soldati*, a quarter in the south of Buenos Aires. My informant thought that this article was remarkable, because one of the Argentinean football players had been cited as saying that in this match only four 'foreigners' were allowed in each team. 'Foreigners' in this case meant Argentineans and other non-Paraguayans.

Grimson notes a similar discrepancy between "absolute and perceived presence" (quoted in Spiegel 2005, 26; *own translation*) in discussions concerning the number of Bolivian migrants in Argentina. Bruno (2007a) expounds the problem of the phenomenon of "imagined figures" and its function within the majority society. On the basis of existing demographic statistics, he argues that since 1869 the proportion of migrants from the neighboring countries has consistently remained at 2 to 3 percent of the total population of Argentina. Nevertheless, the mass media as well as the politicians allege a rising number of immigrants from the adjacent states, thereby aiding and abetting, according to Bruno, racist tendencies that consider immigration from the neighboring Latin American states as a threat to the nation's identity (see also Halpern 2009). At first sight, the presence of migrants from Paraguay seems to have an impact on Buenos Aires similar to the presence of Brazilians on the border region in Paraguay. In one case, parts of Paraguayan territory are 'Brazilianized,' and in the other case parts of the metropolis Buenos Aires are turned into a 'Paraguayan province.' A closer look, however, reveals decisive differences: Paraguayans, in contrast with the agroindustrial *Brasiguayos*, do not normally acquire landed property. To the contrary, their prospects for actually owning living space are precarious and temporary. Their living conditions resemble those of the Bolivian migrants, which Spiegel (2005) has described very vividly. Most Paraguayans and Bolivians in Buenos Aires live in *villas miserias*, i.e., in illegal settlements concentrated in the southern part of town (cf. Maffia 2002), in abandoned houses, on building sites or in the houses of their employers. Their living situation is precarious mainly because they have no kind of legal claim to the place they inhabit. When the city council decides to close a villa or occupied house, they can be evicted and become homeless. The same applies to a domestic worker who lives in the house where she works, or to a construction laborer who has to find another place to stay as soon as his work on a site ends.

The possibilities for appropriating space for leisure activities are, as a rule, also limited. Thus, most public green spaces and parks are used for communal activities. These spaces are then at certain times ethnically marked by cultural practices such as the joint *tereré*†-drinking, so that they become a part of these migrants' particular lifeworld. In those quarters of town where the Paraguayan presence is strong, permanent spaces can also be found. These are used by Paraguayan cultural or sports associations to hold events, and individuals or groups can rent them out. However, the ethno-cultural life of Paraguayans is not only restricted by the precarious living conditions described in the preceding, but also by bans and rules imposed by the administration of the majority society, as the following example will illustrate.

LA FIESTA DE SAN JUAN (THE FESTIVAL OF ST. JOHN)

Every year on the twenty-fourth of June Paraguay celebrates festivities in honor of St. John. For the Paraguayan Iwashita who lives in Buenos Aires, these festivities play an important part in defining her identity, because in her memory they are closely tied to her childhood in rural Paraguay. For her, elementary parts of these festivities are *Judas Kái* (burning Judas), *Tata Py Ari Je Hasa* (walk on fire) and *Yvyra sy* (slippery trunk). *Judas Kái* was symbolized by a larger-than-life doll that was stuffed with everything burnable in order to go up in flames in a spectacular final act. Then, during the *Tata Py Ari Je Hasa*, courageous men, and on rare occasions women, publicly tested their own purity by walking on the fire with bare feet. If the person was not hurt in the process, this was interpreted as a clear sign that he or she was without sin and protected by St. John. Another high point of this festivity for Iwashita was the *Yvyra sy* competition, during which the trunk of a tree was sanded and polished with animal fat. It needed to be slippery enough to impede anyone from trying to climb up. All kinds of delicacies were then tied to the top of the erect trunk. Those who were courageous enough to climb up the slick trunk could snatch the delicious rewards.

Iwashita has only attended one *Fiesta de San Juan* in Buenos Aires, and it was a major disappointment. To begin with, it was celebrated in a chapel. Secondly, there was no burning Judas or slippery trunk. Worst of all, hardly anyone walked on fire. The only 'Paraguayan' aspect was the food. According to Iwashita, even in the rural areas of the Gran Buenos Aires district the fiesta was celebrated in this very limited and for her altogether uncharacteristic way. She says that the security restrictions imposed by the local authorities make it impossible to properly practice these Paraguayan customs.

Iwashita's description indicates that the *Fiesta de San Juan* is transformed in the course of migration by the power relations between the majority society and the ethnic minority. The elements and practices that for her characterize the festivities are prevented by constraints imposed by the Argentinean authorities, so much so that the essential character of this customary Paraguayan event is watered down. The migration version of the festivities features neither the symbolic execution of the traitor Judas nor the fire test distinguishing between sinful and innocent believers. Instead, the event is held in a chapel, meaning that the religious aspects of the event are reduced to the place where it is held. The social aspects, as expressed, for example, in the *Yvyra sy*, are here reduced to the communal meal. It could even be said that this representation of Paraguayan culture is reduced to those aspects that can be consumed by the majority society as well. The festivity that had originally catered to the needs of the ethnic minority is now turned into a kind of tourist attraction for the majority society, which molded the cultural otherness of the festivities into a culinary form and thus made it consumable. Panagakos arrives at a similar conclusion in her study of the Greek diaspora in the Canadian town Calgary: "Activities are focused on the celebratory aspects of Greek culture, such as food, entertainment and shopping, while education, politics and history are nearly absent" (2003, 206). The author concludes that the political reality of multiculturalism in Canada is less a politics of acceptance than of the construction and consumption of the culturally other. She emphasizes that "public displays of Greekness embodied in cultural festivals reinforce the Canadian ideals of ethnicity and not necessarily the self-identity of the community" (ibid.). Against this background, Iwashita's observation is not surprising, that far more Argentineans than Paraguayans had attended the *Fiesta de San Juan*.

"PROUD AMERICAN-USA"—THE TRANSLOCAL COMMUNITY 'CARAGUATAY'

The US is also a favored migration destination for Paraguayans. But here the immigration threshold is more difficult to cross than, for example, in Argentina. Only a minority of people in Paraguay can raise the necessary financial and educational means needed for migrating to the US. The example that follows is an exception that helps prove this rule, insofar as it involves migrants from Paraguay doing undocumented work in the US as unskilled laborers on building sites or as gardeners or helpers in private households. Despite some geographic and legal constraints on their mobility, translocal relations that visibly influence life in Caraguatay have been established between the small Paraguayan town of Caraguatay and the distant relatives of its inhabitants in Brooklyn, New York.

LA 'REPÚBLICA' CARAGUATAY

Caraguatay—in the vernacular 'República Caraguatay'—is a small town about fifty kilometers from the capital Asunción with roughly seventy-five hundred inhabitants. However, about forty-five hundred of them spend only their holidays in Caraguatay, spending the rest of the year in the US, namely, in Brooklyn, New York.[24] Caraguatay has a conspicuous number of newly built, grand houses and large shiny cars. Most of the latter display a stars-and-stripes sticker with the inscription "Proud American-USA." A big church in the center of town, as well as the streets and parks, are conspicuously well tended and clean. A lot of signposts are emblazoned with "Caraguatay" or "Western Union": the black-and-yellow label of the global currency exchange company adorns, for example, the rubbish bin on the children's playground next to the church and the company's local currency exchange, where the inhabitants collect their relatives' regular transfers. "Nearly every household in Caraguatay has a member who is living abroad. Most of them live in New York, some in New Jersey and Colorado. And right now many go to Spain," explains the administrator of *Radio Evolución*,[25] a local radio station, which is broad-casted via the Internet and connects many Paraguayan migrants with their families in their country of origin.[26] He has two brothers in the US himself. Last year he and his wife visited them. He thinks the US is "a wonderful coun-try," especially the material possibilities on offer there. He says that in contrast to Paraguay, one can earn so much money—even as a gardener, bricklayer or household helper—that one can even afford to buy a good car and a house of one's own. When I remark that Caraguatay looks deserted, he explains that at daytime during the week it is very quiet, but on the weekend, especially at Christmastime, I wouldn't recognize the town. When the relatives from the US come home, he says, it's very lively with parties at every street junction.

Such descriptions are familiar to transnational migration research. Smith (1998), for example, reconstructs the development of a "transnational com-munity" that connects the local population of *Ticuanis*, a village in Mexico, to the relatives of the village people who migrated to New York. The relatives who have migrated have organized themselves in New York in order to sup-port the community's development from afar. The successful completion of community-oriented projects has led to the following development: The local population trusts the *Ticuani-Committee* in New York more than its very own local community administration, which is embedded in the national administration system with its long record of corruption. Thus, over and above private relationships, this form of migration can have political and social effects on the local community, which orients itself more to a translo-cal civil organization of migrants than on the nation-state bureaucracies to which it is formally tied. In the case of the translocal community Caraguatay, it is possible to infer individual migratory success from the splendid houses and the cars 'of good quality.' But in addition, there are numerous symbols that illustrate the influence of migration on the community: a new roof for the church, a school built with the funds collected by the *Caraguatay Centro Social* in Brooklyn and, last but not least, the many "Proud-American-USA" stickers on cars and buses, suggesting that the Caraguatayans feel less related to the Paraguayan than to the US-American nation.

THE RELATIONSHIP BETWEEN PARAGUAYANS' GEOGRAPHIC AND SOCIAL SPACES

The representation of Paraguay's history and its social space configura-tion definitely contradict the dominant presumption of transnationalism research, that the alignment of physical and social space has been a valid description of societies framed by nation-states and that this alignment is only now—in the face of current globalization phenomena—in need of revi-sion. Rather, Paraguay can be described as a territory that accommodates a conglomerate of sociocultural forms of organization with historically grown translocal or transnational relationships and loyalties, which resist attempts at national frontier demarcation. Appadurai (1998) clarifies the relativeness of space when he writes: "locality is ephemeral unless hard and regular work is undertaken to produce and maintain its materiality" (180–81). Pries (2006) conceives of social space as a permanent and dense intermingling of social practices, symbolic systems and artifacts. Thus, relational space does not exist per se, but it is interactively generated and preserved. The meaning of the respective space is dependent not only on the social practices, but also the availability and applicability of symbol systems and artifacts.

As the example of the *Fiesta de San Juan* in Buenos Aires demonstrates, the interactive construction of the local is embedded in power structures within a societal order, which is framed by the nation-state. These power structures drastically restrict the possibilities of migrants to participate in shaping the social texture of a town. The disposition of architectural artifacts that are able to mark a space as permanently one's own[27] and the possibility to deploy cultural symbol systems are restricted by the interpretational patterns of the majority society. The same applies to the exercise of the respective social practices, which in their entirety generate and attach meaning to the social space in the first place.

However, the example of the Mennonite colonies illustrates how a practically autonomous social organization can develop on the territory of a nation-state, with an administrative structure that deviates from official nation-state structures. And the practices of the transnational agroindustry in the frontier region *Alto Paraná* illuminate quite vividly the influence of the global economic system on local practices of the appropriation of space, which—in accordance with world market demand—is transformed from living space to agroindustrial space for export production. Finally, the example of Caraguatay shows how, due to migration, a local community can be detached from its national context. Caraguatay may stay put geographically in Paraguay, but it is duplicated to some extent in Brooklyn in the form of the *Caraguatay Centro Social*. And Brooklyn is now turned into the central reference point for the future plans of the Caraguatayans as well as for the development of their local community.

The constitution of the Mennonite colonies or the Caraguatay community, the 'Brazilianization' of the *Alto Paraná* region and the practices of Paraguayan commuting migration cannot be adequately described with categories like 'transnational social space' or 'transnationalization.' Here, the issue is not just one of the transcendence of national boundaries by cross-border relations and practices. Rather, the constitution of social space is embedded in an asymmetric power structure in which the weak state Paraguay loses its sovereignty—or, more precisely, was never able to develop a sovereignty—under the demographic, cultural, economic and political pressure of transnational influences. Although Pries (2006) does start from a concept of relational social space, his concept, indicating a lasting pluri-local configuration across several national societies, is too static and simplified and too near the original myth of the nation-state society to understand the diverse and progressive nature of the described phenomena. By maintaining that globalization weakens the social integration power of the nation-state and adding that transnationalism is an effect of this weakening, transnationalism research presupposes the centrality of the nation-state societal model and thereby adheres to the same methodological nationalism it sets out to oppose. Clementi's concept of the 'living frontier' is not just ideally suited for comprehending the development of the nation-state model of society (in Latin America) within a global historical perspective. The semantic content of this concept also suggests a further development in the framework of interaction theory, because it expresses the tense relationship and the dynamics of the frontier as an interaction space. Also, the diversity of the social organizations and the progressive nature of the border demarcations, both of which arise in the context of migration, can be described equally well by Clementi's concept. As one focuses with the historical-analytical lens of Clementi, Paraguay appears as a *living frontier* between the territories of the two competing (post)colonial powers. Zooming in on particular local situations, like in the example of the *Fiesta de San Juan*, not only reveals that social spaces are mobile, but it also opens up a clear view to the social practices of construction, dissolution, alteration and dislocation of social spaces and their boundaries, wherein migration definitely plays a decisive role.

Paraguay is a country that corresponds to the standardized form of the nation-state only as a statistical construction. On world maps, Paraguay can be found as a geographical demarcation, and its representatives are present in global organizations and even in world exhibitions, World Cups and the Olympic Games. But neither the statistical nor the geographical

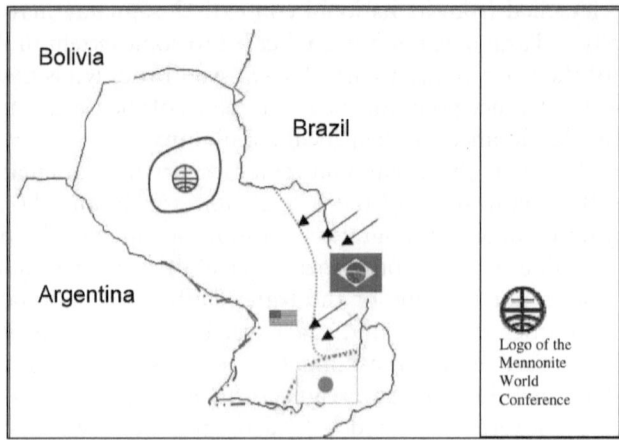

Figure 10.3   Paraguay as a socio-spatial construction.

constructions correspond to the empirical reality. A map of Paraguay that would come close to the social space reality sketched in this study would look more or less like Figure 10.3.

MIGRATION AND NATION BUILDING

A look at Paraguay's current situation in the context of the historical developments of the region can explain why in Paraguay it was never possible to develop a nation-state as defined by Adam Smith: "A named community of history and culture, possessing a unified territory, economy, mass education system and common legal rights" (Smith 2004, 183). As several examples have demonstrated in the preceding, neither a homogenous national culture nor a common statehood has been established in Paraguay. Its geopolitical role and position in the region, recurrent themes throughout the area's history, can essentially be explained by the competition between Brazil and Argentina. "Within this complex structure of alliances within the Cono Sur, the so-called 'weak states' played an important role as a balancing factor in the subregional power balance" (Tini 2004, 6; *own translation*). Paraguay's national sovereignty was therefore limited from the start by the two former colonial powers' competition and eagerness to expand. The colonial history as much as the neo-colonization of the young nation-state Paraguay as a result of the lost war against the powerful neighboring states, in a sense, laid the foundation for sustained marginalization. In the course of this marginalization, Paraguay became not only the country with the worst land distribution, but also one of the most corrupt states in the world (Bareiro 2004). Despite its multiple transnational and translocal linkages, it also turned out to be, interestingly enough, one of the least known countries of the earth.

The report about the human rights situation in Paraguay, annually published by the umbrella organization of Paraguayan human rights associations CODEHUPY, deplores the continuous rise of corruption by the state's administration and the extremely unequal distribution of resources and income. In point of fact, nearly half of the population was living below the poverty line in 2004. These people had limited access to education and health facilities. If they lived in the rural areas, their access in societal resources was even more restricted. Meanwhile, the control over resources like land, raw materials and income was concentrated in the hands of a tiny minority (cf. Molinier 2004). CODEHUPY's analysis of the present social and political situation in Paraguay states a lack of collective attempts at tackling this profound social crisis. However, according to the authors, at the same time an increasing number of people sought *salidas individuales*—individual solutions to avoid or escape from the crisis. *Salidas individuales* alludes both to the rising number of suicides and to rising rates of migration (Bareiro 2004, 14).

The relation between poverty and the lack of prospects, on the one hand, and migration, on the other hand, is a frequent topic both in Paraguayan mass media discourses and in everyday life. During my field research in Paraguay, hardly a day went by without media reports about the numerous Paraguayans leaving for the *madre patria*, the mother of the fatherland, as Spain is called in the media, in memory of the colonial legacy. Paraguay's capital was increasingly depopulated, particularly in the upper-middle social stratum quarters, where more and more houses were put on the market and shops closed down. Despite the high costs of a journey to Spain, it was not only the economically well-off who were selling their houses to finance the flight and the necessary papers. The rural population who tended to migrate to Argentina was suddenly forced to look for new horizons in the course of the latest economic crisis in Argentina. After the deflation of 1999, when their earnings were suddenly reduced by a third from one day to the next, numerous Paraguayans who had formerly financed their lives in Paraguay with their work in Argentina were looking for new sources of income. Many completely lost their work opportunity as a direct result of the deflation. The simultaneous economic boom in Spain and the massive demand for cheap labor, especially in the building, agroindustrial, health and private servicing sectors, motivated people to resort to distant Europe.

The constitutive meaning of present migration practices for the national development of Paraguay has up to now largely been ignored by the political and administrative authorities. Considering that migrants are systematically excluded under constitutional law from participation in Paraguay's political processes, one is tempted to entertain the suspicion that this is not so much a case of administrative ignorance, but a political strategy. In this connection, Halpern points out that Paraguay is "the only state worldwide, where the constitution determines that the right to vote is tied to residence (Article 120)" (2002, 40; *own translation*).[28] Alvaréz-Fleitas suspects that the self-interests of the agroindustry and the large landowners are behind this constitutional exclusion of an ever-larger part of the population:

> Paraguay is a country whose economy is based on large ownership, the majority of migrants constitute the rural population and Article 120 of the constitution prevents us voting from outside the country. This shows that the causation of migration serves the stabilization of law and order in Paraguayan territory. (2002, 37; *own translation*)

According to this argumentation, it seems that the order of the Paraguayan territory is threatened primarily by the existence of the rural population and its claim on living space. So one could conclude that in the context of the extent to which the Paraguayan territory is transformed into agricultural land for the world market, its own inhabitants become a disturbing factor. Is Paraguay therefore in the process of becoming a nation-state façade lacking in content?

Another glance at the migration history of Paula and Jimena may bring us nearer to an answer to this question. Even though the sisters live far away from their family, they remain integrated in the family and in close contact with their relatives. Their regular remittances secure the family's existence and contribute to a certain degree of prosperity. The importance of the remittances has of late been discussed not merely in transnational migration research, but it has also recently found its way into global development–related discourses. This comes on the basis of the realization that the annual currency transfers of migrant families or translocal communities far surpass the total amount of international development aid (cf. Global Commission on International Migration [GCIM] 2005).

Because of the increase of migratory movements to Spain, the economic impact that remittances have on national development has recently been brought into sharper focus in the public discourse in Paraguay. For example, the most recent study on human trafficking in Paraguay (a study commissioned by the International Organization for Migration) emphasizes the importance of the remittances for national development as "the most important national income after the export of soybeans" and "the second most important source of income for Paraguayan families" (Luna Nueva 2005, 45; *own translation*; cf. also Cerruti and Parrado 2007). According to the Paraguayan daily newspaper *Noticias* about 3.7 million Paraguayans lived abroad in 2006.[29] Their regular currency transfers to their families in Paraguay, estimated in 2007 to be between US\$340 million and US\$700 million, were the most important source of foreign exchange for the national economy.[30] If these estimations are correct, about half of the Paraguayan population lives outside Paraguay. Although the estimations diverge considerably, it is undisputed that the migrating populations in Argentina, the US and other countries between 1989 and 2008 have grown enormously in relation to the population growth within Paraguay (cf. Halpern 2009, 87–88). It seems like a paradox that exactly this part of the population contributes most decisively to the maintenance of the nation.

But how is the lasting integration and loyalty of the absent family members secured? As discussed earlier in a more general way, global communication technologies play an essential part in this process. The Paraguayan sisters, too, use the Internet to communicate regularly with their children and other relatives. The combination of private and public communication spaces offered by the Internet enables Paraguayans wherever they are not just to maintain their existing relationships, but also to get in contact with other compatriots in and outside Paraguay. Virtual spaces like the Cibervalle Forum imaginatively connect the participants with their place of origin and in a sense create the nation as a virtual construction. The users of the Cibervalle Forum live in Paraguay, Argentina, the US, Europe, Japan and other parts of the world. Cibervalle's social landscapes thus stretch across social spaces that reach far beyond Paraguay. Not only are the physical lifeworlds of the users, but also the shared virtual communication spaces integral parts of these social spaces. Cibervalle's meaning, however, differs according to the lifeworld context of the users. For this reason, the following chapter will illuminate Cibervalle from the perspective of its users. Part D will subsequently present an examination of Cibervalle's socio-technological structure. This examination will be conducted with the help of communication analysis, thus, in a sense, from the inside.

11 Where and With Whom to Drink *Tereré*†
Cibervalle 'Multi-sited'

A SOCIALLY SHARED VIRTUAL SPACE

The last chapter introduced the common geographical reference of the social formation Cibervalle. That is to say, the country to which the members of Cibervalle feel attached. The communicative center of Cibervalle is an online discussion forum, which as part of a commercial Paraguayan web portal is free of charge and publicly accessible online. The portal is designed as an Internet guide for Paraguay and its range is aimed at persons searching for contact addresses, news and other information about Paraguay. According to one participant, with its twenty-five thousand visits per day, www.cibervalle.com was at times the most frequented Paraguayan site on the WWW,[31] with the only competitor being the online version of the Paraguayan daily newspaper *ABC Color*.

www.cibervalle.com

Accessibility	potentially global, publicly available
Inhabitants	> 1000
Visits	> 25.000 per day
Global on-site reference	Paraguay
Local on-site references	Asunción, Buenos Aires, Ciudad del Este, New York, Madrid and others
Official language	Jopará
Currency	textual and pictorial contributions
Participation status	
-passive	Lurker (anonymous reader/audience)
-active	Nick (registered member)
Administrative organization	Central administration, elected moderators

Figure 11.1 Paraguay as a virtual construction.

The discussion forum of the portal is used primarily by Paraguayans, a relatively small number of whom actually live in Paraguay. The majority are dispersed amongst different regions of the world. According to its moderator, the Cibervalle Forum had more than one thousand registered users in June 2004. The main language spoken in the Forum is *Jopará*, albeit interspersed with a considerable amount of Spanish words/formulations, so that Spanish speakers can follow most discussions even if they do not have any command of *Guaraní* or *Jopará*. The textual and pictorial contributions published in the Forum can be read without registration. But membership is required for active participation. All one needs to become a member is a valid e-mail address and a nickname for signing one's own contributions to the Forum. The technological platform that runs the discussion forum is centrally operated and administered by the company of the web portal. A moderator elected by the users is responsible for observing the rules.

GEOGRAPHICAL DISTRIBUTION OF USERS AND LOCAL SUBGROUPS

Research on the inner structure of membership is a difficult matter—such as the exact number of users, their geographical distribution or gender relations within the group. Although I was able to ascertain the number of registered nicknames ('nicks'), this figure is misleading in several ways. For a start, it does not encompass those users who—even though they are not registered as active members—belong to the social context of Cibervalle, because they regularly read items in the Forum and may even be connected with the active Cibervallers in the Forum and/or come to the local gatherings. On the other hand, there may be an indefinite number of nominal members ('card index corpses') who might have registered once, but then never opened the site again nor contacted any members. Furthermore, it makes sense to distinguish the virtual from the actual 'incarnate' participants, because multiple registrations are technically possible and occur in practice. Those nicks who have been temporarily excluded from participation in the Forum also belong to the category 'card index corpses.' The person concerned can, however, undermine this sanction by registering with a new nick. The old nick might then never be used again, even if the sanction is lifted by the host. In addition, there are nicks who are active on the virtual level, but never appear at any of the local meetings. Most of these only exist on the virtual level. They are so-called *Clons†*, i.e., additional *personae*, who arise from the practice of one person registering under several nicks and using them simultaneously.

The geographical distribution, too, is not easy to ascertain. Nevertheless, the localization of their communication partners is of great interest for the users, so this question is almost always raised during the initial address of a new Cibervalle member. And it is also subsequently raised again during the course of technological updates. For the reasons discussed earlier, the following account of the membership structure is meant as an approach to the shape of Cibervalle as it appeared to me during the time of my research. It must be emphasized that the composition of Cibervalle is subject to constant change.

At the time of research the Cibervalle Forum was one of the most important Paraguayan websites on the WWW. As a public site, it was accessed by users from all over the world. The most active users, however, were concentrated in South and North America, Europe and Japan. The geographical distribution of Cibervallers thereby reflected the current migratory movements of Paraguayans. A consolidated group of users has formed in Europe. Its members live in France and Switzerland. They are active on the virtual level and organize local meetings. Access from Spain is relatively frequent, but prone to much fluctuation. Repeatedly, initiatives can be observed to connect the users in Spain with each other and to organize local gatherings. But so far these attempts have not been successful, at least insofar as there have been no indications in the Forum of regular group activities on the physically grounded local level. Possibly, this reflects the situation of Paraguayans in Spain, the majority of whom not only immigrate without documentation, but also have to be extremely flexible and mobile due to the requirements of the informal labor market. Consequently, they do not have the opportunity to participate regularly and intensively in Cibervalle's virtual activities. The topics raised by the users in Spain concentrate on such existential matters as the risks and precarious conditions of their residence status and working situation.

Very few users in Canada participate regularly and individually in the virtual activities. There is no sign in the Forum of any transformation of virtual into physically grounded local relations among the Canadian users. This is different in the US, where a local community has formed whose members meet with increasing regularity despite geographic distance and then feed these meetings back to the virtual level. With ten to fifteen members, this group is relatively small, but on the virtual level it gives the impression of being larger because the individual members not only participate intensively in the discussions, but also because they boost their virtual presence by using *Clons*†. The group of Cibervallers resident in Paraguay takes up the largest space, especially on the virtual level. However, taking the number of participants in local meetings this impression must be adjusted, because on the physically grounded level the size of the group is comparable to that of the Cibervallers' group in Argentina. In addition, the group of users resident in Paraguay can be divided into two local groups. One of them organizes its meetings mainly in the capital Asunción, whereas the other group meets in Ciudad del Este. However, there are close relations between them and they meet regularly. At the time of my research, the Argentinean group comprised some fifty people, but here, too, internal differentiations developed in the course of time. As a rule, their meetings are held in Buenos Aires. In contrast to the Cibervallers in Paraguay, these Argentinean members are more active on the physically grounded level, but less noticeable on the virtual level.

THE SOCIAL STRUCTURE OF CIBERVALLE
AND ITS USERS' LIFEWORLDS

How can the discrepancies between virtual and local presence of these two groups (Argentinean versus Paraguayan Cibervallers) be explained? The characters introduced in the ethnographic *docu-fiction* "Tragedy in the Supermarket *Ycua Bolaños*" in Part A of the study illustrate the diversity of the lifeworld contexts of the Cibervalle inhabitants. Maríana, for example, lives and works in the US and thereby makes an essential contribution towards her family's upkeep in Paraguay. She has a computer with Internet access at home, which she uses mainly in the evenings and on the weekends, i.e., in her spare time, in order to communicate with her family and friends and also to keep up with current developments and events in her home country. Eduardo, however, who lives in Paraguay and works in the IT division of the public administration, is not online when the tragedy of *Ycua Bolaños* happens because he has no Internet access at home. Like most Cibervallers in Paraguay, Eduardo has regular access only while at work. Carlos is yet another case: As an unskilled laborer at a building site in Buenos Aires without a regular place to live, he frequents an Internet café near his place of work (which doubles as his home) whenever he wants to join the Cibervalle activities and communicate with his friends.

Thus, the place of access influences the practices of membership with regard to time of usage, intensity of participation as well as accessibility. Participants like Maríana, who have access via a dedicated Internet connection at home, can always be online. As long as they stay in their place of residence they are always within reach—even if they are not actually sitting in front of the computer. On the other hand, the participation of those with access at work is mostly limited to the normal business hours and more or less restricted due to the conditions of the user's work contract and the control exerted by supervisors. The visual presence of participants can also be influenced by (feared) restrictions imposed by employers. Some members abstain from participation in local meetings or at least try not to be seen in photos of the event, so as to avoid the danger of later being identified by their employers. Moreover, the virtual existence of the workplace users is dependent by and large on the kind of employment conditions they are faced with. Frequently, the sudden disappearance of a Cibervalle member in Paraguay is explained by the person having changed his job.

The participants with limited Internet access are constrained economically because they have to pay for each minute they are online. In order to enter the virtual room Cibervalle, they have to go to an Internet café and leave it again after they have finished communicating. In other words, the virtual communication is separated from the rest of the user's lifeworld. On the basis of these economic and social conditions of Internet use, it can be assumed that the time Internet café users spend at the computer is shorter, and their usage more concentrated and less integrated into their everyday routines compared to those Cibervalle participants who can access the Internet at home or at work while being simultaneously engaged in other everyday activities.

If we now compare the local contexts of access and the lifeworld situations of Cibervalle inhabitants, certain cultural and socio-structural differences become apparent. In Paraguay, the Internet is a comparatively young medium, the use of which tends to be reserved for the privileged social strata. Even though the number of Internet users in Paraguay between 2000 and 2008 rose dramatically from 20,000 to 530,000, the percentage of individuals with direct access to the Internet has only reached 7.8 percent.[32] This is mainly due to the extremely high telecommunication costs in relation to both the cost of living as well as income structures in this country. The shareholder company *Compania Paraguaya de Communicaciones S.A. (Copaco)*, owned entirely by the state, was responsible for the national supply of landlines and Internet access until March 2009 when the Fernando Lugos government took the first steps towards deregulation.[33]

The number of Internet users is comparatively low, and the availability of Paraguayan data online is rather limited. With its 19,691 Internet hosts in 2008, Paraguay possessed in the context of South America by far the least number of computers connected directly to the Internet where they supplied access to databases.[34] These results confirm earlier studies, which discovered a close relation between the proliferation of the Internet and telephone connections (teledensity) as well as the nature of the competitive situation (free versus monopolized market) with regard to telecommunication and, last but not least, the Internet host density (Warschauer 2003).

Nevertheless, it is easily observable in the growing number of cybercafés that the Internet spreads in Paraguay, too. Similar to other Latin American countries (cf. Herzog, Hoffmann and Schulz 2002, 25), the Internet in Paraguay establishes itself less in private households than via collective accesses, most of which are commercial ones. This form of Internet usage does not, however, seem to be characteristic only of Latin America. More recent studies of local Internet practices in other regions of the world, for example, Morocco (Braune 2008) or the Philippines (Pertierra 2006), emphasize the central importance of collectively used Internet access. Whereas Chen, Boase and Wellman (2002) forecast strong similarities with and an alignment to the practices of Internet access in North America, the developments elsewhere in the world suggest that the model of individual access remains exceptional.

According to Herzog, Hoffmann and Schulz, the high costs of Internet technologies "prove to be a decisive obstacle to their dissemination in all studied countries" (2002, 26; *own translation*). The authors emphasize that the quality of access is also important, as slower connections and frequent interferences tend to raise the price of usage. What they ascertain for Latin America as a whole seems most notable in Paraguay: The standard Internet rates, measured in terms of the cost of living and the earning capacities of Paraguayans, are very high indeed.[35] The rather low quality of access in combination with ever-growing masses of data prove to be additional impediments to Internet usage in Paraguay. High-quality Internet connections are concentrated in the shopping centers of urban centers like Asunción and Cuidad del Este. These cater primarily to the upper income groups. Even though a cybercafé can be found in each of the provincial towns, the best place for those members who live in Paraguay to regularly take part in the Cibervalle activities without any time pressures seems to be their place of work, unless they belong to that tiny minority with access at home. Only highly skilled employees of the public administration as well as those employed by business companies actually have a place of work equipped with a computer and Internet access. This group of people has a higher education and income.

The fast-paced growth of Internet access in the countries of the periphery have tempted many an author to predict that the present discrepancies regarding access potentials to the worldwide communication network would gradually decrease: "The data for 1995 and 2007 suggest that every single one of the world's regions is closing the gap with North America" (Robison and Crenshaw 2010, 37). A closer glance, however, reveals a striking contrast between the *Organisation for Economic Co-operation and Development (OECD)* countries and the rest of the world: Whereas between 72.5 and 62.81 percent of the inhabitants of the OECD states had private Internet access in 2007, a mere 19 percent of the population of the rest of the world were equipped with their own Internet connection (Drori 2010). In addition, existing social inequalities are reproduced by the unequal distribution of Internet connections: "access and use of ICT came first and foremost to the socially privileged" (ibid., 66). With 3.5 percent in 2006 and 7.8 percent in 2008, the penetration of the Internet in Paraguay is far below the average of the peripheral countries. Furthermore, the sociogeographic distribution of high-quality access and the user profiles of the Cibervalle discussion Forum reflect an unequal intrastate distribution of Internet connections. This by and large corresponds to the social inequalities in Paraguay.

The initial costs of attaining Internet access in relation to income and cost of living are much lower in the main destinations of Paraguayan migrants, i.e., in the different regions of the US, Japan, Europe and in Buenos Aires. Also, the distribution and quality of access are more developed (see Table 11.1). As a result, an Internet café with affordable prices can be found on nearly every street corner. Migrants (often female) working in the private service sector can in some cases use a connection in the house of

Table 11.1 Internet Penetration in Paraguay and Argentina

Internet users (2008)	Paraguay	Argentina
total (in proportion to the total population)	530,000 (7.8%)	20,000,000 (49.2%)
with broadband (2009)	15,000 (0.3%)	3,185,300 (7.8%)
monthly costs for 1 Mb/sec	92 US$	22 US$
gross national income/per head	1,679 US$	6,050 US$

their employer, or they are even given their own in the same house. With permanent residence the installation of a personal connection in a private house is also comparatively easy.

The living conditions of Paraguayan migrants, however, differ considerably from those Cibervallers resident in Paraguay. As discussed earlier, migration often has paradox effects on the social status of participants. This applies especially to the economic situation, educational opportunities and the social regard for the family, on the one hand, and its migrating members, on the other hand. Betrisey (2000), for example, demonstrates how the open discourse in Argentina construes these migrating persons as cultural others who threaten the society's value consensus. Although Argentina's self-conception is that of an immigrant destination, its national identity is constructed mainly on the basis of the imported cultural values and practices of European immigrants. The discrimination of Paraguayan, Bolivian or Peruvian migrants is predicated on a racist distinction between people of European origin and the offspring of native South Americans.[36] In an ethnographic study of the living situation of young Bolivian women in Buenos Aires, Spiegel (2005) has observed how experiences of discrimination and the construction of ethnic differences between Argentineans and the different migrant groups are produced by means of ethnic markers like skin color and accent, and how these constructions are reproduced again and again. Halpern (2009) has described similar tendencies in his study of exiled Paraguayans in Argentina.

Most Cibervallers who live in Buenos Aires encounter experiences of discrimination, too. Most of them work in the low-wage sector as sales assistants, cleaners, house helpers, nurses or unskilled laborers on building sites. Very often they are not in possession of a work contract nor are they insured. As a result, they are exposed to arbitrary acts by their employers, and without a work permit cannot even claim their rights after having been mistreated. While working, many try to simultaneously make use of the free education system in Argentina. But their living and working conditions often prevent the successful completion of a course or university degree. Moreover, schools and universities in Argentina are institutions where migrants are stigmatized (cf. Spiegel 2005). Most Cibervallers, like a large portion of Paraguayan migrants, originate from the rural areas, especially from *Misiones* and *Itapúa*. Even though as their access to public facilities tends to be limited, migrants describe the infrastructural conditions in the Argentinean capital, including the opportunities for a good education and income, as far better than in their place of origin in Paraguay. Although as migrants they don't feel socially appreciated in Buenos Aires, the Cibervallers can use the difference in income and cost of living to contribute to their own and their families' social esteem. Actually, this paradox dynamic is reflected in their chances to access and use the Internet, and it leads to interesting socio-structural modifications in their virtual communication. In Cibervalle, members of different social classes and lifestyles come together, whereas in Paraguay's physically grounded social space they would either live in different milieus or their relations would tend to be structured hierarchically.

"A WINDOW TO PARAGUAY"—VIEWS
ON CIBERVALLE FROM ABROAD

Those Cibervalle Forum users who live abroad often call this site a window to Paraguay that gives them an opportunity to remain integrated in the everyday life of their country of origin despite being physically absent. The Forum presents a chance to speak their language, ease their homesickness and participate in current social events as well as exchange experiences with compatriots in a similar situation. According to each user's background, participation in Cibervalle is compared, for example, to a spontaneous outing to the pub down the road where one can meet familiar people, talk and have a nice time. The encounters Cibervalle members can have in the Forum differ from a visit to the pub in the current place of residence mainly regarding language, topics of conversation, interests and musical tastes. Users emphasize that everyone has the option to choose between the social relations in the place of residence and the mediatized relations that are tied in his or her imagination to the place of origin. However, Cibervalle can sometimes become the center of a member's lifeworld, wherein most of this person's social relationships are kept, partly as substitutes for physically grounded friendships and practices.

> I feel better when I sit here and talk to you than if I take a stroll, for example, through NYC doing window-shopping or whatever. [. . .] There may be people who say that's like locking yourself up in your own room, but that's not how I see it. [. . .] If something remains of our conversation after we have been logged out for a few hours, then for me that means it hasn't been lost time. [. . .] To the contrary, then I have learnt something and that's what counts [. . .] and if you have learnt something too, so much the better. (Condor, New York, log file, IM conversation)

At the time of research Condor had been living and working in New York for several years without a residence permit. He interprets his current social life, which he conducts primarily in virtual space, in the context of his biography. He says he has always lived a bit reclusively, even when he actually lived in Paraguay. Nevertheless, he puts a lot of effort into meeting up with other Cibervallers who live more than one hundred kilometers away in neighboring US states. But beyond that, Condor is nearly always online. He gets up in the morning and his very first act is to boot up his computer and log into the instant messaging client. Measured by the high degree of networking, his self-description appears contradictory. Condor does not in fact live reclusively. He compensates his social isolation in his physical place of living by computer-mediated relationships and by participating in local meetings with other Cibervallers.

Those members living outside Paraguay often emphasize that without the Forum they would not have much chance to get in contact with compatriots or be able to maintain their language and cultural practices of origin. However, as the descriptions in the preceding indicate, this does not apply to Paraguayans in Buenos Aires. Nevertheless, the members of the local group with whom I became acquainted during my field research in Buenos Aires claim that the important role Cibervalle plays in their lives is the opportunity to meet fellow countrymen/women and form friendships. Either they have lived a rather isolated life with hardly any social contacts before they discovered the Forum, or almost all of their friends were Argentineans. In any case, all respondents similarly emphasized that they came in contact with other Paraguayans through Cibervalle. How can this phenomenon be explained in light of the described presence of Paraguayan social life in Buenos Aires, which the Cibervallers themselves recognize and occasionally refer to jokingly ("Buenos Aires is a province of Paraguay")?

At the time of my field research, a seemingly important event for the *colectividad paraguaya* (the collectivity of Paraguayan migrants in Buenos Aires) took place: The arrival of the *Virgin of Caacupé*[37] was celebrated. The statue of the Virgin is brought over from Paraguay to Buenos Aires, where she is carried from one chapel to the next, to stay there for a while before she is returned to her home church in Paraguay. On the day of her arrival the Cibervallers organized a meeting in one of the public parks. This meeting bore no reference to the Paraguayan festivities. The members did not object to the chosen date and nobody appeared to have the desire to welcome the Virgin. How can it be explained that the Cibervallers had no interest in an event that is of central importance to the *colectividad paraguaya*? Why do they not use such an event or one of the many Paraguayan associations to get in contact with fellow Paraguayans in Buenos Aires?

As mentioned earlier, Iwashita's visit to the *Fiesta de San Juan* in Buenos Aires was a disappointing experience for her. Her disappointment was related to the restrictions imposed by the institutions of the majority society that curtail the exercise of Paraguayan cultural practices and appropriation of social space. In my conversations with Iwashita she clearly set herself apart from Paraguayan life in Buenos Aires: She does not share the musical tastes of the Paraguayans there and criticizes their conduct with each other, especially between the sexes. She despises the Paraguayan *machismo* as much as the culture of *callarte* (Spanish for 'keep your mouth shut'), which she associates with the experiences of Paraguayans under the Strössner dictatorship. During the first period of her life in Buenos Aires she deliberately kept away from the places and activities marked as 'Paraguayan,' because to her they appeared to be dirty, shameful and mortifying. At the time of my research, Iwashita studied educational science at the state university and identified with the young techno-scene in Buenos Aires, where she met her boyfriend with whom she lived at the time of our conversations. Together they were actively engaged in a local health project.

Iwashita became aware of the group activities in Buenos Aires through her participation in the Cibervalle Forum and went to a meeting "because I was curious to find out which persons were behind the nicks." In doing so, she presumed that these other Paraguayans would also set themselves apart from the local Paraguayan life, which she had deliberately avoided. "I thought they had Internet, so maybe they would be more open-minded and progressive than the rest." Like Iwashita, other members also went in for the occasional attempt to contact Paraguayans in Buenos Aires, but only to soon turn away again in the light of the misery they saw in the *villas miserias*, the shantytowns where most of the Paraguayans live. Carlos, for instance, for whom the Cibervalle group is like a family, visited his aunt shortly after his arrival. She lives in one of the *villas miserias* in the southern part of Buenos Aires. Afterwards he never went there again, because he did not like the *ambiente* as it was dominated by violence and drugs.

The initial interest in Paraguayan associations, clubs and localities in Buenos Aires that the newly arrived Paraguayans often approach shortly after their arrival soon changes into shame and disgust in the light of the social and cultural misery that they encounter. So, if the Cibervallers in Buenos Aires consciously set themselves apart from what they conceive as the life and culture of the *colectividad paraguaya*, why do they nevertheless emphasize the value of the Forum as an opportunity to come in contact with fellow Paraguayans? Or, to put the question differently, why is it important to get together with compatriots if mutual verbal communication with the majority society does not pose a problem?

During a computer-mediated conversation with Ariel, a member of the Cibervalle group in Buenos Aires sent me an article that had just been published in the Argentinean daily newspaper *El Clarín*. The article summarizes the results of a survey on practices of discrimination against migrants in Argentina and emphasizes that *Paragua* and *Bolita*[38] were among the most popular cusswords used by children in the slums of Argentina. Ariel, who has lived in Buenos Aires since he was thirteen and finished school there, relates the results of this study to his own experiences:

> The Argentineans discriminate a lot, for example if you have slightly darker skin or something like that. It is true, what they say (in the study), it has happened to me when I came here. I did not have a name for them, I was *Paragua*, that's what they called me. Everywhere they say *Paragua* to you, or *Bolita* if you are Bolivian. And if you have a different accent they treat you as *mal hablados* [bad speaker; *note H.G.*]. Only because you have a different accent from them, that does not mean that you speak the language badly. What the report says is also true, that the Argentineans believe they get fewer jobs because there are so many migrants here. They say "the fuckin Paraguas take away our jobs." But there are many Argentineans in Paraguay, too, they just don't see that. I think this is very unfair. At school I looked for someone who speaks like me, but there was none. At least not in my class. Because if you are like that, they do not want to be with you. It was very difficult for me at first. It really wasn't easy. (Ariel, Buenos Aires, log file, IM conversation)

In search of the individual, social and societal conditions that enable individuals to "conceive of themselves as belonging to a context as well as recognize and respect themselves" (Mecheril and Hoffarth 2004, 229; *own translation*), what at first seems most obvious is the ability to speak the local official language. This is indeed relished by integration courses as a prerequisite for integration. But in Ariel's account of his own experiences it is apparent that the command of the local official language does not suffice to be accepted as an equal communication partner. Paraguayans as much as Argentineans speak Spanish (to be more precise, Castilian). In other words, it might be inferred from this that Paraguayan migrants fulfill the linguistic qualifications that enable them to become members of the "natio-ethno-cultural" (Mecheril 2003) context of belonging in Argentina. However, the legitimate way of speaking in Argentina is not Spanish but *Argentinean* Spanish. The Paraguayan variation of the Spanish language is not only conceived as a deviation but debased as linguistic incompetence ('bad speaker'). "Natio-ethno-cultural membership is recognized phenotypically and para-phenotypically. The symbolic order at the base of this recognition can be denominated as a *physiognomic code*" (Mecheril 2003, 154; *own translation, emphasis in the original*).

In Buenos Aires, the 'slightly darker skin' and the deviant accent are signals that make Paraguayans 'recognizable.' The classification as 'Paragua' or 'bad speaker' not only throws them back to their culture of origin, but it also stylizes them as "natio-ethno-cultural others" (Mecheril 2003). This 'natio-ethno-cultural' identity that is pinned onto them is also rated as inferior in relation to 'being Argentinean.' The racist discrimination in everyday life in combination with the restrictions described earlier, namely, the restrictions regarding the exercise of cultural practices and the availing of social resources, impress themselves on the life of Paraguayans in Buenos

Aires. The humiliating shape in which 'being Paraguayan' in Argentina is perceived here, thus, reflects not so much natio-ethno-cultural idiosyncrasies of the culture of origin, but rather more the social impact of structural discrimination and the precariousness of migrants' living conditions.

Despite their attempts at setting themselves apart, Cibervallers are perpetually construed as other due to their appearance or way of speaking. Thus, they are thrown back to their Paraguayan origin, as Ariel's example has shown. In this situation marked by social exclusion, Cibervalle turns into a chance to build a context of belonging that is based on the revaluation of an (imagined) mutual culture of origin.

> Contexts of belonging are empirical approaches to ideal typical interrelations, in which each individual can experience him or herself as an equal among equals (dimension: membership), wherein they develop and apply the power to act (dimension: effectiveness) and, finally, with which they can be affiliated (dimension: solidarity). (Mecheril and Hoffarth 2004, 234; *own translation*)

The local meetings of the Cibervallers in Buenos Aires generally take place in public places, for example, in parks or in ethnic semipublic localities like the *Casa Paraguaya*, a Paraguayan cultural center. They are used for giving a warm welcome to new members and for intensifying the relationships that have been seeded virtually in order to make them more lasting. One has a good time with one's peers and appreciates the opportunity to be Paraguayan in Buenos Aires, for example, by speaking *Jopará* and drinking *tereré†* without being exposed to the *othering* of the majority society.[39] One talks a lot about personal matters, one's own biography and (hi)story of migration. Worries are shared concerning both one's current personal situation as a migrant and the political and social situation in Paraguay. The self-descriptions of the group characteristics underline the mutual affiliation to the Paraguayan place of origin and to the rural areas. Rural culture is associated with the image of the simple farmer, who is poor, never locks his door, shares everything with everybody even if he does not own anything and welcomes strangers with his arms open wide. This tenor is clearly mirrored in the group's identity and expressed, for example, in the emphatically warm and open mood of the local meetings. Each newly arrived member is made to feel very welcome by the older members and accepted into the group with great interest in his or her person and history.

Considering the life situation of Paraguayan migrants in Argentina, the explicit and repeated practice of welcoming and integrating the newly arrived, the demonstratively warm attention and caring for each other that can be observed on the local level of the Cibervalle group in Buenos Aires, appears to make sense in connection with their everyday experiences of discrimination as migrants who are excluded from equal participation in resources and met with suspicion and rejection. The mutual history of origin and belonging, shared cultural practices—although they differ from the dominant representation of the *colectividad paraguaya*—and a shared current situation as migrants are the main attributes that characterize the Cibervalle group in Buenos Aires. Whereas they are prevented from belonging to the natio-ethno-cultural context of the majority society, they find an instrument for creating a context of belonging that is based on (an imagined) common history and culture of origin.

But for its users in Buenos Aires the Cibervalle Forum does not merely function as a platform for locating one another and forming local communities. Firstly, local events take place in the awareness of their subsequent 'virtualization.' Thus, the place where the local meeting is held can lose importance in relation to the virtual space where the event is later retold. Secondly, the virtual retellings present an opportunity for the participants to, in a sense, apply corrections to the event. For example, the positive aspects of the shared experiences are emphasized during their retellings in the Cibervalle Forum, whereas not very pleasant incidents can be kept quiet. In this respect, the practice of the virtual retelling of a local meeting has similarities to a private slide show, during which photos of the family holiday are presented to friends.

Moreover, for its users in Argentina, the Forum also has the importance of a window to Paraguay—despite geographic proximity, commuting migration and the highly visible Paraguayan presence in Buenos Aires. It offers these users a chance to keep in touch with their country of origin, a chance that they sometimes even prefer to local activities, because it allows more distance and enables them to design their country of origin in their imagination in accordance with their own conceptions. Iwashita, who had been hoping to fulfill her need for ethnic community life in the Cibervalle group in Buenos Aires without being confronted with those elements of Paraguayan culture that she dislikes, was disappointed. So she has turned her back on the local group and returned to the computer:

> Paraguay is here in the computer, in Cibervalle. For me this is Paraguay because of the language and the news that they use to tell us. [. . .] What is keeping me near to Paraguay, what represents Paraguay for me is Cibervalle dot com and not this community that is here and that brought these idiosyncrasies with them, because of which I have fled Paraguay. I lived in one such mediocre place, with this ideology of 'keep your mouth shut' (*callarte*). But I don't like keeping my mouth shut, I never liked keeping my mouth shut. That is what I told those guys in Cuidad del Este. I always had problems at school, because I voiced those things, those problems that bugged me. I do not buy that fairy tale of the dictatorship that you 'should not speak about certain things.' I think one should speak, especially when it is about a topic that causes bad feelings. If it makes me feel anxious or afraid, then I have even more reason to speak about it. Why should I shut up and be stuck with that? No! I am me. I do not like this hypocrisy. That is why I am not pleased with this side of Paraguay, I really don't like it, that is why I chose Buenos Aires and I will stay here in the

capital. And those are my contacts here [*she points to the computer screen*]. (Iwashita, Buenos Aires, recorded face-to-face conversation)[40]

For the Buenos Aires group Cibervalle is therefore, firstly, an opportunity for forming ethnic communities in opposition to the negative image attached to Paraguayan life and culture in the Argentinean capital. Simultaneously, Cibervalle also offers a chance to approach the geographic context to which the Forum members feel attached, albeit in a reserved imaginative manner. Cibervalle thus does not only facilitate the construction of *local contexts of belonging*, but also of *virtual contexts of belonging* for its migrant members. According to Spiegel, the lifeworld of a migrant Bolivian woman in Argentina is characterized by the constant pressure to "imaginatively belong to the place where she neither lives nor wants to live" (2005, 114; *own translation*). The Internet provides an opportunity to ease this pressure. One can approach places of belonging imaginatively and take part in their construction as often and as long as one likes, but one can also turn away from them simply by logging out of the website.

For those users who live farther away in places where Paraguayan life is not as present as it is in Buenos Aires, as well as for those users for whom local Paraguayan life seems too precarious, Cibervalle is a window into Paraguay through which they can look any time and observe pieces of Paraguayan everyday life. In addition, Cibervalle can be used to organize a rather large part of their social relations. For the users *in* Paraguay, however, other needs are more important, even though the needs of their geographically distant fellows appear to be reflected in their practices.

"A GATEWAY TO THE WORLD"—PERSPECTIVES FROM THE SEDENTARY POPULATION

For the Cibervallers resident in Paraguay, the Forum is avowedly a chance to extend their reality. In the sense of a virtual field for experimentation, it serves for some of its users as a platform to playfully try different personalities and modes of behavior. According to one user, Cibervalle corresponds to an "imagined world that forms in our heads and in which each nick represents another role acted out in this scenario. The real persons behind the nicks are scriptwriters or directors" (Juanes, Asunción, Cibervalle Forum).

For other users, the foremost aspects are in connection with the opportunity to access global networks and discourses. The Forum is thus not only a helpful network when it comes to preparing possible migration schemes. Also, the Internet in general presents a chance to extend one's horizon; to acquire knowledge; and to gain access to other lifeworlds, experiences, opinions or cultures when physical forms of mobility are restricted.

Whereas holidays to geographically distant regions are hardly affordable for Paraguayans, the Cibervalle Forum (and of course access to the Internet in general) facilitates virtual journeys around the world. One user describes the value of the Cibervalle Forum as, for example:

> the chance to meet other people who, because of the distance, I would not have gotten to know in my surroundings (I did not even get as far as Clorinda,[41] hoho). Through other people from other towns, countries, continents etc., I got to know different ways of thinking, other realities and visions. (Eduardo, Asunción, Cibervalle Forum)

Even though he spends his "everyday life exclusively in one local context" (Werlen 1996, 99; *own translation*), Eduardo's lifeworld is globalized by his participation in Cibervalle, because it is in a sense "embedded in global processes" (ibid.). The Cibervalle membership extends Eduardo's options both to "relate the world to him" and to acquire "his (social and spatial) position in the world" (ibid., 110). In addition, his "selection horizon" (Stichweh 2004, 6; *own translation*), which constitutes the framework for local decisions, turns global through his Cibervalle membership. Eduardo told me in a personal conversation that he got to know people all over the world and theoretically he now had places where he could stay everywhere and knew people who would support him during migration. He said that an acquaintance in Canada had in fact sent him blank forms for the immigration and work permits, but he did not want to live anywhere else. Eduardo made this decision not to live elsewhere on the basis of a global selection horizon, in other words, a radius of options "that is characterized by the alternatives taken into consideration that embrace spaces all over the world" (Stichweh 2005, 17; *own translation*).

With reference to the relationship between Cibervalle's virtual and physically grounded levels, different tendencies can be discerned when comparing the group in Buenos Aires with the Asunción group. Whereas the participants in Buenos Aires use the meetings to intensify the computer-mediated social relations and to integrate them into their physically grounded lifeworld, the tendency is vice versa in the Asunción group. During meetings the participants in Buenos Aires address each other with their real names, but continue to use the nicks in the Forum's communication. Often, the Cibervaller's partners and children are present at meetings, whereas they are not active on the virtual level. In contrast, most of the group members in Asunción only know each other by their nicks, and as a rule only those who are active members of the Forum come to meetings. The personal background of most participants usually remains unknown and excluded from the online part of their lives.

Whereas the group in Buenos Aires seems primarily self-oriented, with meetings being held primarily to have a nice time with each other, a strong orientation on the geographically distant members in the US, Europe and

Japan can be observed in the Asunción group. The latter group organizes meetings to welcome those who announce their stay in Paraguay beforehand. Also, local meetings can be dedicated to an absent member, as the following example demonstrates.

NORA'S VIRTUAL BIRTHDAY PARTY

Sandra informs me about a meeting that was announced in the discussion forum and is to be held on the evening of the same day in a shopping center in *Villa Mora*, an affluent part of Asunción. The occasion is the birthday of Nora, a Cibervaller living in the US. The organization of the birthday celebration is coordinated with Nora herself and the party is carried out by Juanes and Carolina in Asunción. Nora has ordered a cake in a pastry shop in Asunción: She will pay for it and Carolina will pick it up. Juanes takes on the invitations of the Cibervallers. He has opened a Tópico for this purpose in which he announced the place and time of the meeting and has asked members to confirm their participation. I accompany Sandra and Eduardo to this meeting.

When we arrive, we meet up with a group of nine people who sit around a table in the *Patio de comidas*, the open dining area of the shopping center. Juanes welcomes us. Two of those present I have never met personally, but I have communicated with them via the Forum. We introduce ourselves and relate to situations we mutually experienced in the Forum. After he has served drinks and food, Eduardo talks to Nora's cousin, who is taking part in a Cibervalle meeting for the first time. Most of the other people appear to me to be as bored and disinterested (almost impatient) as the participants of my first meeting in Asunción: agitated shifting glances around the room, fidgety legs and hands that play with objects, very little mutual attention between those present, hardly any conversations. Juanes is constantly moving around the table, shooting pictures with his digital camera. Or he asks others to take photos of him and the fellows around him. Then another member arrives and brings the *bandera*, a white sheet roughly one meter squared with the Cibervalle logo imprinted in the middle. Grouped around this logo are handwritten signatures of the individual nicks, including those of members whose residence is geographically distant. Group photos with the *bandera* are taken. At midnight Nora phones on her cousin's mobile. He talks to her first and then hands the mobile on. It travels around the table, so that in the end everyone has talked once to Nora ("Happy birthday!" "I am nick so-and-so," "guess who I am," "Are you having a nice time celebrating?"). Juanes and Eduardo capture these scenes with the digital camera, including the moment when Carolina appears with the cake, which is impressively large and bears the name *Nora* in the middle, opulently decorated with little roses made of pink-colored meringue. The cake is cut and the pieces are distributed to and eaten up by everybody while the events are captured in digital photos. Then the group disperses. Like last time, everyone takes leave with words like "nos seguimos leyendo" or "nos leemos en cualquier momento" ("read you again" transferred to the script-based interaction in the sense of "see you again").

The next day Juanes introduces a new Tópico in the Cibervalle Forum. Nora is again congratulated for her birthday. The participants report on the meeting, make comments on the photos Juanes has posted in the Tópico and

Nora thanks everyone for the beautiful party. Others, who have not been to the meeting, also congratulate Nora and comment on the photos. In contrast to the actual meeting, the virtual retelling appears amusing and exciting. On the virtual level the participants communicate far more with each other than in the face-to-face situation.

Similar to Nora's birthday party, during the local activities of the group in Asunción the impression arose that the participants relate less to the moment and to the local group than in a kind of performance to those who cannot be physically present at the place the participants feel they belong to. The social meaning of the meeting becomes evident not so much through the face-to-face contact than through the online preparation of the meeting and its subsequent virtual retelling. Even those who could not participate in the actual physical meeting can thus become a part of the retelling process. These observations are reminiscent of the literary letters of migrated Polish peasants to their families (cf. Thomas and Znaniecki [1918–20] 1958), which were publicly read for the relatives at a suitable occasion. In comparison to the situation described here, it becomes apparent that the permanent enhancement of practices designed to *synthesize presence* is a central aspect of media usage in migration contexts. The Polish letter readers as much as the Paraguayan birthday party guests lend their bodies to the absent members of the community in order to substitute their physical presence.

Apart from the fact that the communication in the case of the Cibervalle community is much more dense and complex due to the temporal compression, visual elements and combined media usage, the main difference between the two examples lies in the relation between the local event and its mediatization. Whereas the gatherings in Poland presumably end with the reading of the letters, so that the local event takes the center stage, the meetings in Paraguay are from the start engendered online: The meeting described in the preceding would have made no sense without the possibility of the preparation and follow-up online.

It becomes apparent that the dissimilarities in the lifeworld contexts of the Cibervalle users are reflected in the plurality of Cibervalle's meanings for its inhabitants. In the following section, the different dimensions of Cibervalle will be discussed with regard to the question of how a social formation that has to deal with a literally far-reaching plurality of contextual relations can be held together.

GLOBAL NETWORK OR NATIONAL COMMUNITY? DIMENSIONS OF A TECHNO-SOCIAL FORMATION

As discussed in the previous section, the social formation Cibervalle stretches far beyond the discussion forum: It connects people who live all over the globe and it conjoins different physically grounded locations with computer-mediated social spaces. But what terms can be used to describe this strange social formation? Social sciences continue to discuss the possible descriptions of Internet-based forms of relations. They distinguish between socio-electronic networks (Wellman 2000) and virtual groups (Thiedecke 2000), and the latter are discerned from virtual communities (Rheingold 1993). Differentiations are also made concerning the number of participants, the degree of belonging and the ties between members, whether their communication is oriented towards tasks or towards relationships, whether it is bi- or multilateral, whether there are formal membership rules, whether the communication is stable and regular or spontaneous and short term. However, according to Heintz (2000), the social world of the Internet cannot be adequately described if one tries to subject it to fixed sociological categories. Her research results[42] lead the author to revise the sociological category of community: "Instead of conceiving community as a specific form of living, which is characterized by solidarity and strong ties between members, I take community as a continuum that ranges from loose networks to group-organized relations" (2000, 189; *own translation*).

The social formation Cibervalle also has different dimensions that must be described using a flexible concept of community. Cibervalle bears the properties of a global network because it allows not only weak ties, but also an enormous scope. At the same time, a differentiation into subgroups that are formed via spatial or temporal synchronization can be observed. For those members whose participation in Cibervalle has become an essential part of their everyday routine, and who organize a major part of their everyday life via this socio-electronic network, Cibervalle is a synonym for a community in the classical sense. But how does Cibervalle, despite its global scope and different dimensions, reproduce itself, and what exactly holds this social formation together?

Apart from the mutual geographic reference, Paraguay, the main structuring elements of the social formation Cibervalle are *information* and *solidarity*. The first dimension one comes across when opening the Forum pages could be described as a *global socio-electronic network for Paraguayan concerns*. Basically this information and contact network is open and accessible to anyone who has the necessary resources and skills. There is, however, a thematic bias on topics related to Paraguay. The network is used by Paraguayan migrants in order to stay in contact with their country of origin beyond all geographic distances and to receive information on a daily basis. In addition, the Forum presents the option to localize fellow countrymen/women near the member's present place of residence. Persons who live in Paraguay but plan to leave their country or are interested in an exchange with their countrymen/women abroad also make use of the Forum in terms of an information and contact network. In the latter case, the Forum offers the chance to compare one's own preconceptions about

Table 11.2 Tópico "Voy a España"

Yo voy a España y vos? te vas también?	I will go to Spain, and you? are you going, too?
Yo me quiero ir y me gustaría saber que onda† con el laburo allá, no tengo problemas en trabajar en lo que sea. Si alguien me puede orientar.	I will go and would like to know, what it is like (que onda†) there, workwise, I have no problem to work, whatever it is. If someone could advise me.

possible migration destinations and experiences with the actual experiences of compatriots who have already migrated. Also, Cibervalle enables the prospective migrant to get in contact with people at his destination.

Apart from this rather noncommittal relational level, another dimension that has already been mentioned can be identified, in which Cibervalle presents itself as a *virtual context of belonging*. 'Natio-ethno-cultural' (non)belonging is marked linguistically, for example, by using *Jopará* and the 'correct' keypad mode, i.e., the keyboard that takes account of Spanish characters. A comparison of the photos made during the local meetings and subsequently published in the Forum reveals that Cibervallers living far away tend to 'Paraguayanize' the social context. For example, there are national symbols in the photos, like a Paraguayan flag as a background to a group having their photo taken. Similarly, the representation of the preparation and subsequent consumption of typical dishes takes up an important role in photos. Those depicting meetings of the subgroups living in Paraguay, however, do not show national symbols, as the context of these local meetings is self-evident and permanently a Paraguayan one.

There are numerous Tópicos in the Forum that are invitations to mutual imaginative journeys into the past, wherein the members involved collectively refresh their memories of the habits, places, music and literature that they associate with their own biography (see Table 11.3).

Mecheril calls this "remembering of activities and experiences" (2003, 249; *own translation*) a central moment of "biographization," which in turn is constitutive for social affiliation. "People belong to a context of social affiliation as soon as they—as effective members—are able to perceive their own history as an affirmatively integrated part of the context in question" (ibid., 247; *own translation*). The places, landscapes and habits one remembers are woven into the context of belonging to one's own history and thereby establish solidarity with this context. Affirmative responses from other participants turn the individual experience into a collective history. That is to say, the answers to Laura's Tópico relate to her experiences and enrich them with more details, thereby affirming that they know exactly what the other person means, that they are as familiar with, for example, the smell of coconut tree flowers as they are with the taste of *Clericó†* or the long Christmas evenings with the family.

Table 11.3   Tópico "La Navidad de Flor de Coco"

que delicia por lo menos imaginar la navidad de flor de coco . . . los vecinos con sus pesebres . . . y degustaciones de *Clericó*† . . . que delicia de recuerdos . . . chipa guazu. . sopa paraguaya . . . bombitas y estrellitas y la famlia reunida hablando hasta muy tarde o muy temprano cómo se quiera!! un beso mi PARAGUAY!	What a pleasure it is to at least imagine the cocos flower blossoming at Christmas . . . the neighbours with their nativities and the tasting of the Clericó† . . . what a pleasure these memories are . . . chipa guazu . . . sopa paraguaya[43]. . firework crackers and rockets, and the family united, talking to late at night or the early hours if they feel like it!! A kiss for my PARAGUAY!
Nick: laura	Nick: laura
E-mail: 6—8 @T*L*S*RF.COM.PY	E-mail: 6—8 @T*L*S*RF.COM.PY
IP: 80.77.23.*	IP: 80.77.23.*
Respuestas: 21	Answers: 21
Última respuesta: 07/01/2004	Last answer: 07/01/2004

Ana from Buenos Aires explains that the Forum section "Music, Literature and Culture" is particularly important for her, because there she can talk with the others about the rock music of the 1980s that she used to listen to in her youth in Paraguay. The music that was popular at the same time in Argentina feels strange to her, so she cannot join in any discussions of this. Ana lacks the biographical experiences necessary to mutually remember Argentinean music of those days and to identify with the 1980s Argentinean generation. But when she exchanges memories of the Paraguayan rock music of the 1980s in the Cibervalle Forum she finds 'her' 1980s generation. As a Paraguayan one is the norm in Cibervalle, whereas as a non-Paraguayan participation in Cibervalle needs an explanation. One 'speaks' *Jopará* here and everyone knows how and when to drink *Tereré*†. And here one can share one's own biography as a collective history with others.

But even in Cibervalle the belonging of the physically absent can be questioned. In conversations with Cibervallers in Paraguay the allegation was repeatedly heard that the migrated compatriots would leave their country only to speak badly about Paraguay. When Esther demonstrated her daily use of the Internet to me and the way she takes part in Cibervalle, she explained why she hardly ever visited the section of the Cibervallers abroad: "Because they rail against us too much. [. . .] If you live abroad in better conditions, it is easy to criticize. Why don't they contribute ideas, suggestions or get involved in improving the situation?" (Esther, Cuidad del Este, field diary, face-to-face conversation).[44] Similar reactions to critical remarks about the social and political situation in Paraguay can also be found in the Forum. For those far away from their country of origin the call for loyalty and constructive contributions, which is mostly coupled with the repudiation of the criticism, provides opportunities to show solidarity.

Thus, solidarity turns into a form of *practiced belonging*. Donations in favor of charitable institutions in Paraguay are regularly initiated through the Forum. At the time of my field research in Paraguay I had the opportunity to attend a Christmas collection for a children's refuge in Asunción. The Forum served as a platform for the organizers in Paraguay and for those Cibervallers in geographically distant places who wanted to participate actively in the campaign for donations. Suggestions were invited and discussed, and finally, a vote for the best institution was taken. The organizers in Paraguay visited the institution, collected information about its mode of operation and its concrete needs, shot photos and placed these at the disposal of the Forum. The collection was then coordinated via the Forum and the current level of donations was announced regularly. The official handover of the donations took place in the children's refuge on January 6 ('día de los reyes'), when the children in Paraguay usually get their Christmas presents. The photos documenting the ceremonious delivery were published in the Forum almost simultaneously, where they were commented upon by the participants.

Solidarity, however, is a decisive characteristic of the Cibervalle formation not only in relation to the mutual national context of belonging. The following example (Table 11.4) is part of a Tópico that tells the history of Cibervalle from the subjective perspective of a long-standing member.

In her narration Esther describes Cibervalle's transformation process from an anonymous electronic network to a 'real'—i.e., a mutually supportive—community. Cibervalle's first generation of users agree that the activities arising from the birth of Mayra were a key event in this transformation process. Mayra, the daughter of a Cibervalle user who lived in Paraguay, had been born prematurely. She needed the kind of expensive medical assistance her parents could not afford. When the other Forum users heard about this emergency, they initiated several donation campaigns involving also those users who lived abroad. Together they raised the money for Mayra's treatment in hospital. In the course of the organization of these collections some users got to know each other personally. Finally, it was Mayra's baptism that prompted the first local meeting of the Cibervallers in Paraguay. The solidarity, which had developed spontaneously in the context of the emergency aid campaign for Mayra was soon

Table 11.4 Tópico "Mayra"

Aqui hay bautismos . . .	*There are baptisms here . . .*
Nació Mayra. y decidí salir del anonimato e ir a conocer a los padres, quien diría hoy Mario es mi compadre† REAL y Eduardo quien para mi era un escritor de novelas pasó a ser el puntal en las campañas que se hicieron para la bb de cibervalle y aquí estamos . . .	Mayra was born and I decided to step out of the anonymity and get to know the parents, who today are, I would say, Mario is my REAL compadre† and Eduardo, who to me was an author of novels and then developed into being the bearer of the campaigns organized for the Cibervalle-baby, and here we are . . .

institutionalized by Forum members taking on the role of godparents for the newly born children. Thus, the daughter of an anonymous conversation partner became a 'Cibervalle-baby' whose helplessness in a sense laid the foundation stone for the materialization of a virtual network and it's self-conception as a community based on the principle of mutual solidarity. Especially recurrent activities such as the application of terms that imply blood relationships and the godparenthoods for newly born babies of other members, as well as the donations in favor of Cibervallers in emergencies or the blood donation for a member's forthcoming operation have a symbolic character that casts Cibervalle as a *family-like community.*

Whether it is related to the mutual geographic reference Paraguay or to the relations between members, solidarity in any case becomes crucial in terms of bonding. Solidarity intertwines communication with action, it links virtual and physically grounded spaces together and it ties the geographically dispersed members to the Cibervalle community as well as to the mutual context of belonging named Paraguay. In Cibervalle the members meet on the (imagined) common ground of a shared 'natio-ethno-cultural' context of belonging. In other words, they communicatively construct themselves as a national community. The nation Paraguay, which—from an ethnographic point of view—turns out to be a bureaucratic fiction fortified with social scientific terminology, is now, in a virtual form, generated by the actors themselves. Natio-ethno-cultural belonging thus becomes an elementary modus for the construction and reproduction of community in Cibervalle. This community is global in scope, but refers imaginatively and by means of practiced solidarity to the geographic space Paraguay. The example of Cibervalle refers to a seemingly paradox process that is enhanced by media usage in migration contexts: Whereas the nation-state loses its integrative power or—like in the case of Paraguay—has never been able to develop such a capability, in global virtual space national identity acquires a durable shared meaning. This common ground obliges its members to be loyal and facilitates their mutual solidarity.

Part D

Cibervalle's Communicative Architecture

The following part of this study will examine the communicative architecture of Cibervalle with respect to the question of how *global togetherness* is technologically and practically possible. A methodological reflection on the type of data at hand is then followed by a description of the communicative evolution of Cibervalle. Following on from that is a discussion of the genuine practices of media usage that have developed in Cibervalle and THAT provide the socio-technical frame in which global togetherness takes place. Finally, communication in Cibervalle is examined with respect to another dimension of globality, a dimension related to the potential global accessibility and the public availability of the Forum.

Part D

Chevalle's Communicative Architecture

12 How to Analyze Computer-Mediated Sociality

As has been presented earlier, the development of the methods used in this study adheres to the principle of ethnomethodology's 'unique adequacy requirement.' Essentially this request for a methodological concept that befits the subject matter is based on the assumption that there is a strong rapport between the research subject and the instruments used for its scientific examination; that research subject and methods are mutually constitutive. In other words, the way one perceives a scientifically interesting matter largely depends on one's methodological eyeglasses. The data analysis from Part C was primarily based on reconstructive data gathered by ethnographic methods. The concept and reflection of the ethnographic procedure have been thoroughly discussed in Part B.

This part is concerned with another data type, which must first be defined. The data consists of archived websites as well as log files that preserve the course of written communications between users of the online discussion forum Cibervalle. Not only is the communication form itself relatively new, but also the data type it generates; the discussion about the adequate analytical tools for such data is still young. What we have seen in Part B regarding ethnography also applies to the handling of other methods in qualitative Internet research: Conventional methods are transferred to the Internet, so that, for example, an interview is turned into an online interview, a group discussion into an online group discussion (cf. Mann and Stewart 2000) and a textual analysis becomes a hypertext analysis (cf. Moes 2000).

Log files of the Forum communication could entice the researcher into assuming that conversation analysis is an excellent tool for analysis, firstly because we are concerned here with conversations, albeit written ones,[1] and secondly, because the data are formed from communicative processes and have 'occurred naturally' (Silverman 2007). In other words, they are spontaneous and detailed representations of courses of communication that would have taken place exactly like this even if the researcher had no interest in recording them. So, one could conclude that log files are in a sense natural transcripts that not only save the researcher the tedious task of transcription, but also preserve the richness of the data, which is something that otherwise could be lost in the course of transcribing audio or video recordings.[2] But are these really natural transcripts? Let us first look at the premises of conversation analysis, so that we can verify in the next step whether a method developed for the analysis of audio data can be applied to the data type in question.

CONVERSATION ANALYSIS AND INTERNET COMMUNICATION

Conversation analysis operates with audio(visual) recordings of real inter-actions, "which can be said to be 'natural' insofar as they are kept in their original habitat and would have occurred if the researcher with his recorder had not been present" (Bergmann 2003b, 531; *own translation*). Tradition-ally, conversation analysis is based entirely on audio recordings of conver-sations and their transcripts. The latter should contain all linguistic and paralinguistic elements, even if (or rather precisely because) their sense is not immediately apparent to the researcher. Conversation analysis thereby adheres to the principle of "order at all points" (Sacks 1984), forbidding selection during transcription, which is why slips of the tongue, phonetic elements and pauses are not omitted. The "order-at-all-points" principle maintains that speech interactions adhere to an inner orderliness on which the speakers orient themselves and that they construct communicatively, as it were, in the act of doing so.

Sacks, Schegloff and Jefferson (1974) have developed an elementary system of the organization of a conversation, which mainly identifies the following functional mechanisms: The basic unit of a conversation is the turn of speech. A conversation has a sequential, i.e., temporal progres-sion, wherein the allocation of rights to take the next turn ('turn-taking') is regulated by (among other features) the specific connection of utter-ances. The adjacency pair is one of the most important organizational elements in a conversation. Talk is largely organized in responsive pairs. Typical adjacency pairs are greetings and question/answer. The realiza-tion of the first utterance ('opening turn') implies a normative expecta-tion for the subsequent one ('closing turn'). To take a case in point, if one person greets another person, this other person's failure to greet back is perceived as a turn-taking violation, just as if someone reacts to a ques-tion by greeting the questioner. Thus, the first part of an adjacency pair not only renders the second part conditionally relevant, but it also deter-mines the content of the second part (cf. Bergmann 1988). Conversation analysis ascertains the sequential order of talk in interaction by analyzing transcripts line by line so as to identify the typical functional mechanisms for particular types of conversation.

However, the strong orientation on conversation and the preference for audio recordings leads to a tendency to neglect elements of communica-tion that are not conveyed linguistically (e.g., direction of gaze, gestures, facial expressions). Conversation analysis is thus extremely well suited to the analysis of telephone conversations (Bergmann 1993), but rather less for the analysis of Televisión programs (Ayaß 1997) or—like in the "studies of work"—for the analysis of working environments, wherein the everyday practices of a particular field of work are being examined (cf. Bergmann 2003a, 129ff.). The exclusive concentration on audio material is equally problematic if the research focus is on human–computer interactions (Krummheuer 2010). In all of these research fields, video recordings that also capture nonlinguistic elements of communication as well as context information are deployed.[3] Ethnographic methods can also be applied in these research fields, and they can be usefully combined with conversation analysis (Suchman 1987; Goll 2002).

Despite the differences in relation to the data density of audio and video recordings, the analytical principle essentially remains the same in both cases. The meticulous and systematic transcription of the recordings follows the sequential analysis of the transcripts. The systematic transcription procedure is already part of the analytical process because the process of abstracting the raw material into writing and textual symbols facilitates the identification of recurring patterns and structures of order in the data. The sequential procedure facilitates tracing what Garfinkel calls the interactive "accomplishment" of social reality. Even if the researcher, unlike in the live interaction situation, is presented with the opportunity to manipulate the data chronologically, e.g., to jump from here to there in the text or to repeat a particular sequence or to view it in slow motion, he or she should initially refrain from doing so in order to retrace the way in which the participants mutually produce the meaningful orderliness of the studied social situation. As the participants themselves cannot explain an utterance through recourse to passages that appear later in the text, it is analytically questionable for the researcher to do so. In this context Bergmann (1985) warns of falling into the trap of naïve realism by interpreting one's recorded data as a mirror image of reality. He emphasizes that social reality is essentially ephemeral, and that this basic property of the social world is eliminated in the very moment of its documentation.

ARE LOG FILES NATURALLY OCCURRING TRANSCRIPTS?

Bergmann (1993) argues for the special suitability of conversation analysis for studying telephone conversations by pointing to the lower density of this form of communication in comparison to face-to-face encounters. According to Bergmann, a telephone conversation is, in a kind of natural reduction of data, inherently freed of visual cues, meaning that the analytical process can be focused on the spoken word. At first sight, Internet-based written forms of communication such as e-mail, forum or chat communication appear to be, to an even greater degree, naturally reduced data. Facial expressions, gestures and phonetic elements (e.g., loudness, pauses and intonation), which conversation analysts transcribe and translate into signs, are not transmitted. To the contrary, chat communication is a hybrid form of speech falling somewhere between speech and writing.[4] Here, participants themselves are in a sense engaged in transcription when they take physical and phonetic elements of communication as well as pieces of contextual information, all of which are invisible/inaudible for their counterparts, and abstract into signs the ones they consider relevant for the coparticipant. At this point, the assumption that conversation analysis is suited extremely well to examine log files of Internet-based communication appears to be correct. But let us take another look at the structural organization of Internet-based communication.

As opposed to face-to-face or telephone conversations, both of which have a sequential order on which all participants orient themselves and that can therefore be reconstructed by means of conversation analysis, the sequential order of Internet-based forms of communication is broken by several structural characteristics. For Orthmann, the suitability of conversation analysis for chat communication is limited: It is not able "to ascertain the organizational social principles and procedures guiding the chatters' conversation, i.e., the principles and procedures that structure their interaction" (2004, 158; *own translation*). Her study of the log files of a web chat for children and young adults concludes that chat communication differs considerably from spoken conversation. The assumptions relating to the sequential order of communication; the way in which the turn-taking is organized; the meaning of paralinguistic elements such as pauses, overlaps or self-initiated repairs of the speaker's own utterances; and conversation analysis' methodological procedure based on these assumptions simply cannot be applied to the sequential order of chat communication. "Due to the technical nature of the 'distribution system' of chat-messages, consecutive turns rarely bear reference to each other. In contrast to spoken conversation, coherence can hardly be interpreted by means of the sequential order" (ibid., 153; *own translation*). Orthmann summarizes that the participants in chat communication are more oriented towards the topicality of contributions than on their sequentiality. As a result, contributions frequently remain unanswered because they simply disappear in the overabundance of potential options that arise due to the multitude of messages the different parties send simultaneously.

With regard to the online discussion forum communication format, there are two additional features to be observed. Firstly, it is an asynchronous form of communication, wherein the social reality, which we investigate here, is in a sense fixated by the communicators themselves. Secondly, the hypertext structure and the multimedia structure of the electronic bulletin board, as well as the specific practices of this particular user culture, suggest a multitude of different kinds of interpretation. This further complicates the production of a sequential order to which all participants can adhere, as we shall see in this section. Concerning the data analysis, the question also arises as to how far particular hypertext linking schemes or visual elements of the communication should be taken into consideration (cf. Bergmann and Meier 2003, 432; Moes 2000). In other words, the process of natural data reduction caused by the auto-transcription on the part of the communicators conflicts with a variety of contextual references, concepts of order and the hypertext and multimedia nature of this communication form. All of these have to be tackled by the users of the online discussion forum and by the researcher. In the case of Cibervalle, not just the written communication, but also the placement of photos play a central role the analysis must take account of.

For some time now, genre analysis has been applied in the study of Internet communication. Other than conversation analysis, which focuses on the internal structure of talk in interaction, genre analysis establishes an analytical link between particular speech events and the sociocultural embedding of speaking practices, i.e., social structures, norms, rules, expectations and ideologies. Genre analysis thus has the advantage of relating the different structural levels, which constitute "culturally patterned speaking practices" (Günthner and Knoblauch 1995). In the case of mediated communication, this includes the structural features of the medium. But what exactly is a communicative genre and how can genre analysis be applied to the present research subject?

GENRE ANALYSIS AND INTERNET COMMUNICATION

Communicative genres denominate a level of social communication, which settles intermediately between the social mediation of knowledge ("linguistic, code-related level") and its institutionalization in historically specific social structures ("institutional, social-structure-related level"; Bergmann and Luckmann 1995). They are solutions to specific communicative problems and support the maintenance of a cultural group's social order. Different societal types come with a diverse repertoire of communicative genres. However, culturally and historically comparative research illustrates "the universality of communicative genres as an organizational principle of social communication but also remarkable similarities in many of their specific historical forms" (ibid., 291). One can thus refer to the particular repertoire of communicative genres and other, weaker patterns of written communication as the "meaningful and activity-oriented interior architecture of a society" (Knoblauch und Luckmann 2003, 546; *own translation*) or of a cultural group, the analysis of which affords an inductive approach to their patterns of interpretation and structure of order.

Genre analysis suggests that communication is analytically divided into two levels. The *external structure* comprises all characteristics arising from the relation between communicative action and the respective social structure. Characteristics with respect to milieus, social categories of participants and the social relationship between them are incorporated here, as are the conventions for the use (or nonuse) of certain communicative genres. Here we analyze their relations to the social environment, cultural, ethnic, institutional or gender-specific traits and—in the case of mediated communication—the structural features of the media in use. The *internal structure* comprises linguistic phenomena, like prosodic and (non)verbal elements or stylistic devices that constitute the respective communicative genre. Günthner and Knoblauch, however, suggest a third level of analysis; the *situational realization level*, which consists of those elements that are part of the ongoing interaction, i.e., the 'interaction order' (Günthner and Knoblauch 1995). This relates to features of the interactive process of communication, such as turn-taking rules, adjacency pairs, social relations of the interactants and spatial-temporal aspects (cf. Knoblauch and Luckmann 2003).

As mentioned earlier, genre analysis methods have been used for quite some time in studies on Internet-based forms of communication. However, some problems with this process have arisen and are discussed in the following section. This discussion is designed to specify the communicative form at hand and the appropriate methods for its analysis. For this reason, some select characteristics of the social formation Cibervalle are raised in the following discussion before a deeper look into the communicative organization of Cibervalle is presented in the section after.

IS THE ELECTRONIC BULLETIN BOARD A GENRE?

Frequently genre analysis is applied to the study of Internet communication by way of defining these communication tools themselves as genres. By doing so, the structural features of a communicative tool are elaborated and the specific features that are ascertained are interpreted to be results of the tool itself. Examples include a study on chats (Schmidt 2000), a personal homepage (Dillon and Gushrowski 2000) or a blog[5] (Miller and Shephard 2004). Androutsopoulos (2003) criticizes this approach by pointing to the increasing differentiation of communication technologies and styles on the Internet. The author emphasizes that, even within these new communication tools brought forth by the Internet, different styles and user-specific cultures are formed. Thus, a hosted chat with politicians differs considerably from a chat dedicated to counseling or a role-playing game. According to Androutsopoulos, one has to therefore discern between a communicative tool and a communication genre. In the case of Cibervalle there is indeed a wide variation of communicative patterns comprising elements of chatting and blogging as well as topic-centered discussion groups. A specific user culture has developed that combines several tools and forms of communication, as we shall see in the following. The practice of linking different communication tools here actually forms the basis for the consolidation of communicative patterns or genres rather than for the communication formats themselves.

In the case of Internet communication it is difficult to discriminate the structural levels of communication, especially with regard to the typification of certain groups of participants and their social contexts. In many cases the participants of an online chat or discussion forum cannot see each other and often reside in mutually unfamiliar spatial and social environments. As a result, social context information is hard to come by both for the researcher and for the participants, and cannot be presumed as relevant per se. On the other hand, information concerning gender and social status, for example, cannot necessarily be considered irrelevant because, unlike the visions suggested by the first decade of Internet research (cf. Turkle 1995; Poster 1997), virtuality does not guarantee egalitarian social relations or free choice of alternative identities. Instead of presuming the basic relevance or irrelevance of social context information, it appears more useful to me to examine the communication with regard to how and to what effect the participants supply context information into the communication themselves, as well as how they mark socio-structural, gender-related or ethnic differences or similarities. For a more thorough genre analysis of online-forums similar to Cibervalle that define themselves by means of a mutual geographic reference, an interesting question could be, how is 'natio-ethno-cultural' (non)belonging organized communicatively?

In the case of Cibervalle, the transnational practices of the users spawn interesting socio-structural modifications. As has become apparent in the ethnographic part of this study, transnational migration is not linked only with somewhat paradoxical changes of social status, but also usually leads to a facilitated access to the Internet. Contrary to the geographical migration destinations of most Cibervallers, Internet access is relatively expensive in Paraguay and therefore largely limited to the privileged groups of the population. Paraguayans living in migration who, due to their financial and lifeworld-related situation in Paraguay, had scant access to the Internet, can now find, for example, a cheap cybercafé at nearly every street corner in Madrid or Buenos Aires. Even the ownership of a personal computer with Internet access is possible when living in migration, meaning that communication with relatives can take place from home and participation in the Cibervalle activities can be integrated into day-to-day life. Through its transnational structure Cibervalle becomes a social space in which members of different social classes and lifestyles interact, although in the physical grounded Paraguayan space they mostly live in separate milieus or interact within relations that are hierarchically structured. In the framework of a further genre analytical approach to Cibervalle's communicative architecture, the question arises as to whether or not the socio-structural modifications resulting from the social formations' transnational character are communicatively constructed (and if so, how).[6]

Ultimately the technological conditions of communication can hardly be separated from the communicative practices. Thus, elements of the situational realization level and internal structure are modified by the respective medium and can therefore not be examined separately from the external structure. The spatial and temporal context, for example, that Schmidt (2000) in her study on the communication form chat assigns to the situational realization level is in electronic communication very much determined by the technological preconditions of transmission. Baym (1995) therefore suggests focusing more on the influences of the medium on the social forms of its appropriation. In her study on the Usenet discussion forum r.a.t.s. she takes the case of the fan community of a soap opera to examine the social dimensions of computer-mediated community-building. She defines system infrastructure and temporal structure as medium-specific levels. According to Baym, the level of system infrastructure should be included, because the hard- and software with which individual participants are equipped, and also the server-dependent bit rate, exert their influence on the communication at hand.

On the level of the temporal structure Baym distinguishes synchronous and asynchronous forms of computer-mediated communication. Here again, interesting interrelations between system infrastructure and social structure can be observed in Cibervalle, which on the global level appear as a mirror image of unequally distributed opportunities for participation in the global communication network. Thus, Cibervallers in Paraguay in general have to make do with lower bit rates and more obstacles than, for example, their counterparts in the US. This is due in part to the fact that the website is hosted on a server in the US, but also because of the performance specifications of equipment available to the participants, namely, processing speed, system configurations and respective network capacity. Global social structures of inequality thus do not merely affect the unequal distribution of technological resources, but also influence the opportunities for participation in global discourses.

The differentiation of synchronous and asynchronous forms of communication makes sense in Cibervalle, too, insofar as it allows for conclusions about the different practices of usage and patterns of interpretation. Nevertheless, it can also be observed here that it is not only the medium that determines whether a communication is synchronous or asynchronous. Rather, it is the specific practices of appropriation of the communication tool that play a decisive role in this definition. Baym writes: "Rather than being constrained by the computer, the members of these groups creatively exploit the system's features so as to play with new forms of expressive communication" (1995, 159). The interrelations between technological tools and the practices of their appropriation are of special interest in this study because they provide insights into the types of relations, communities and sociality that in transnational migration contexts can emerge through the everyday usage of the Internet.

A MODEL FOR ANALYZING CIBERVALLE'S COMMUNICATIVE ARCHITECTURE

The analysis of the communicative organization and social order of the mutually shared virtual space named Cibervalle aims at understanding the inner logic of social processes that occur in connection with migration and the use of global communication technologies. It can therefore only be understood if it is embedded in the ethnographic description of the social spaces and everyday life of the Cibervalle inhabitants as detailed in the preceding. Conversation analysis, which focuses primarily on "the inconspicuously small, microscopic molecular forms of sociality" (Bergmann 2003b, 536; *own translation*), might inspire and sharpen the focus on the present research subject.

However, in order to fully describe such a complex social formation as Cibervalle, an analytical procedure that also turns its attention to the interrelations between communicative, socio-structural, media-related and contextual elements of the construction of social reality is needed. If one perceives communicative genres as "historically and culturally specific and formalized solutions of communicative problems, which have been consolidated within the respective society [. . .] the function of which lies in the accomplishment, mediation and tradition of intersubjective lifeworld experiences" (Günthner and Knoblauch 1997, 282; *own translation*), then genre analysis—despite the problems discussed earlier—is advantageous for the analysis of the specific culture of a computer-mediated social formation.

The next chapter will take a closer look at the communicative architecture that allows the inhabitants of Cibervalle to live together despite geographic distance. While taking into consideration the problems of applying genre analytical procedures, structure and characteristics of the electronic bulletin board and the instant messaging client will be described and the socio-technological evolution of the Cibervalle Forum will be examined. This evolution will serve to distill the reciprocal effects between technological features and their social appropriation by the participants. Using the ethnographically generated data, the specific media-based practices and the techno-social forms on which global togetherness in Cibervalle rests will then be elaborated.

13 Structure and Techno-Social Evolution of the Cibervalle Forum

The communicative organization of Cibervalle is based primarily on the combination of three communication systems.[7] Besides the publicly accessible online discussion forum, an instant messaging client is used for private communication between two or more participants. In addition, regular local meetings are held in the participants' respective places of residence, which in turn are communicated back to the global public level of forum communication. The social formation Cibervalle is thus based on a complex interplay of different media-based and copresent forms of communication, interaction and mobility that are presented and analyzed in the following.

CONTENT, CONTEXT, ROLES AND MODES OF PARTICIPATION

Exterior Context and Embeddedness of the Forum

The discussion forum is part of the communication environment of a commercial Paraguayan website that is globally accessible via the WWW. This website offers different online services, all of which relate to Paraguay. These services include a search machine, a social network service,[8] a national and international news feed, regional/national information and important national addresses. The range of information and services offered come in a package with advertisements for Paraguayan firms. During the first period of my research, the interactive communication environment of the Cibervalle website was restricted to a discussion forum and a chat. Following substantive renovations to the website towards the end of my data collection, Cibervalle.com supplied free of charge the option to open one's own e-mail account and a personal blog. Links to the websites of Paraguayan cellular phone franchises that supplied free SMS services to Paraguay were also established.

Necessary Resources for Participation

The Cibervalle Forum is public and potentially accessible worldwide; anyone can read the discussions without registration. Nevertheless, access is limited on several levels, as one has to have certain resources (namely, a computer equipped with Internet access), information and know-how in order to gain access to the Forum. One also needs to have some level of competence in working with a computer and the Internet, as well as the ability to read and write. To make sense of the communication in the Forum, the ability to speak Spanish (the main language of the Forum) is of absolute necessity, although it is infused with the linguistic hybrid *Jopará*. English, German and French occasionally appear, either in single words or very rarely in complete conversations, mainly between participants in the US, Australia, Germany and France. But as the following example (Table 13.1) illustrates, this deviation from the implicit rule is usually criticized quite quickly by other participants who demand Spanish/*Jopará* as the language everyone can understand.

The commentary is part of the welcome-Tópico, in which I presented myself as the new participant "Mafalda." During the course of my self-introduction I was welcomed by another participant in German and I answered in German. This short exchange was subsequently interrupted by Luis's contribution. His first turn[9] contains a twofold message: First, Luis demonstrates that he knows some German. Simultaneously, he makes clear that the exchange in a foreign language will not be understood by the community and that there is a general claim to linguistic comprehension. The latter is implied when he demands in the next turn that this communication should be continued "in the language of the poor," the folk respectively, and thus in Spanish/*Jopará*. After my communicative exchange with the first participant in German, the communication switches over to Spanish/*Jopará* following the request from Luis.

If nothing else, one has to actually find the Cibervalle Forum within the endless depths of the WWW—either by chance or by being informed about its existence or by knowing its URL or at least its name so that the website can be accessed. Given the system of linking of the WWW, the likelihood of discovering Cibervalle by chance is greatest when one is searching online for information about Paraguay. In other words, apart from linguistic proficiency and media-specific skills, interest in Paraguayan topics also plays a role in access to the Cibervalle Forum.

Table 13.1   Welcoming Tópico "Mafalda"

He!Das Volk wie wir will wissen, was sie ist, darüber sprechend. Irgendwie, Samuel, Herr-Liebe	He!The folk like us want to know, what she is, talking about it. Somehow, Samuel, Mister-Love
Jejejeje aulen na un poko en el idioma de los pobres, jejejeje	hehehehe, please do whine a bit in the language of the poor, hehehehe
Luis	**Luis**
IP: 200.85.34*	**IP:** 200.85.34*
10/09/2004	10/09/2004

Roles and Modi of Participation

The roles of participation that constitute Cibervalle can be differentiated according to, firstly, the density of participants' addresses and, secondly, the right to intervene in the communicative flow in the Forum. Address density here means the extent to which participants are addressable by other participants. Whoever restricts his participation to anonymous reading is not personally distinguishable, and thus not addressable as a communication partner, but rather only as an indistinct part of a diffuse and imagined audience.[10] To register, one must supply a nickname (nick) with which one presents him- or herself to the other participants. Furthermore, an e-mail address that is known at least to the host and the administrators of the Forum is necessary. However, even as a registered member, one is only perceivable if one contributes his or her own Tópicos or comments. Thus, the address density on the level of the Forum communication increases the more frequently participants contribute their own posts. Beyond the communication system, the Forum provides the opportunity to publish personal information like age, date of birth, zodiac sign, place of residence, e-mail address and photos. During registration it is usually recommended that the new member open a special e-mail account in order to use the instant messaging client that most other members also use. Frequently, the participants also ask for each other's e-mail addresses in the Tópicos in order to extend communication to instant messaging. The public Forum communication is closely tied to the private communication via IM, as will be illustrated in the following section. Another possibility to increase the address density results from taking part in the regular meetings in the participants' places of residence.

Concerning the right to intervene, the role of the participant differs from that of the host or administrator, as both of the latter have the option to erase individual contributions or complete Tópicos, as well as to prevent individual nicks from active participation. Moreover, only the administrators have the right to make modifications to the communication system. As mentioned earlier, the Forum is part of a commercial website. Given the status differences in relation to intervention rights, the commercial orientation of the company as opposed to the primarily social interests of the Forum community is worth mentioning. The construction of this antagonism or, to be more precise, of a community's own identity in dissociation with the corporate management will be discussed later in the context of reconstructing the development of the Forum's code of conduct.

The Tópico

In order to open a new Tópico, the respective thematic category is first chosen. The title and opening text of the new Tópico can be entered in an electronic form found at the end of the list of current Tópicos in the category.

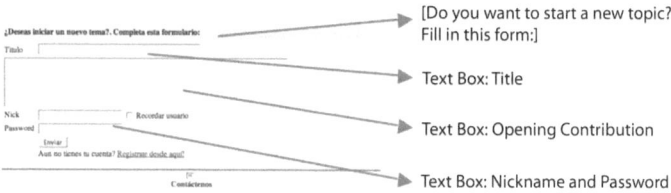

[Do you want to start a new topic?
Fill in this form:]

Text Box: Title

Text Box: Opening Contribution

Text Box: Nickname and Password

Figure 13.1   "New Tópico."

Depending on the technological capacity of the computer, the location of the provider or the server's bit rate, it can take several minutes for the Tópico to be uploaded and for its title to appear in the list of currently discussed themes. If one clicks on the title, the page of the discussion thread opens and one can read the introductory text, which includes further information about the author.

Besides the name of the author and his encoded e-mail address, one can deduce his or her whereabouts, or to be more precise the provider location from his encoded IP-address.[13] Furthermore, the opening sequence provides information about the number of answers in the Tópico and the 'freshness' of the discussion. In other words, one learns when the last contribution was made (Table 13.2). The answers appear in chronological order below the opening post, so that the last comment is situated at the bottom of the page. If one wants to participate in an ongoing discussion one has to scroll to the end of the page, where an electronic form invites commentaries.

Table 13.2   Tópico "Alguien por Alemania"

Alguien por Alemania	*Anybody in Germany*
Lo hago por una hermana que vive alla, no conoce a nadie y acaba de volver de Paraguay donde estuvo de vacaciones, es mas para los interesados que quieren comunicarse con una compatriota que llevo yerba, coquitos, rosquitas, chipitas para compartir.(jijijiji)	I am doing this for a sister who lives there, she doesn't know anybody and she has just come back from Paraguay, where she spent her holidays, it is directed at all interested persons, who want contact with a fellow country-woman who has brought yerba[11], coquitos, rosquitas, chipitas[12] to share them. (hihihihihi)
Nick: David	**Nick: David**
E-mail: d-vi-sm-r-c @*m**l.com	E-mail: d-vi-sm-r-c-@*m**l.com
IP: 138.82.28.*	**IP:** 138.82.28.*
Respuestas: 23	Answers: 23
Última Respuesta: 28/01/2004	Last answer: 28/01/2004

Table 13.3   Tópico "Alguien por Alemania"

Yo estoy en Alemania hace mas de un anho. Es dificil al comienzo, por donde esta tu hermana? Cualquier ayuda, consejo que necesite a las ordenes. Jóse **IP:** 134.111.342.* 26/01/2004 (#136489)	I have been in Germany for more than one year. It is difficult in the beginning, where exactly is your sister? For whatever help, advice she might need, I am there for her. Jóse **IP:** 134.111.342.* 26/01/2004 (#136489)

Contrary to the opening of a Tópico, there is no option when answering to provide a title or a subject, and the e-mail address is also not displayed; only the IP-address, date and the total number of contributions the Forum counts at this particular time are shown (Table 13.3).

TIME STRUCTURES OF VIRTUAL SPACES

Synchronicity and Asynchronicity

Contrary to other Internet-based forms of communication such as chat or e-mail that provide, respectively, for either synchronous or asynchronous communication, the Forum accommodates both. As the contributions are transmitted nearly in real time, participants who are online at the same time can answer their geographically distant counterparts immediately. In fact, many Forum conversations can be found that are more similar to an everyday conversation than to a discussion in the sense of a topically centered exchange of factual arguments. In these Tópicos, content and structure of the text are similar to the synchronous communication form chat, as the following example (Table 13.4) illustrates.[14]

Chaot marks his sudden presence in the Tópico with a salutation and demonstrates communicative openness to all participants by asking a question not addressed to a particular person. Similar to communication in a chat room, he tries to get into an ongoing conversation. Sandra, who is online at the same time and who has opened the Tópico, catches the ball thrown into the court by Chaot and answers his question. Thus, a short, synchronous exchange commences between the two before the contributions of other participants interrupt the two-way communication and guide the conversation into a thematically different direction.

General greetings, quick changes of themes and participants, short contributions and verbal exchanges between individual participants are typical for this synchronous form of usage (cf. Schmidt 2000), which lends a chat room character to the Cibervalle Forum. Contrary to a chat, however, all contributions of a discussion are saved and the course the discussion has taken can be

Table 13.4 Tópico "Dinosaurio"

Hola buenas tardes como estan Alguien vio a mi Dinosaurio en patin por hay Chaot IP: 65.198.43.* 23/04/2004	Hello, good afternoon, how are you Has anyone seen my skateboarding dinosaur here somewhere Chaot IP: 65.198.43.* 23/04/2004
recien pasó, iba de bajada, creo que hacia al puerto este es? sandra IP: 200.85.34* 23/04/2004	He just passed by, he was on his way down, I think he went in the direction of the harbour, is this the one you are looking for? sandra IP: 200.85.34* 23/04/2004

read later in chronological order, at least as long as the discussion as a whole lasts, and, at least during my research period, at the latest ten days after the last text contribution to the respective Tópico.[15] It is possible, then, for participants whose activities in the Forum are temporarily (or financially) limited, or who cannot be online at the appropriate time, to reconstruct ongoing discussions and either join in or simply enjoy reading them.

Sequentiality

The technological conditions do not only frame the communication and social organization of Cibervalle, but they also affect them in a more intensive way. With regard to the sequentiality of the communication, both the lack of nonverbal means of turn-taking in a 'many-to-many' communication structure (as in chat communication) as well as the medium itself and its technological embeddedness lead to sequential disorder. Because one cannot see one's communication partners, and thus cannot judge who is preparing to make a contribution or how many participants are taking part in the discussion, contributions are not tied together in such a way that they meaningfully relate to one other. This lack of a meaningful order of appearance of individual contributions is due in part to the technologically determined difference in the speed with which they appear. Therefore, how the individual contributions relate to one another cannot be reconstructed by means of the sequential course of the communication at hand.

An important feature of the Forum communication is the degree of its fleetingness, which arises from its temporal structure and leads to a number of methodological as well as social consequences. The social life happening in the Forum is less ephemeral than face-to-face or chat communication because all contributions in a Forum discussion can be seen on the screen for as long as the discussion lasts. The ephemeral character of the spoken word implies that participants arriving late to a conversation cannot reconstruct on their own the course it has taken. To join in a meaningful way, one has to rely on other participants helping out in reconstructing what has been discussed so far. Usually, the participants who have conducted the conversation agree to a shared interpretation, and in doing so reassure themselves of what they are actually discussing. The Forum communication, however, provides the opportunity—and this, in a sense, is one of its structural characteristics—for new participants to inform themselves by reading the course of the conversation to date. In other words, this medium presents the participants with the opportunity to reconstruct on their own the developed course of a discussion. Contrary to face-to-face conversations, there seems to be an expectation of the participants of online-forum discussions to independently reconstruct the course of the communication. Participants have been observed to neither start their participation by asking what the discussion is about nor to be welcomed with the kind of summary explanations often found in face-to-face communication. The option of asking, "What's going on here?" as a way of constructing coherence appears not to exist in this kind of persistent social reality.

The Forum discussion, however, cannot be reconstructed in its temporal course by those joining in later, as temporal disruptions or longer pauses cannot be meaningfully interpreted.[16] Pauses due to technical factors can hardly be distinguished from socially caused pauses. Thus, the temporal development of the interaction differs according to the actual activity of each participant. If one communicates synchronously, one experiences temporal lags and pauses, but does not know how the communication continues. If one reads a discussion afterwards, then one as a rule does not, while reading, reconstruct the actual temporal course. Instead one reads the Tópico as if the contributions were written consecutively and without a pause. Also, while reading, one does not have to adhere to the sequential order of the text, but rather can skip around and read selectively. In other words, the participants are highly dependent on their own individual interpretations. Very different readings can result—each according to the person's lifeworld and time context of reception. The next section will examine how the participants attempt to construct coherence, or at least keep the flow of the communication going, despite sequential disorder and the structurally determined multitude of individual readings.

In comparison to the nonelectronic text genres, online-forum communication is much more fleeting. Due to its hypertext structure, it is more complex and its analysis is therefore more complicated. When a Tópico receives no contributions for longer than ten days it is erased. In other words, it is not accessible anymore via the website of the Forum, but it could quite possibly be found by an Internet search engine. In some cases the Cibervalle administration or the moderator decide to erase a Tópico for other reasons, even if the discussion has not ended. In particular, contributions are erased if individual participants feel they or the Cibervalle community as a whole has been insulted or hurt. At this point—due to the public accessibility of the Forum—the triadic communication structure is foreshadowed, which decisively molds Cibervalle's social life on the Forum level. The removal of a contribution does not turn the clock back on the insult that was the cause for its elimination. However, as it was an insult in front of others (on a public stage), the necessity arises to erase contributions in order to keep their distribution as low as possible. In other words, the imagined anonymous audience is an intrinsic part of the communication. This point will be revisited in Chapter 15.

In any case, it is characteristic of this communication system that an opening turn is structurally stipulated, but no closing turn indicates the end of the discussion. For archiving and analysis of the data generated online, this entails, firstly, that a discussion one has observed for a long time but not yet saved can suddenly disappear, and, secondly, that one cannot determine the exact time at which to archive these data. During the subsequent analysis of the discussion, the lack of a sequence that marks the end of a discussion makes the texts appear unfinished; it is as if the communications had abruptly ended without a conceivable reason or as if one had archived them too early, having not been patient enough to wait for the end.

The degree of fleetingness, the lack of a closing turn as well as the hypertext format require the researcher to always "ascertain where a text begins and where it ends" (Moes 2000, 7; *own translation*). In order to guarantee a meaningful delimitation of the text and the order in which it is analyzed, Moes suggests that in website analysis the structure of the site should itself be the focus. In the case of Cibervalle, it must be noted that the external structure of the website is determined by the designers and administrators of the site, neither of whom are representative of the users themselves. Thus, I suggest taking a more critical look at the relationship between the internal and external structure of the communication system. The actual readings of users can only be reconstructed to a limited extent from the course of the communication. It is difficult to ascertain whether a participant has actually read the complete discussion thread before he or she contributes a comment, whether the person has been informed about the state of the discussion via another communicative channel or whether it is simply coincidence that this person's contribution fits into the discussion in a meaningful way. Also, the question of orientation within the hypertext structure of the site is difficult to detect by means of the analysis of the website alone. Whether the links placed by other participants in a Tópico have been followed or not can be deduced only insofar as the content of the linked site is in any way referenced in the subsequent discussion.

Within the framework of an ethnographic study in which the local perspectives and practices of the actors are taken into consideration and in which the researcher's own experiences as a member are utilized as an additional resource, different patterns of interpretation can be reconstructed and analyzed with regards to their impact on the communication course taken in an online discussion forum. So the question in the first place is not how a hypertext can be delimited and brought into a meaningful order. Rather, we are asking how the participants orient themselves in the hypertext structure and how they achieve coherence or at least ensure that the communication continues. By means of the evolution of the Cibervalle online-forum, we can now reconstruct how the technological features of the communication system, which cause sequential disorder and throw users back onto their own individual readings, are met with specific communicative practices and, last but not least, how these practices are subsequently integrated into the technological environment.

"ONCE UPON A TIME . . ."—THE EVOLUTION OF MEDIATED SOCIALITY AT A DISTANCE

The quotation in Table 13.5 is taken from the Forum. It is the opening sequence of a Tópico in which Esther, the author, narrates the history of Cibervalle from her own subjective perspective. Esther is one of the long-standing members. She helped in shaping Cibervalle's transformation process from an anonymous virtual communication space to a global mutually supportive community. She also played an active part in the evolutionary development of the Forum's communication and witnessed several technological renovations. Her comment not only emphasizes the multiplicity of communicative subject matters and practices that are characteristic for the Cibervalle Forum, but also, in stressing the condition of anonymity as much as the scarce means of expression in its beginnings, Esther also points towards the connection between informational richness of communication and the quality of social relationships.

As part of my analysis I reconstructed the process of mutually advancing technological tools and their usage for the time between 2002 and 2005. For this purpose I used the Internet Wayback Machine,[17] an archival website that enabled me to find older versions of the electronic bulletin board and to examine the website renovations made over time. Via the ethnographic data I determined that the technological development of the electronic bulletin board was strongly shaped by the users' needs and communicative practices. Furthermore, through my own participant observation, I was able to grasp the meanings of those technological renovations.

The Forum first appeared on the archived pages of the Cibervalle web portal in 2002, four years after the website was established. At that time, the interactive communication had been restricted to a chat (since late 1999) and the option to send SMS to the mobile phones of a Paraguayan mobile telephony network (since 2002). According to one of the first registered members, the Forum was set up by the designers of the website and left to its own devices: "When I first entered the Forum, there were only 5 users, I had the number 6, hehe, there was nobody there, nothing happened. I started sending e-mails to my acquaintances and so little by little more people arrived" (Manuela, Asunción, e-mail communication). Slowly

Table 13.5   Tópico "Erase una Vez"

Erase una vez . . .	*Once upon a time there was . . .*
un foro más, donde muchos Nicks entraban a leer, opinar, divagar, hacer catarsis, enviar poemas, aprender tags†, contar chistes, pelearse, escribir novelas, relatos, dar clases de sexo, en fin . . . yo también quise formar parte de ese grupo, los leí como 3 meses y empecé a hacerme una idea de como era realmente cada uno de ellos . . . en aquel tiempo no había album de ciber-valle, y nadie manejaba casi el html y mucho menos subir una foto en el foro . . . o sea era algo tan impersonal . . .	just one more electronic bulletin board, entered by many nicks in order to read, to argue, to maunder, to calm down, to forward poems, to learn tags†, to joke, to write novels and tales, to teach sex education, in short . . . I wanted to be part of that group, I read them for about three months and started to imagine what each one of them would be like in reality. At that time there were neither a photo album nor member pro-files, and hardly anyone had proficient usage of html, and we knew even less how to upload photos . . . I mean every-thing was very impersonal . . .
Postear dirigiendote a alguien era como un tiro en la oscuridad, porque no sabías si como te respondería o si lo haría.	Writing to someone in particular seemed like a shot into the dark, because you never knew whether and how he or she would answer.
Imaginarse entonces, su sonrisa o su voz, o su rostro era una utopía. Y saber sus puntos fuertes y débiles ni soñar.	To imagine the smile, voice or face of your counterpart was utopia. Knowing his or her strengths and weaknesses you could not even dream of.
Nick: Esther E-mail: -lg-.-h-r-.f-lt-s@mol*ns.com.py Cantidad de posteos: 1204 IP: 200.85.34.* Respuestas: 164 Última respuesta: 13/07/2005	Nick: Esther E-mail: -lg-.-h-r-.f-lt-s@mol*ns.com.py Number of posts: 1204 IP: 200.85.34.* Answers: 164 Last Answer: 13/07/200

the hitherto rather lifeless Forum was populated with users from all over the world who were more or less ignored by the administration that ran the website at that time. The users settled there and experimented with the communicative means at their disposal, extended them or adapted their communicative practices to the technological conditions.

CHANGING MODES OF TEMPORALITY

The evolutionary development of the Forum between 2002 and 2005 can be documented by comparing the archived front pages of each year on the basis of different renovations to the systems infrastructure. As Figure 13.2 illustrates, the front page of the Forum in 2002 has a rather simple design.

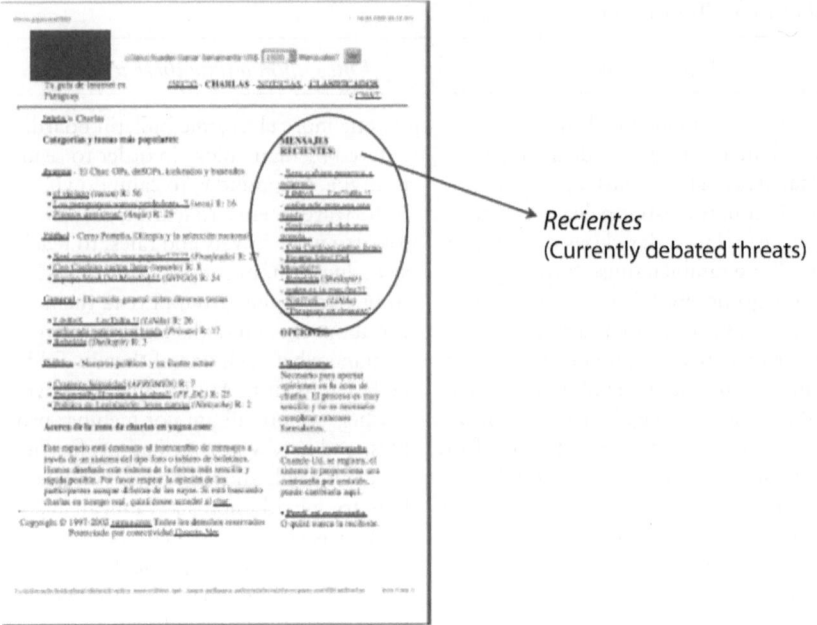

Figure 13.2   Cibervalle Forum 2002.[18]

The Forum is thematically divided into four categories that are defined by a title and a short description: *1. Cibervalle:* According to its description, this category is meant to be a communicative connection to the chat, wherein incidents from the chat can be discussed, and those users who have been temporarily excluded from the chat can raise their voice. *2. Football:* This category avowedly serves the discussion of Paraguayan football. *3. General (issues):* No restrictions here as regards to content. *4. Politics:* This is designed to be a forum for public discussions of current political issues, or for commenting on the conduct of official political representatives.

The front page also contains some details regarding the code of conduct. Firstly, the forum communication is explicitly dissociated from the synchronous form of chat communication, including a link leading directly to the Cibervalle chat. Furthermore, the users are asked to respect other participants' opinions, even if they do not correspond to one's own point of view. Finally, the navigation bar on the right side of the front page includes a category called "latest messages" (*Recientes*), in which the currently debated threads are listed regardless of their thematic affiliation. The *Recientes* displays a selection of the currently debated threads in chronological order from newest to oldest, where the date is taken as the date of the last post. When a member posts in a thread it will jump to the top because it is the latest updated thread. Similarly, other threads will jump in front of it when they receive posts.

Comparing the front pages between 2003 and 2005 shows that the *Recientes* over the years has become the most important part of the electronic bulletin board. In 2002 the *Recientes* contained no more than the thread's title and its author's nickname. Already in 2003 it had twice as much room and displayed not just the title of the Tópico and the name of the author, but also the number of replies the Tópico received so far. In the next year, a rule was added that states Tópicos that do not receive an answer within ten days are to be erased. In 2005 the *Recientes* was expanded even further: Tópicos then remained marked with a certain annotation as long as they had not been answered. Also, a distinction was introduced between 'replies' (*respuestas*) and 'visits' (*visitas*). By means of a small square symbol in the respective national colors authors of Tópicos can be assigned to a certain country, normally the national context of the message author. In summary, participants now find out with a mere glance at the front page who is currently contributing to which Tópico, from where and how much attention the respective thread has received so far.[19]

Participants orient themselves not just on the content but even more on the timeliness or topicality of the discussions. "What is happening right now in Cibervalle?" seems to be the primary question. The practices of usage can be interpreted accordingly. Especially for those users who have unlimited access to the Internet, participation in Forum activities can be described as the opening of an additional techno-social space. During an online inquiry, I asked Cibervallers about the time they spend in the Forum per day. When I

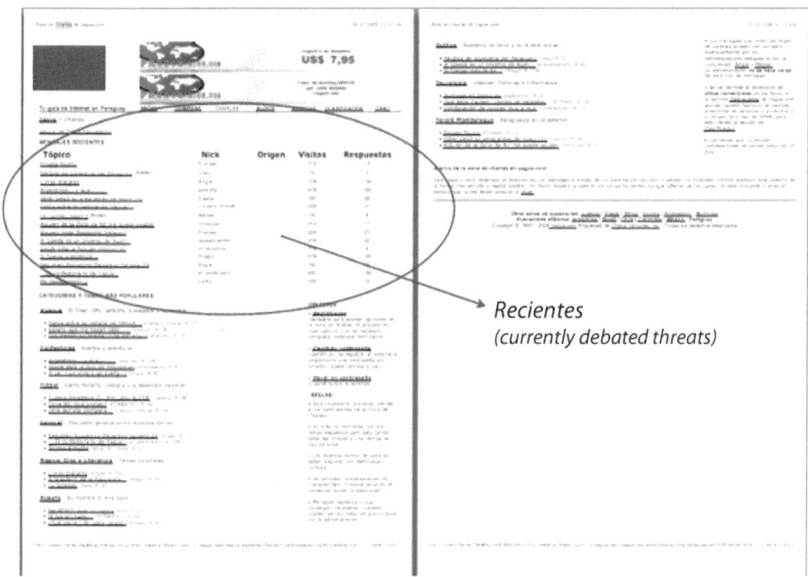

Figure 13.3 Cibervalle Forum 2005.

formulated this question, I presumed a certain kind of participation, namely, one in which users would purposefully enter the page in order to read or write in it and subsequently close it again. So the answers were rather surprising, as the majority described a completely different kind of participation.

For a start, those questioned found it extremely difficult to specify the time they spent in the Forum. Instead they described their practices as "I go in and out" or "I keep the page open but do not read." Many participants set the Forum as the homepage of their browser. Whether these users work with their computer or leave it to do other things, the website is either kept open or consulted repeatedly during the day, in order to keep up with the current goings-on. In doing so, they mainly orient themselves on the *Recientes*, as Eduardo from Asunción describes: "I update the top ten as often as I can to see the news." When choosing a Tópico to turn to, they actively orient themselves on the data apparent from the lists. It may be the title of a Tópico that raises the interest of a participant; however, a high number of answers may deter him or her from having a closer look. Similarly, there may be a preference for or against the contributions of certain nicks or geographic contexts. The *Recientes* appears to be the place where the Forum's movements become visible and observable. Here one can experience Cibervalle's own social life, which is taking place parallel to the physical everyday life of the participants and independently from the activity of each individual.

The lack of a closing turn marking the end of a discussion reinforces the impression of ongoing social activities. It is worth mentioning another renovation regarding the number of contributions. Originally, the Tópicos were limited to seventy-two contributions each, after which they were closed with the notation: "Discussion ended due to too many contributions." Instead of replacing this automatic closing turn produced by the system with meaningful utterances by the participants themselves, since 2005 the threads simply remain unfinished. During the course of a day they slowly change their position and move from the *Recientes* down into the depths of Cibervalle's collective short-term memory. From there they can be updated and again be discussed at any time by any active member, until they eventually vanish for good. Meanwhile, however, communication in Cibervalle is continued elsewhere, in other Tópicos. When a Tópico starts its downward path from the *Recientes* into the lower places of the top ten, only the theme or the participants have changed but the communication never ends.

ENRICHING INFORMATIONAL
THICKNESS OF COMMUNICATION

As Esther describes in her history of Cibervalle, the facilities for expression were rather limited in the early Forum. It was only possible to produce pure unformatted text, and the user specifications were confined to the author's nick, his or her encoded e-mail and IP address and the date of the contribution. Users were learning by practice and through virtual exchanges with more proficient users how to deploy HTML tags†, which now enabled them to format their own text and to utilize different typefaces, font sizes and colors. By means of tags† they could also integrate into the Tópicos not just links to other websites, but also photos and other visual elements and even audio content later on. The users themselves thus changed the internal structure of the Forum communication to a considerable extent. This in turn led to a change in the external structure. At first, 'technology' was included in the Forum as an additional category, in which new or technically nonproficient users were imparted with HTML know-how and taught how to use tags†. During the next technological renovation, the operating company adopted these practices by augmenting the forum with a user-friendly input mask that facilitates formatting text and adding elements and links. In other words, the increased complexity of user options, which the users developed themselves, was integrated as constituent parts in Cibervalle's communication environment.

But what do Cibervallers express when they utilize different colors, typefaces, font sizes and photos? Different character styles and colors can be used for coordination purposes, for example, to accentuate the receiver of a contribution. But they are also deployed for the simulation of intonation. Thus, a written commentary can be amplified (similar to a spoken word being boosted by a raised voice) by means of larger script or garish colors.

Figure 13.4 Tópico "Local meeting *Cumpleaños Ana*."

The example (Figure 13.4) shows a section of a discussion in which Iwashita, the initiator of the Tópico, addresses a conflict she had with the Cibervaller Ana at Ana's birthday party—a conflict Iwashita wants to resolve via the Forum. The commentary highlighted in blue is by Lisa, Ana's friend. She was also present at the party and now accuses Iwashita of lying in her description of how the conflict arose. Lisa also criticizes Iwashita for using the public Forum rather than talking personally to Ana about the problem.

Lisa uses capital letters for her contribution, which she highlights with a potent blue. The meaning of her words is rather aggressive, too. As a result, a number of members raise their voices primarily to complain more about the form of Lisa's contribution than about the content. Irén chooses a similar format for her contribution, simultaneously expressing her alarm at Lisa's contribution being so aggressive: "ouch! my eye!" Some exchanges later she makes her interpretation of Lisa's commentary more explicit: "Lisa nearly made me blind." Another contribution asks Lisa to repeat the same words but to use less conspicuous lettering, thereby demonstrating that the criticism is not directed at the content but at the form of her contribution.

The written text here seems to serve as a context for the interpretation of the chosen expressive means, because garish colors and capital letters are not always taken as a sign of aggression and criticized as such by the communication partners. Still, in the same Tópico another contribution appears in a similar format, but this one calls for the group to make up and stop quarreling. In contrast to Lisa's contribution, this commentary only receives answers relating to its meaning rather than its form. We have discussed earlier how, due to the multimodality of speaking in face-to-face communication, the spoken word and its vocal and physical frame mutually serve each other as interpretation contexts. Similarly, in script-based communication, the construction of meaning is also dependent on the interplay of verbal and visual expressions.

The adoption of visual elements is also utilized by Cibervallers to sharpen their own profile, for example, by creating avatars and inserting them in their signature. This may be someone's self-portrait, the picture of a comic-strip character or personal writing as a signature.[20] In addition, virtual greeting cards are employed, which are chosen from the WWW and integrated into the respective Tópico. Also widely practiced is the publication of photos of the physical surroundings of the members—especially in connection with the local meetings.

These technological advancements of the Forum communication are not invariably welcomed by all participants. For the Cibervallers resident in Paraguay, these advancements entail lower rates of transmission because of growing data volume, because in terms of technological facilities and bit rate, Paraguay is underprivileged compared to the technologically more advanced places of residence of the migrants. In other words, the desire for a higher communicative density here competes with the need for real-time communication. At this point, technologically produced socio-structural inequalities that relate to the chances of participation in the communication of Cibervalle again become apparent. Because of the better technological facilities Cibervallers abroad tend to have at their disposal, and because the Forum has a server based in the US, Paraguayan users are clearly at a disadvantage.

THEMATIC EXTENSION AND COORDINATION OF COMMUNICATION

A first glance at the thematic development of the categories on offer in the Forum reveals a growing diversity of subjects in Cibervalle. The number of categories rose from four in 2002 to nine in 2005. In 2003 the thematic variety in the Forum was at first extended by the categories 'sex' and 'Paraguayans abroad.' In the same year the general rules for communication in the Forum were first established, and two members of the group of users were appointed as moderators to make sure these rules were observed. Initially, the rules were oriented on the *netiquette*,[21] i.e., the customary rules of Internet communication. They forbade insulting other participants, demanded a diplomatic and polite discussion culture and they granted the moderator the right to intervene when necessary and erase individual Tópicos or contributions of members who have not abided by the rules.

But why is it necessary in a virtual discussion space to make such rules explicit and to oversee their observation when all of this should be self-evident? In discussion groups of copresence it would be a source of irritation if such rules of politeness were explicated. Asserting such rules and threatening sanctions if they are not obeyed implies that there are persons present who are not able or willing to apply the respective 'ethno-methods.' Do we therefore have to assume that Cibervallers have no command of such rules of politeness? This question initially leads us back to the problem of constructing coherence in the Forum's communication.

The technological preconditions cause, as I have outlined in the preceding, sequential disorder in the course of communication. The possibility of informing oneself about the course of a discussion throws the participants back onto their own individual constructions of meaning. Thus, it seems reasonable to assume that the Forum communication promotes conflicts between the participants because, compared to face-to-face conversations, there is a higher risk for contradictory interpretations and misunderstandings. At the same time, however, it can be observed how Cibervallers develop communicative patterns over time—i.e., practical solutions to the structural problem of the sequential disorder of communication—in order to explain the context of their own contribution. The specification of the recipient is one such example, which is also used in face-to-face communication with more than two participants. In the Forum communication the name of the addressed person is prefixed to one's own contribution—sometimes also highlighted in a different color.

Table 13.6   Tópico "Plagueate un Ratito"

no por el hecho de ser hispana naci bailando salsa	Only because I am Hispanic American I was not born dancing salsa
panambí IP: 64.62.221.*19/04/2004	panambí IP: 64.62.221.*19/04/2004 [22]
Este es un dilema legalmente. Yo para bailar soy un desastre, unas cuantas veces fuì a "ballare latinoamericano" . . . En la pista eran todos expertos, menos . . . adivinen!!! Y no falta quien te hincha.	It is a real dilemma. I am a disaster when it comes to dancing, I went to a „Latin-American Dance" a few times . . . Everyone on the dancefloor was an expert, except. . . . you guess!!! And there is no lack of people poking fun at you.
terry	terry
IP: 80.33.176.*	**IP:** 80.33.176.*
20/04/2004	20/04/2004

A second option, enabled by the fact that forum communication is less ephemeral than face-to-face conversations, will be discussed as follows (Table 13.6).

Terry relates his commentary to a remark by Panambí, which she made the day before in her Tópico "Plagueate un ratito (Let's complain for a minute)." In her Tópico she invited the members abroad to talk to each other about the dark sides of life in migration, as she explained in her opening contribution. When Terry decided to answer her, the Tópico had already received quite a number of comments. But Terry relates to Panambí's second contribution without commenting on any of the other contributions. He clarifies the connection of his remark by taking the part of Panambí's comment that his answer relates to, as well as the signature of the author, and copying and prefixing these to his own comment. In doing so, he helps safeguard the coherence of communication—despite the sequential disorder and temporal discontinuity that this course of communication takes.

This option to safeguard coherence does not always work, for example, when arguments are developed collectively within one Tópico, or when the theme of the discussion changes so that the opening contribution is no longer suitable as a reference for an answer. Also, even though the conservation of a text allows selective reading, the normative orientation in Cibervalle seems to tie the reception of a Tópico to its chronological course. The exterior structure of the forum format already suggests such an interpretation. The majority of communicators orient themselves on this chronological reading and comment on deviations from this rule. In other words, it is expected of the Forum participants that they know the progressive course of a discussion so that they can meaningfully connect their own contribution to the present stage of the ongoing communication.

As Figure 13.5 depicts, the external structure of the Forum stipulates a chronological order of contributions, placing the opening contribution at the first position and the latest contribution at the last position of the list. The text box for a new contribution is placed directly below the last

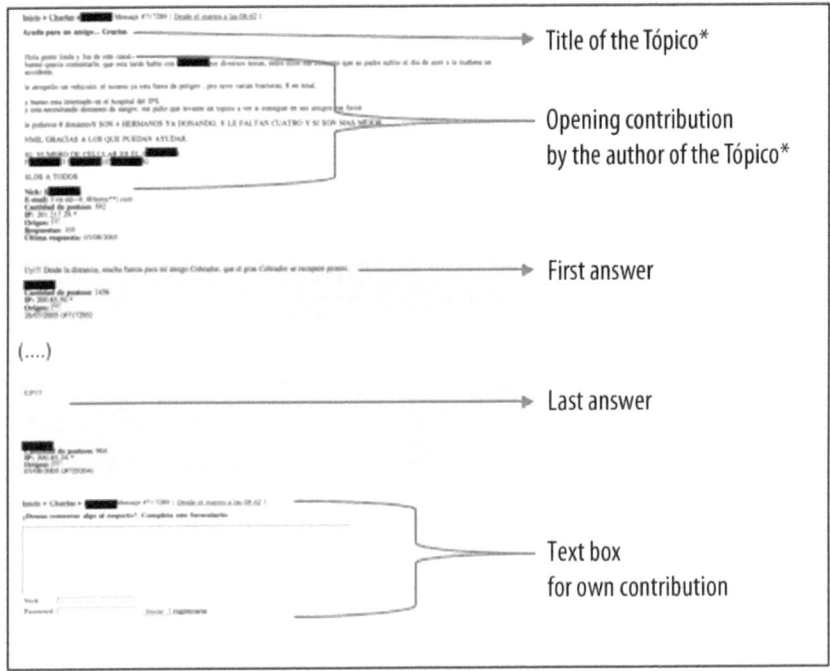

Figure 13.5 Chronological structure of the Tópico.

comment, meaning one has to scroll down through the whole page in order to get to the field for one's own comment. Thus, the external structure strongly suggests that participants first read the whole discussion before writing their own commentary.

An alternative possibility of organizing the Tópico might be establishing a chronological order in reverse. In that case, the latest contribution would be positioned below the opening text and the box for one's own comment would be placed right next to the opening contribution. Such an order would suggest that one's own comment relates directly to the opening text without having to plow through the whole discussion. The external structure of the Tópico has remained intact during several renovations of the Cibervalle Forum. Also, Cibervallers' descriptions of their own practices support the impression that the normative orientation corresponds to the external structure. It is being decided quite frequently merely on the basis of the number of replies a Tópico has received whether or not one should contribute to an ongoing discussion or not (Table 13.7).

The renovation on the Forum's homepage as discussed earlier can be interpreted in this connection: The list of *Recientes* indicates the number of contributions a Tópico has received. Thus, a mere glance at the *Recientes* suffices to decide which Tópico to contribute to and which to ignore.

Table 13.7 Tópico "Definir lo Virtual"

Me gusta el tema, pero no puedo ko yo ponerme a leer tooooodo eso. Y no quiero opinar sin leer porque puedo mea fuera del vaso	I like the topic but I cannot start read it aaaallll now. And I do not want to comment before I have read it, because I could fail to piss into the glass *[in the sense of 'missing the subject', H.G.]*
gerardo IP: 200.85.34* 05/04/2004	gerardo IP: 200.85.34* 05/04/2004

"DISCUSSION OVER!"—RULES AND RIGHTS OF/TO DEBATE IN CIBERVALLE

Let us now have a closer look on the development of explicit rules that govern participation in the Forum discussions. The rules concerning the discussion culture have hardly been changed between 2002 and 2005. However, at the suggestion of users, another category was established in which the general rules of polite conduct (e.g., the ban on personal insults) do not apply. In this category participants can quarrel endlessly until the cows come home without risking a ban from active participation. New rules were decreed after the takeover of the web portal by a new company in 2005. From then on, advertisements for commercial pages, products and services were prohibited in the Forum. This rule is placed on the Forum's main page, including a reference to the premium area of the website, which is designed for commercial purposes. With this rule the commercial character of the web portal came to the fore and into the Forum, which the former owners had hardly taken any notice of. Moreover, the new administration reserves the right to end discussions, i.e., to close Tópicos, whenever they are under the impression that the comments of participants are being twisted or skewed, or discussions are being corrupted. The rules thus emphasize not only the ties between the Forum and the company's management, but also newly define the roles and rights of the participants. The role of a Forum user is decidedly equated with that of a guest who is expected to behave respectfully by the "head of the household," i.e., the administrators and moderators.

The emergence of these rules can, in a sense, be understood as the climax of a conflict that arose in the Cibervalle Forum while the change of ownership was taking place. Initially the Cibervallers expressed their delight with the new owner. They approved of his announcement to implement some modifications of the Forum, which users had demanded for a long time. But the mood changed when it became apparent that the new owner would expand his commercial interests to include the Forum and would thereby also exert his influence on the activities within the Forum community. Consequently the Cibervallers began to discuss the new company policy in the Forum. A banner ad placed at the head of the Forum's main page led to open criticism of the management. This ad depicted the faces of two girls whose lascivious look encouraged the reader to seek them out in a pornography website. As a result, one of the users living in Canada started a Tópico in order to draw attention to the contradiction between the Forum rules and the content of this banner ad: On the one hand, Tópicos with a pornographic content were ruled out in the Forum; on the other hand, the company management was earning money with commercials for pornographic sites, thereby giving the web portal Cibervalle (and therefore also the Forum) an image of the same sort. This Tópico attracted the attention of many other participants. Even the owner of the web portal piped in and presented his position. He could not, however, satisfy the Cibervallers, and the discussion dragged on for a long time. Finally, the owner was again asked to present his position. But suddenly the Tópico disappeared altogether from the *Recientes*. For a short while it could be seen in the thematic category to which it belonged, although it could not be activated with new contributions. The administration had closed the Tópico and announced this closure with the words "discussion closed." Several new Tópicos emerged wherein Cibervallers were complaining about this procedure, until the administration finally issued the rules discussed earlier.

In summary, the evolution of rules is conducive to reconstruct essential characteristics of the Forum community in the process of change. At first, the Forum was no more than a meaningless virtual space that, as a part of an electronic communication environment, had been launched in the WWW where it was left to its own devices. During their virtual travels, the first users came across it more or less accidently and began to settle there. They appropriated this virtual space and interactively negotiated its meaning and social order. As the first owner of the site did not tend to it much and hardly ever affected any changes of his own, an autonomous community with its own interests and its own identity as Cibervalle developed within the virtual space of the Forum.[23] With the change in the company ownership and management policy, the primarily social interests of the Cibervalle *community* clashed with the primarily commercial interests of the *company* Cibervalle. This resulted in a need for negotiating participation status and the meaning of the techno-social space Cibervalle. The executive management prevailed, according to formal law, as it clearly articulated by its insistence on rules. But the practical might of the Forum users cannot be underestimated, as they have clearly increased the popularity of the web portal by the frequency of their participation and have thereby also augmented the economic success of the company.

The Cibervalle Forum is not a discussion forum in the classical sense; the topic-driven exchange of arguments is not its main purpose, even though this form of communication is practiced as well. Rather, the description of the structural characteristics of the Forum illustrates a multitude of different social activities as well as an experimental handling of the technological conditions and particularities of this communication space. The inhabitants of Cibervalle, who have accidentally met in the Forum, converted this hitherto meaningless virtual space into a techno-social space grounded on their own social needs. They have thereby transformed this space, in which the attributes of different Internet-based communication formats are combined, in a manner that allows them to live together and share a part of their everyday life with one another.

14 Global Togetherness in Cibervalle

Coming back to the communicative practices constitutive for social life in Cibervalle, we note that computer-mediated everyday life is far from restricted to the public level of the Forum communication. For more private chat, as well as for specific requests that need to be discussed instantly, the inhabitants of Cibervalle also use instant messaging. IM clients facilitate synchronous communication between two or more persons over an electronic network like the Internet. Most client programs can be downloaded from the WWW as freeware and can be installed on one's own computer if it complies with the necessary system requirements. By means of an IM client, individual socio-electronic networks can be established. The IM client program used in Cibervalle enables one to add and remove the e-mail addresses of contacts with whom one would like to network. When logging into the IM client, a window pops up (the so-called 'buddy list': Figure 14.1) in which the collection of names shows which of the contacts are currently online. As soon as one of the offline contacts logs on, a corresponding message appears on the screens of the other users and the status of this contact changes from offline to online in the buddy list.

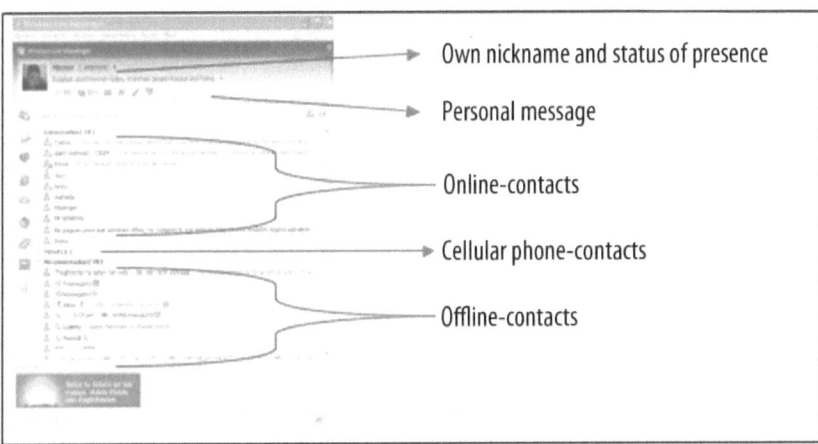

Figure 14.1 IM client buddy list.

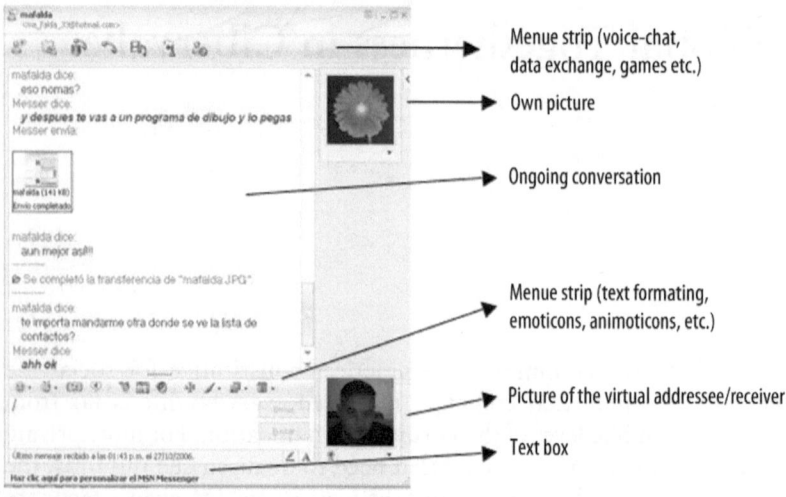

Menue strip (voice-chat, data exchange, games etc.)

Own picture

Ongoing conversation

Menue strip (text formating, emoticons, animoticons, etc.)

Picture of the virtual addressee/receiver

Text box

Figure 14.2   IM client private conversation window.

If the user clicks one of the contacts marked as online, a private conversation window (Figure 14.2) pops up on her or his computer screen, wherein a message to the other person can be posted. On the screen of the addressed counterpart another box pops up displaying the message that has been sent.

Whenever a message is received or a buddy from the list logs in, the IM client emits a sound. The communication is private in the sense that other persons cannot follow the conversation even if they are online simultaneously and connected via the buddy list.[24] However, any number of people can be added to a conversation. Newer versions of the IM used by most Cibervallers also allow—besides the script-based form of chatting—the use of webcams, voice-chats (a kind of Internet telephone), the exchange of data and the use of online games. In addition, several cellular phone companies offer their customers the option to log into the IM client via their mobile phone, and the IM client itself provides an SMS service. In this case the users appear in the buddy lists of their contacts with the corresponding reference and they can send short messages between their mobile phones and IM clients. Accordingly, Schneider et al. (2005) referred to a merging of the communication forms SMS and IM. In the course of my field studies I observed that usage of IM clients is closely tied to the Forum activities. The media practices of Cibervallers spawn hybrid forms of presence and interaction that can hardly be grasped by means of classical sociological concepts—at least insofar as the classics focus on physical presence and solely conceive of lifeworld in terms of territorial space. The following section will introduce the observed practices and discuss some conceptual implications.

BUDDY LISTS AS INTERPRETING COMMUNITIES

Initially it can be ascertained that private communication via the IM client promotes the differentiation of the whole complex of Cibervalle into a multitude of individual social networks that constitute themselves in buddy lists. Not all Cibervallers are linked to each other via the IM client, nor do they all communicate regularly and synchronously with each other, so that the buddy lists of the users can differ substantially. It can be observed that private IM communication is capable of influencing what is happening on the Forum level. For example, users send the link of a thread they have just started to one or more of their contacts, asking them to contribute to their Tópico (Table 14.1).

Such a short instant message to a user's contacts can contribute to a Tópico receiving answers fast and thus staying in the list of currently discussed Tópicos. This in turn increases the likelihood that a Tópico will attract the attention of other participants. IM is also deployed to talk to one or more of one's contacts about the current goings-on in the Cibervalle Forum. Before one divulges one's opinion on a particular issue, one may try to find out via the IM client what others think about it. In other words, the events on the publicly accessible level of Cibervalle are influenced by the communicative activities of the IM networks—that is to say, 'behind the scenes'—in a way that is not transparent for the public. On the other hand, the meaning of what is happening in the Forum is negotiated interactively inside the techno-social networks of the IM clients. Thus, contributions are prepared together or the meaning of an event is communicatively constructed in retrospect.

The participants playfully and experimentally appropriate the new communication technologies. The "house of horrors," a game collectively developed and tested in the Forum by a group of five participants, is an example of the way in which this combination of private and public levels of communication works. According to one of the participants, the game consists of opening Tópicos in the Forum and occupying them as a group, in order to then by all means prevent nonmembers of their group from lingering in this Tópico. In other words, when a participant unsuspectingly strayed into the "house of horrors," this person was continuously attacked by the members of the group until he or she stopped contributing to the Tópico. The

Table 14.1 IM-Log File "Perro"

Diabolo dice:	Diabolo says:
http://charlas/cibervalle.com/topico. php?id=6532	http://charlas/cibervalle.com/topico. php?id=6532
Diabolo dice	**Diabolo says**
opina† ahy sobre mi perro	write [opina†] something about my dog

group utilized the IM client to reach agreements and to coordinate concerted action on the Forum level. For the Forum users who were not able to see behind the curtain of these activities, i.e., who could not recognize the alliance between different nicks nor the purpose behind this alliance, an utterance in one of these Tópicos was indeed similar to entering a house of ghosts in which unfathomable and frightening things happen and in which one is best advised to leave as soon as possible.

Thus, interpreting communities constitute themselves via IM communication, namely, buddy lists. These communities influence what happens on the Forum level and each one of them negotiates its own interpretation. In this process, the combination of different media supports the differentiation of interpretational patterns, which in turn differ according to their belonging, address density and the degree of users' involvement. The synchronous communication via the IM client and the simultaneous presence in front of the computer are decisive for the formation of these interpretational communities. The differentiation into partial communities continues on the Forum level, so that certain collections of users reappear in different Tópicos.[25] For those users who confine themselves to the practice of anonymous reading, a lot of what they observe there remains unexplainable or appears to them in a different light.[26]

On the other hand, activities can be observed that are contrary to this differentiation, aiming to reproduce the global entity through the combination of IM and Forum communication. Thus, there is another game played in Cibervalle that aims at gathering as many Cibervallers as possible in a Tópico in the shortest possible time. For this purpose, a thread is opened requesting a specific participant, and the task of those reading the Tópico is to find this person and convince him or her to post an answer in the Tópico. The sought-after person then names another user who is to enter the Tópico. Users usually search for these people via IM, but if the required person happens to not be logged on, he or she is often reached by phone so that the game can proceed. Thus, this game searches for and tests Cibervalle's communicative channels while at the same time activating and defining the current limits of the socio-electronic network.

The specific combination of IM and Forum communication in Cibervalle reinforces a process that is marked by the simultaneousness of two contrary dynamics. On the one hand, there is an ongoing differentiation into local subcommunities, which, on the other hand, conceive of themselves as parts of a global entity they reproduce again and again.

JOINT TRAVELING THROUGH THE EVERYDAY WORLD OF CIBERVALLE

Often it is not the purpose of IM conversations to make an active contribution to the Forum or to prepare this interactively. Users are frequently

Table 14.2   IM-Log File "Maricones"

Albert Einstein dice:	Albert Einstein says:
JAJA . . . JUAZZZZ . . . VIERON EL TEMA DE MARIO. . . . . . JAJAJA-JAJA . . . EN ALUCION A QUE EN CIBERVALLE LOS HOMBRES SON TODOS MARICONES???	HAHA . . . HUASSSS . . . DID YOU SEE THE TÓPICO OF MARIO . . . HAHA-HAH . . . INSINUATING THAT IN CIBERVALLE ALL MEN ARE FAG-GOTS???
Corinna dice: y el tambien pio ?	Corinna says: Him too?
Corinna dice: jajajajajja	Corinna says: hahahahha
Albert Einstein dice: QUE LOKOOOO!!!!!!!!. . . . JAJAJAJA JAJAJAJAJAJAJA. . . . EL TIPO SALE EN UNA FOTO HACIENO DIBUJI-TOS.	Albert Einstein says: HOW CRAZY!!!!!!. . . . HAHAHA HAHAHA HAHAHA . . . THERE IS A FOTO OF THE GUY PAINTING LITTLE PICTURES
Albert Einstein dice: NAAA . . . EL MISMO SALE HACI-ENDO MANUALIDADES. . . . JAJA-JAJAJAJA	Albert Einstein says: MYY . . . NOW HE IS DOING NEE-DLEWORK . . . HAHAHAHAHA
mafalda dice: si lo vi es supersimpatcio	mafalda says: yes, I've seen it, it's really funyn
mafalda dice: simpatico	mafalda says: funny
Albert Einstein dice: JAJAJA . . . A VER COMO LO TOMA RAFAELO, . . . SE LO DEDICA A EL	Albert Einstein says: HAHAHA . . . LET'S SEE HOW RAFA-ELO TAKES IT . . . IT IS DIRECTED AT HIM
Corinna dice: upsssss mientras no se enoje	Corinna says: oohpsssss as long as he is not peeved
Albert Einstein dice: POR AHI SE ARMA DE VUELTA UNA SANGRIENTA, DESTRUCTIVA Y MORTAL DIALOGO	Albert Einstein says: IN THE END THERE IS ANOTHER BLOODY, DESTRUCTIVE AND DEATHLY DIALOGUE
Corinna dice: jajajajajja	Corinna says: hahahahahha
mafalda dice: o se lo tomara con soda	mafalda says: or he takes it cooly
mafalda dice: y se rie	mafalda says: and laughs
Albert Einstein dice: JIJIJIJI. . . . OJALA. . . . . . MASIADO LECHE HERVIDA YA ES	Albert Einstein says: HEHEHEHE . . . HOPEFULLY. . . . TOO MUCH MILK HAS BEEN BURNT ALREADY

content with communally watching the events from the lurker position, and then commenting on them to each other, interactively negotiating the meaning of these events, getting steamed up about them and poking collective fun at other participants. Table 14.2 presents an extract from a longer conversation between three Cibervallers who discuss a quarrel between other participants in the Forum. Rafaelo and Maribel were the protagonists of this quarrel. Rafaelo felt insulted by Maribel, who had criticized and affronted him in his function as moderator of the Forum. Maribel had called him a maricón (Spanish for "fairy") and complained about his moderation, which she thought interfered with and censored the ongoing communication. Rafaelo had subsequently erased the Tópico, arguing that it contained prohibited personal insults. Albert Einstein, Corinna and mafalda are discussing this incident with each other while navigating through the Forum and skimming through the different threads concerned with this quarrel, while not getting involved in it on the Forum level. Suddenly Albert Einstein discovers a new Tópico he associates with the quarrel. In this another participant with the nickname Mario has published photos of himself depicting him in activities considered to be typically feminine.

Albert Einstein, who lives in Paraguay, navigates through the Forum while chatting with his two conversation partners in front of their computer screens in Middle America and Europe. At the same time he tells them which part of the Forum he is currently viewing so that they have the chance to enter the same Tópico. For this purpose users often simply send the respective link via IM. By means of the private IM communication, the inhabitants of Cibervalle are now able to observe the same things happening and jointly stroll through their virtual everyday world. They do not, however, restrict themselves to merely commenting on the current state of events or laughing about Mario's joke, thereby communicatively determining the meaning of the event. With his remark "let's see how Rafaelo takes it," Albert Einstein refers directly to the future development of this event. Corinna relates to this with her "oohps, as long as he's not peeved," thereby sketching a possible scenario of how the quarrel might continue. Albert Einstein then takes up Corinna's suggestion and exaggerates it with his "bloody, destructive and deathly dialogue." He ridicules the quarrel by insinuating that a virtual verbal dispute can hardly end in death and destruction. Thus, he topicalizes the relation of virtual and physical reality and emphasizes the limitations of virtuality that, he claims, the warring parties disregard when they attribute too much importance to what is happening in virtual space ("too much milk has been burnt already"). Most notably, in this sequence the conversation of Corinna, mafalda and Albert Einstein clarifies that the social happening in Cibervalle has a life of its own, which will continue independently from a particular member's own active participation. If these three decide to now turn to other things and leave Cibervalle, they do so in full awareness of the fact that social life there will continue during their absence and the situation will be changed when they next decide to enter.

Whether the Forum activities are ironically commented on or members collectively fret about another participant's utterances or whether they share their delight in a Forum event, by means of the IM conversations with which the Cibervallers coordinate the joint observation of the Forum they produce collective relevance and transform the Forum into a shared social space. Thus, the Cibervalle Forum becomes an everyday world that describes "a sector of the outer world [that] is equally within the reach of each partner, and contains objects of common interest and relevance" (Schütz [1953] 1967, 16). Furthermore the specific combination of the two media (IM client and online-forum) as practiced in Cibervalle enables the actors to synchronize inner time lapses by means of an exterior event that they watch communally.

> If you and I observe a bird in flight [. . .] I do know that, whatever your experiences during the flight of the bird, they were contemporaneous with mine. [. . .] Since we are growing older together during the flight of the bird, and since I have evidence, in my own observations, that you were paying attention to the same event, I may say that *we* saw a bird in flight. (Schütz 1964, 25)

Like in Schütz's tableau of a bird in flight, the issue here is not the communal observation of an exterior event but the possibility to intervene in the situation so as to become part of it. Similar to the ornithologists who do not only watch the same bird, but may shoot him if they so decide, the Forum observers are also in the position to interfere in the event at any time.

THE VIRTUALIZATION OF PRESENCE AND INTERACTION

In the everyday world of Schütz, the human body is still the center for defining social 'we'-relations that are based on the simultaneous physical presence of two or more individuals in the same space of time and territory. The mediatized everyday world of Cibervalle is not so much based on physical presence, but rather more on purely communicative accessibility and mutual perception as an address. But how can this hybrid form of presence be grasped with sociological concepts that tie interaction and copresence down to the simultaneous physical presence? In the mid-1990s, when the extensive spread of the Internet was already in full swing, Berger (1995) predicted that the continuing development and dispersion of communication technologies was going to increasingly replace presence with accessibility. One need only think of telephone communication to agree with this forecast. Communication is here indeed enabled by having a telephone connection, an actual telephone in working order and a telephone number by means of which one can be potentially reached by others.

With respect to the growing importance of information and communication technologies in workplaces, Boden and Molotch (1994), on the other hand, emphasize the special quality of face-to-face communication. These authors predict that task-oriented communication cannot—even in the long term—do without copresence. They argue that copresence is irreplaceable not only "because copresence is biographically and historically prior to other forms of communication" (1994, 258), but also especially because the high degree of its complexity and informational density, which, according to the authors, cannot be attained by mediated communication, makes face-to-face communication so indispensable. "Communication is a managed physical action as well as brain work" (ibid., 262). Nonverbal elements of communication, like gestures and facial expressions, but also paralinguistic expressions like laughing, "mmph," "O," etc., are equally involved in the construction of the meaning of a speech utterance. The most dependable part of a message does not, according to Boden and Molotch, lie in *what* is said, but in *how* it is said. Body language elements are therefore considered to be the more reliable part of a message and can be seen as the parameter for establishing trustful relationships. Also, the participants can demonstrate and perceive the respective degree of mindfulness and attention most easily and effectively in copresence. Because merely by arranging to meet the other person or by spontaneously approaching someone and thereby interrupting one's daily routine, one demonstrates heedfulness to that person, the authors argue. The organization of turn-taking in face-to-face communication has a multitude of facets by means of which the actors orient their speech acts and interpretations on each other and by which they develop the conversation as an interactive process.

However, Knorr-Cetina and Bruegger (2002) use the example of virtual communication flows in the global foreign exchange market to show that computer-mediated communication is able to organize work routines without having to resort to copresent interactions. Financial markets are interactively organized by currency traders whose workplaces are situated all across the globe. Despite geographical distance, the actors are able not only to observe their own activities and that of all the others on the screen, but also to temporally coordinate these activities and relate them to those of the other actors. According to the authors, such global work arrangements facilitate intersubjective experiences and 'we'-relations on the basis of collectively observed events. Knorr-Cetina and Bruegger argue that these communication flows can be described as variations of interactions and presence, even though they cannot be grasped with the classical microsociological categories that tie copresence and interaction to the physical body and that conceive of locality exclusively in terms of territorial space. The authors therefore suggest that "embodied presence" and "response presence" should be distinguished, and they describe the latter as "situations in which participants are capable of responding to one another and common objects in real time without being physically present in the same place" (Knorr-Cetina and Bruegger 2002, 909).

But the results of this ethnographic study of global financial markets contradict the assumptions of Boden and Molotch only gradually. As Knorr-Cetina and Bruegger concede, the smooth flow of the globally coordinated interaction results from the high degree of standardization and of the simplicity of communication in global financial markets. Thus, a strong measure of standardization in the form of communicative routines is capable of replacing what Boden and Molotch identified as the nonmediatable aspects of communication without permanent instances of misunderstanding and communicative breakdowns.

The results of the present study finally suggest that computer-mediated communication cannot replace presence with accessibility. Rather, they call for a fundamental revision of microsociological concepts. Communication in Cibervalle is anything but standardized and simple. Cibervalle is, rather, a complex social formation with a wide variety of communicative patterns that are far more similar to everyday life than to work routines. Nevertheless, the observed practices suggest that here, too, forms of presence are constructed that—even though they are not physical—can still bring about 'we'-relations and a globally shared everyday life. Global microstructures based on global interaction systems would therefore not only be possible in the minimalistic version of standardized work routines in global markets as described by Knorr-Cetina and Bruegger. In this context, one could even speak of *global forms of living together* that are constituted via keyboards and screens of at least two computers. A bold thesis?

GLOBAL INTERACTION: COMMUNICATION AMONG THOSE VIRTUALLY PRESENT

Systems theory's precisely defined concept of interaction shall serve as an instrument here to ascertain whether it is in fact possible to speak of interaction systems in the case of Cibervalle. Systems theory conceives of interaction as a special form of communication that is tied to physical copresence because it is based on reflexive perception. An interaction is only possible if "several people are perceivable for one another and therefore begin to communicate" (Kieserling 1999, 15; *own translation*). So interaction is composed of the elements of perception and communication. Both are information processing. They differ in that perception does not have to discern information and message, whereas communication happens to be based on exactly this difference. Mutual perception can thus not be equated with communication. However, Kieserling qualifies that a social situation in Goffman's term[27] almost inevitably leads to communication because the information supplied by one's own body can be interpreted by the observers who are present in a way

> that is unpleasant for oneself, and whoever wants to avoid this has to add messages to the information on which the unfavorable impression is based. These messages are supplied in the hope that they amend the unfavorable impression. In order to limit the symbolic damage caused by representational mistakes and inconsistencies, pure perception is continually being progressed in the direction of communication. (Kieserling 1999, 122; *own translation*)

Thus one does not merely perceive of another, but the act of mutual perception is reflexive, i.e., one's own perception is mirrored in the perception of the other person. Put simply: Because I perceive my communication partner registering what I perceive, I align my own behavior to the anticipated expectations or interpretations of my behavior.

In Cibervalle, practices of media usage can be observed that point to exactly this process of reflexive perception. Unlike in telephone communication, users usually do not log into the IM client only when they wish to communicate with their contacts directly. In particular, the members with temporally unrestricted access to the Internet log into the IM client as soon as they have switched their computer on. Then they throw a glance at their buddy list and check who is online, saying hello to one or two of their contacts before they turn their attention to routine tasks for which they sometimes even leave their computer. When they hear the respective sound, they probably return to their screen in order to see who wants to communicate with them and then they answer that person. But they may also overhear the signal or be preoccupied with a task they do not want to interrupt. But the virtual communication partner sees that he or she is online and could therefore misinterpret the missing answer. In the course of its technological evolution an option was added to the IM client program that displays the respective status of the person. The choice is between different options like "busy," "absent," "back in a sec," "on the phone," "lunch break."[28] Furthermore, personal messages can be composed that are sent as automatic answers to all contact attempts. Even if one is not online, a minimal degree of presence can be maintained: The Cibervallers initially used the input box for nicknames for the purpose of sending personal messages. As the nickname always appeared in the buddy list of contacts regardless of whether the user was online or not, messages could be placed here that were read even if one was not online at that moment. So the nickname box often contained, for example, the new telephone number of the user, a tender note for the loved one, a birthday party invitation, good wishes for the weekend, a reason given for a longer absence and so on. In the newer versions of the IM client program, this practice was taken up again and implemented as an additional function. As can be seen in Figure 14.1, besides the nickname and status of presence, a personal message can be posted that is displayed in the buddy list.

Thus, the IM client is not just a medium for synchronous communication that—similar to the telephone—enables potential accessibility and with which one can send instantaneous messages and chat with others. Logging into the IM client, one can see who is presently online. Moreover, logging into the IM client also implies that one knows the others can see that one is online. It also entails that one is conscious that others are aware that one knows that one is perceived by them. In other words, when the users communicate temporary absence via the buddy list, they do so assuming that their contacts comprehend them as present and expect them to answer whenever being addressed. IM thereby produces a reflexive consciousness of mutual perception. It can thus count as a social situation leading to interaction insofar as it is necessary to supplement the information mediated by virtual presence with messages in order to prevent misinterpretations. It is not essential to always remain in front of the screen or to actually communicate with each other: The availability and the reflexive awareness of mutual perception create a feeling of proximity and impart the impression of presence in the same space—a space structured not so much by geographical closeness as by temporal coordination. For Schneider et al., too, the "self-perception and perception of others under the condition of technical mediation" (2005, 84; *own translation*), as well as the possibility to observe the movements of the virtual counterpart, are the essential characteristics of IM communication, which they call "tele-presence." Schneider et al. write:

> The observability of the cyberspace behavior of the contacts on the list (especially when they enter and quit) makes their absence and presence perceivable—it can actually be sensed. [. . .] The possibility to approach those present at any one moment and to simply perceive their tele-presence can intensify relations—even if the frequency of actual conversations is rather low. (2005, 87ff.; *own translation*)

These authors, however, act on the assumption that IM primarily serves the extension of communication options for people who already have regular offline contact, in other words, those who live in relative geographical proximity. In this case, tele-presence is therefore only an extension of copresence. Boden and Molotch's thesis of the primacy of physically grounded copresence thus appears to be correct. Or does it not?

The Cibervallers are scattered across the globe and as a rule did not know each other before they met in virtual space. A look at their communicative practices and the permanent enhancement of the communication forms and media in use detects strong parallels with copresent conversations. In Forum as well as the IM communication, paralinguistic elements are used, body language elements are simulated and gradually even voice-based and visual information are incorporated into the communication. In the case of Cibervalle, tele-presence does not have merely an extending function. Rather, the simultaneous presence in virtual space and the virtual traveling by means of which the participants open up common spaces of relevance to a certain degree substitute copresence. The borderline between physical presence and total absence tends in any case to dissolve and the social relevance of one's own realm of perception changes. Distance is now of immediate relevance for action, which in turn affects the relevance of what is happening locally.

SPLIT ATTENDANCES: WHEN PHYSICAL AND VIRTUAL LOCALITIES OVERLAP

The digital connection with other actors opens up additional relevance systems in everyday life that overlap with the respective physically grounded environment with which they must be coordinated. The actors switch back and forth between the virtual and physically grounded social contexts, whereas, in a manner similar to Televisión viewing, the computer-mediated communication alternates from being the main activity to being a secondary activity. In their conversation-analytical study of recipient communication, Holly and Baldauf illustrate that watching Televisión is often coordinated with other parallel activities, such as "talking while watching," which, according to them, is a kind of "soft-coupling" (2001, 49; *own translation*) to the medium. They emphasize that the recipients interactively negotiate the respective degree of attention they give to the different objects. Therefore, according to the authors, the structure of communication that accompanies the act of watching Televisión differs fundamentally from everyday conversations, but at the same time exhibits similarities with the "open state of talk"[29] observed by Goffman in working situations.

IM communication is very similar to "open states of talk" or "speaking while watching Televisión" because of the presence of temporal discontinuity. One starts a conversation, talks about this and that for a while, until suddenly the conversation breaks off because a pair sequence is not finished. After a while, sometimes even after several hours, a question is answered, which the questioner has possibly forgotten already, because in the meantime he has closed the conversation box and turned his attention to other things. But the person to whom the question was addressed only just now returns to her screen, which she had had to leave when she was called upon by her boss to attend a meeting. Now she sees the conversation window with a question addressed to her. In face-to-face conversation, one does not normally leave a question unanswered without a good reason, because a question is the opening section of a pair sequence that requires a closing turn, in this case an answer. In an open state of talk, this structure is loosened. Because conversation in this instance is not the main activity, the "obligation to answer the other person with a responsive act is reduced" (Holly and Baldauf 2001, 46; *own translation*). Furthermore, "pauses do not have to be perceived as pauses, because both actors are also engaged with other activities" (ibid.; *own translation*).

However, the situation described here differs from open states of talk in Televisión and working contexts. Firstly, conversation partners must coordinate two or more social environments with each other. The respective relevance of these environments can come into conflict because a virtual conversation partner does not have access to all of the counterpart's environments. On top of this, the influence of technology has an impact on the flow of communication. The ample scope for the interpretation of pauses in the present case is not predicated on the fact that one cannot see what the other person is presently preoccupied with. In addition, it is also highly difficult to discern between pauses caused by social reasons and those brought about by technological problems. Different bit rates, software breakdowns, server problems or problems caused by the Internet connection: All of these technological interferences affect the flow of communication. For example, an IM conversation breaks off because the contribution of one conversation partner has not been transmitted to the other partner and both of them assume that it is the other person's turn. Perceiving the other person to be simultaneously engaged in other activities as well, one reasons at best that the partner's contribution is missing because the other person is too busy to answer. Thus, there are many reasons for the breakdown of an IM communication, deliberate silence being only one of them. In the course of time the actors as a rule learn to take the diversity of potential contextual, technological and social disruptions of communication into consideration. Experienced Cibervallers, hence, learn not to interpret communication disruptions as primarily social matters. Instead of taking the missing answer as a personal insult, one tends to ascertain first whether the question has reached the addressed person and then copies the relevant part of the conversation that one assumes has not been transmitted and sends it off again.

Nevertheless, it is necessary to emphasize that the management of the overlapping social environments of the actors impacts the temporal structure of IM communication. More precisely, the synchronicity of the medium is constrained by the extent to which virtual relevance systems compete with physically grounded ones. As shown earlier with regard to forum communication, it is clear that in IM communication a well-defined differentiation between synchronous and asynchronous media cannot be made. Rather, it is always dependent on the context and the practices of usage.

DEGREES OF PRESENCE

The meaning of presence and absence therefore has to be newly defined in the context of computer-mediated communication. Presence and absence are no longer connected with the body as center. Sharing the same physical grounded space can become subordinated to simultaneity.[30] In the case of computer-mediated interaction, presence and absence are no longer mutually exclusive. I would argue that the social meaning of virtual interaction can be more precisely ascertained by discerning degrees of presence and absence, which vary situationally with the technological conditions and the cultural practices of appropriation of a communication media.[31] It has been illustrated here how participants oscillate between different degrees of presence and how the evolutionary development of the technological environment adopts these practices and implements them in the program structure. The following example of a media-driven love relationship that developed in Cibervalle illustrates to what degree geographical distance can be compensated by communicative proximity.

"IT IS REALLY LIKE LIVING TOGETHER, ONLY THE BODY IS MISSING" [32]

Irén and Tomás have gotten to know each other via the Cibervalle Forum. Irén lives in Paraguay, where Tomás was also born and raised. Tomás has now lived in the US for several years. For a while, the two of them communicated via the Forum and IM. Later they telephoned and finally met in person during one of Tomás's regular visits to Paraguay. At the time of the conversation with Irén they had already had a long-distance relationship for one year. For a few months now Irén has had a computer of her own in her room. It was a present from Tomás. The computer is equipped with a headset, a microphone, a webcam and loudspeakers, and Irén has a dedicated Internet connection. Irén and Tomás communicate with each other every day via different media. Irén says that the Cibervalle Forum is more important for her boyfriend than for her because he lives far away, and for him the Cibervalle Forum opens a window to Paraguay. She says that Tomás spends much more time than she does in the Forum and with the social relationships he has made via the Forum. Irén herself uses the Forum primarily in order to locate her friend and to participate in the everyday life he shares with other Cibervallers. The signature under his contributions tells her not only when he was last active in the Forum; the IP address also tells her whether he wrote his comments at home or at his workplace. Moreover, she can guess with whom or what he is currently concerned. Both of them have a cellular phone and Tomás phones her several times a day. When he is outside of his home or workplace, he usually stays connected to the IM client so that Irén can reach him at any time. Via IM they now meet every day at the same time. Both places of residence are in the same time zone. The time lag is between zero and one hour, meaning that the course of the day of the two lovers is temporally synchronous and they can spend the evenings together without any problem. When Irén returns home from work, she enters her room, switches the computer on and logs into the IM. She has also opened an additional account that she shares only with Tomás so that she can communicate with him alone. Sometimes, when they do not feel like conversing, they activate the webcam and simply look at each other, or they play one of the games on offer in the IM. Tomás usually remains logged in continuously and even leaves the webcam on when he is occupied with other things and not sitting in front of the computer. Irén, however, switches the webcam off at the end of the conversation. She would feel uncomfortable being watched by Tomás doing everyday things or while she was sleeping. They have also tried video calling† several times, but they do not do this anymore, as it was unpleasant for Irén and accompanied with feelings of shame.

LIVING TOGETHER IN CYBERSPACE?

The example of Irén and Tomás illustrates one of the most intimate forms of relationship that exist in Cibervalle: the mediated love attachment. For both participants, Cibervalle is a social space where they can meet in order to converse either with a group of other users or in pairs (with the help of an added private communication medium) about everyday life in this social space. As this social space houses a reality, which is not as prone to fleetingness as the physical everyday world, the Cibervalle Forum also serves to reconstruct the traces left by the other participants as a means of participating asynchronously in the everyday life of these others. This example again illustrates that the virtual everyday life is embedded in the physically grounded environments of the actors, and occasionally even competes with them. Irén is able not just to reconstruct Tomás's movements within the Forum, but, by means of his active participation in the Forum and his current status in the IM client, she can also detect whether he is at home or at the office or elsewhere. And the webcam even makes the physical context of the virtual counterpart accessible. Because of the linkage of the different communication media and the temporal synchronization of their daily routine (made possible by the geographical position of both residences in the same time zone), the couple can weave a communicative web between them that is so dense that Irén herself describes it with the words, "it is like living together, only the body is missing."

In summary, in the Forum communication, as well as in the combined usage of Forum and IM, different characteristics can be found that in their totality form the basis of these peculiar techno-social forms of interaction and interrelationships. One might suppose that Urry had just these characteristics in mind when he made the following prediction:

> Virtual travel produces a kind of strange and uncanny life on the screen, a life that is near and far, present and absent, live and dead. The kinds of travel and presencing involved will change the character and experience of 'co-presence' since people can feel proximate while still distant. (2002, 267)

The combination of asynchronous and synchronous communication, which characterizes both IM and Forum communication, is an important precondition for creating global communities. Whereas asynchronicity allows for global communication between individuals living in different time zones (Stegbauer 2000, 25), synchronicity at the same time leads to the compression of time and space, thus enabling real-time communication regardless of geographical distance. The Forum thus builds bridges between temporal and geographical distances, and it is able to unite people who to different degrees play a part in common activities. The oscillation *between* synchronicity and asynchronicity also allows the inhabitants of Cibervalle to coordinate the different relevance systems and the respective duties of being present, while at the same time being 'here' in the physical grounded and the virtual environments. As the discussion of the evolutionary development of the Forum has shown, synchronous communication in Cibervalle has steadily increased over the years. Users are geared more to continuous interactions than to the semantic content of the shared virtual space. The global community Cibervalle is maintained by specific usage practices of the technology. These include being perpetually online, keeping the Forum page open and the IM client in operation, as well as the necessity to constantly shift the focus of attention back and forth between local priorities and those on the screen. This kind of usage supports the impression that Cibervalle is a part of each inhabitant's everyday life, an additional social space that is integrated into the physically grounded environments. The social life of this space continues even if one turns away for a while because it is maintained by a multitude of virtual–local interaction systems. The joint virtual travels and the IM talk about the current happenings in Cibervalle augment the feeling of being together and part of an "ongoing community of space and time" (Schütz 1964, 26).

Boden and Molotch's (1994) skepticism concerning the communicative potential of information and communication technologies and their insistence on the singularity of communication in copresence appears a little antiquated in the light of the communicative practices described in this study. Schneider et al. (2005) presumably underestimate the potential of global social media, as their research was restricted to users in a limited territorial space who were not so much in need of building social relationships across large geographical distances. For transnational migrants, such media appear to offer additional chances.

Considering the active role of users in the act of extending communicative options offered by the Internet, one could say that transnational populations with access to global communication technologies prove to be trendsetters for future forms of interaction and relationships. As Irén and Tomás's example illustrate, the actors manage to gradually compensate for the restrictions of virtual communication by the combined usage of different electronic communication media and the permanent development of Internet-based technologies. The configuration of these technologies is strongly tied to the users' practices, as exemplified by the evolution of the Forum. The development of the IM programs can be interpreted as an attempt to gradually emulate the elements of face-to-face communication. Interactive script-based forms of communication, or "typed conversations" (Beisswenger 2002; *own translation*), were accompanied from the start by so-called *emoticons*, or 'faces' that initially were composed of punctuation marks. Used to express different feelings, emoticons have been differentiated continuously during the last few years and have become more complex. Because of their permanent enhancements, particularly by the users themselves, the typographical signs have been turned into digital animations one can send to conversation partners via the screen to express whatever one cannot say with words alone. With the aid of audio and video calling†, the communicative elements constructed by intonation and facial expression can successively be reintegrated into communication. Also, images of the communication partner and the context he or she is in at the time can be mediated almost in real time by means of the webcam. As Irén's example illustrates, computer-mediated communication is capable of such a high degree of density and complexity that it may even under certain conditions be conceived as too near. Even though the technological conditions allow the simultaneous transmission of sound and vision, Irén appears to prefer the photo image and voice transmission of chat communication and the pure voice transmission of the telephone.

So is there any difference at all between computer-mediated interaction and face-to-face encounters? Or can we assume that the simultaneous embodied presence in the same geographical space is replaced by the simultaneous presence in virtual space? Is it possible to synthesize copresence merely by mediating electronically the participants' local contexts and the voice-based verbal and physical elements of communication? In light of the virtual forms of interaction presented so far, it may come as a surprise that my answer to this question is "No." In fact, the virtual is only one part of the story because the participants meet regularly. Moreover, as has been sketched ethnographically in Part C of this study, the Cibervallers use the Forum to localize each other and to organize meetings in their respective places of residence. The following chapter of the book examines these local meetings and the particular manner of reconnecting them back to the Cibervalle Forum in view of the question of how global togetherness in Cibervalle is attained.

15 "Now the World is Watching You!"
How Cibervallers Once Became 'Global Players'

The previous chapters illuminated Cibervalle's meaning from the perspective of the lifeworld context of its inhabitants before the communicative architecture that enables global togetherness in Cibervalle was scrutinized. The last chapter of the book now examines the genuine organizational structures of the Cibervalle Forum, a globally shared techno-social space the Cibervallers inhabit. This chapter also focuses on the public framing and potentially global and anonymous accessibility of the Forum activities that contrast paradoxically with the privacy of the relationships between users. On the one hand, all activities in the Cibervalle Forum are open to the global public[33] because they can always be anonymously watched, by members as well as total strangers, from anywhere around the globe. On the other hand, Cibervallers relate to one another predominantly through their Forum contributions, reporting primarily on personal matters. But they do so knowing that they can be observed, even though they have no exact information as to who is watching their activities, or from where. Forum communication has a triadic structure in which not only the communicators, but also their imagined audience play a crucial role. In other words, the technological characteristics of the Forum communication, in combination with the social particularities of Cibervalle, tend to move private relations and everyday life into a potentially global sphere of observation.

But although the Cibervalle Forum is potentially accessible on a global scale, its real range is limited. We have already ascertained that, in the context of the necessary resources for participation in Cibervalle activities, a fundamental barrier to access is the difficulty faced when trying to find the website in the endless depth of the WWW. If one has no knowledge of the existence of the Forum, one can find it accidentally while surfing through the WWW and looking for information about Paraguay. But Paraguay is, on a global level, an almost unknown country. So the question arises as to who is searching online for Paraguay in the first place and thereby chances upon the Cibervalle Forum. The following pages will be concerned with this dimension of globality. The possibilities and limitations of reflexive self-perception within a global sphere of observation will be critically examined and scrutinized with regard to their implications for social life in Cibervalle. The connection between media, the construction of images of the world and the possibility of reflexive self-perception within a global frame of reference are discussed within the context of the marginal position of Paraguay and the Cibervalle Forum. Thus, the construction of this dimension of globality will be questioned within the limits of structural possibility and empirical (im)probability. Subsequently, the meaning of globality will be more closely examined with reference to the communication in Cibervalle. The analysis of the "communicative budget" (Günthner and Knoblauch 1995) of Cibervalle will then reflect on the public framing of communication as a structural characteristic.

As discussed earlier, ethnomethodology uses the process of 'becoming a member' to gain access to the intrinsic order of the field and to learn about the practices of its maintenance. In Cibervalle new members are regularly introduced and welcomed. It can even be observed that the welcoming communication is so important that a particular genre of Tópico has been formed with which the introduction and welcoming of new members is organized in an almost ritual fashion. Thus, in order to understand the structures of order by which Cibervallers come to terms with their virtual everyday life, the patterns of the welcoming communication will be introduced and analyzed. As a second step, the triadic communication structure will be examined more closely: Which forms of address are used by Cibervallers and which types of audience do they assume? It is demonstrated that the subcommunities that have formed within Cibervalle at the users' respective places of residence represent a kind of internal public that is of central importance in connection with the practice of local meetings and their media-based reproduction. The relation between potential and situationally realized globality will then be discussed in the context of the analysis of the activities in Cibervalle related to the fire in the supermarket *Ycua Bolaños*. In the closing section of this chapter, the audiences identified in the analysis will be summarized with reference to their inherent dimensions of globality and belonging.

BLIND SPOTS ON MEDIATIZED WORLD MAPS: WHY GLOBALITY IS UNLIKELY

Table 15.1 shows the opening turn of a thread in the Forum, in which Panambí, who is living in the US, invites other members to "complain" about the darker sides of migration "for a minute." It reflects a frequent experience of Paraguayans and, incidentally, researchers on Paraguay: The larger the distance from Paraguay, the deeper the lack of knowledge about the country. The description of an American journalist that Paraguay is a country that is "nowhere and famous for nothing"[34] adequately expresses Paraguay's position in the dominant images of the world.

Table 15.1   Tópico "Plagueta un Ratito"

A mi me tiene re-cansada tener que lidiar con gringos ignorantes de la geografia mundial y tener que explicar por enesima vez que la capital de Paraguay no es Montevideo. Y que, oh sorpresa, Paraguay y Uruguay son dos paises distintos! Tambien que no por el hecho de ser hispana naci bailando salsa, o que como arroz con gandules como dieta diaria o que me encanta Speedy Gonzalez y su novia Rosita.	I am so tired of having to deal with gringos who have not the slightest idea of world geography and having to tell them for the umpteenth time that Montevideo is not the capital of Paraguay. And that—surprise, surprise— Paraguay and Uruguay are two different countries! And also that even if I am a hispana I was not born dancing Salsa and my diet does not consist of rice with gandules, nor am I enchanted with Speedy Gonzales and his friend Rosita.
María IP: 64.62.223.* 15/01/2004	María IP: 64.62.223.* 15/01/2004

In globalization research, increasing global linkages, the mutual perception within a global frame of reference and as a result the reflexive awareness about being part of a global social entity are defined as essential empirical features of globalization. Guillén, for example, recaps the different approaches within globalization research and defines globalization "as a process leading to a greater interdependence and mutual awareness (reflexivity) among economic, political and social units in the world, and among actors in general" (2001, 236). But how do reflexive self-perception and the construction of a global frame of reference come about in the first place?

Any reality outside of that sphere of our lifeworld that is in direct reach, in other words, which we can perceive with our own senses, only gets to us as a media-based construction. The main part of our knowledge about the world outside of the physically grounded sphere of our own lifeworld is nowadays conveyed by the mass media. "Globalized lifeworlds" (Werlen 1996; *own translation*) are therefore necessarily *mediatized* lifeworlds that are by and large mass media–constructed images of the world. However, media constructions of the world only register certain details of what is happening in the world, whereas other places, actors and events are more or less permanently ignored. Whether or not one perceives of oneself as a part of a global social entity is therefore highly dependent on one's own position in the global arena. Paraguayans as a rule inhabit the outer border areas of the dominant images of the world. Paraguay is hardly ever a focal point in the international mass media because it is neither a 'global player' in the political and economic sense nor does it attract international attention as a tourist attraction. How can one relate the world to oneself and position oneself within it when one does not even appear in its mass media representations? And how does one realize at all that one is *not* perceived and observed?

Paraguayans realize that they are not perceived as soon as they change their marginal position. This happens in the case of migration, as María

Table 15.2 IM Communication "No Somos Nadie"

Ariel dice: yo aveces entro en un chat internacional	Ariel says: Sometimes I enter an international chat
Ariel dice: donde hablan ingles	Ariel says: where they speak English
Ariel dice: y les digo que soy de py	Ariel says: and I tell them that I am from py [Paraguay]
Ariel dice: y me preguntan donde queda eso	Ariel says: and they ask me where that is
Ariel dice: eso ya me paso varias veces	Ariel says: that has happened to me several times
mafalda dice: y antes de tener internet no sabias que la gente era tan boluda, supongo	mafalda says: and before you had Internet you did not know that people are that stupid, I presume
mafalda dice: o sea te sorprendio al principio cuando te paso eso?	mafalda says: I mean, did it surprise you at first when that happened?
Ariel dice: si	Ariel says: yes
Ariel dice: pense que la gente sabia poco de geografia	Ariel says: I thought these people did not know much geography
Ariel dice: pero no es eso	Ariel says: but that is not it
Ariel dice: porque si decis estados unidos	Ariel says: because when you say United States
Ariel dice: quien no lo conoce	Ariel says: whoever does not know it
Ariel dice: porque es un pais importante, rico	Ariel says: because it is an important country, rich
Ariel dice: Grande	Ariel says: large
Ariel dice: famoso por sus descubrimientos tecnologicos	Ariel says: famous for its technological inventions
Ariel dice: cosa que no pasa en py	Ariel says: concerning Paraguay it is different
(...)	(...)
Ariel dice: es como que nos ignoran	Ariel says: it is as if they ignored us
Ariel dice: no somos nadie!!!!!	Ariel says: we are nobody!!!!!

describes in Table 15.1, but also by traveling virtually. During these journeys Paraguayans meet inhabitants of geographically distant regions in international chats and discussion forums. The above section of an IM conversation (Table 15.2) I had with a Cibervaller who lives in Buenos Aires is a vivid illustration of this cognition process.

Ariel initially interprets the question "where is that?" (which is repeatedly asked in reaction to his geographical self-identification) as a problem of localization in terms of a lack of geographical knowledge ("I thought these people did not know much geography"). As he said in another conversation, Ariel also uses the Internet to gain access to the online versions of international newspapers and global news networks. He regularly reads mainly *CNN Español* and concludes here, too, that as a rule Paraguay does not feature at all. On the basis of his experiences, he soon realizes that his overseas counterparts do not merely find it hard to place Paraguay on the world map, but that most of them have also never even heard of it. Thus, in the world the Internet opens up for Ariel, neither Paraguay nor he himself as a Paraguayan exists. Eduardo, a Cibervaller from Asunción who has had similar experiences during his virtual journeys, concludes that Paraguay is "an island in the sea of globalization."

Miller and Slater (2000) made a similar observation in the context of Trinidad. Starting from their own geographical and cultural knowledge, Trinidadians are shocked to realize that their island is an almost unknown entity: "Most people are not prepared for the sheer lack of knowledge about Trinidad as they encounter the more global reach of Internet chat, summed up in the question 'What is Trinidad?'" (2000, 98). Thus it could be said that the media-constructed maps of the world are strewn with a number of blind spots like Paraguay and Trinidad. Even though the Internet—due to its technological network structure— is designed to be global and the scope of the Cibervalle Forum can be understood to potentially include the world public, access to the Internet initially causes the opposite effect for members of peripheral regions of the world. Their virtual travels around the world merely underline their own marginal position instead of enabling them to reflexively perceive themselves within a global sphere of observation.

Even if their media socialization entails this disillusioning realization that, in the global scheme of things, they are nobodies, the public framing of communication in the Cibervalle Forum nevertheless reflexively affects the participants' self-perception. They are being observed, this much they know for sure. By means of the kinds of addresses used by Cibervalle inhabitants, it can even be shown that they imagine different audiences. The complexity of the Cibervalle audience is illuminated in the following by means of the welcoming communication, the Tópicos of local meetings and the Cibervalle activities that arose from the context of the fire in the supermarket *Ycua Bolaños*.

EVERYDAY LIFE UNDER SURVEILLANCE: THE PUBLIC AS A STRUCTURAL FEATURE OF MEDIATIZED SOCIALITY

As discussed in Part B, the participant Iwashita describes typical stages in the process of 'becoming a member.' Moreover, her commentary in Table 15.3 alludes to the actual range of the Forum, the different roles of participation (including parts of the Cibervalle audience) and the rules of presenting and receiving new members. Initially, Iwashita discovered the

Table 15.3 Tópico "Definir lo Virtual"

(. . .) Yo estaba una vez aburrida frente a la computadora pensando, internet, internet, mi novio dice que hay todo de todo y para todos, ndeeee† qué cosas no? y yo qué voy a hacer, y bueno google: Paraguay, lo primero que apareció fué cibervalle.com me metí me registré y leía los comentarios, opinaba† aveces y un día decidí abrir un tópico pensando, qué puedo escribir para que llame la atención y me lean así saben que existo porque me daba no sé qué escribir que era nueva, entonces pongo uno de que estaba metida a full con el tema de las drogas y recibí varias opiniones que me gusta-ron mucho, jejeje, muy bueno el tópico, logré escandalizar a unos cuantos! pero pasó el tiempo y yo fuí dejando las drogas (en el armario) fuí conociendo a algunos de argentina, fuí a un encuentro, y así tuve mi primer encuentro con paraguayos en Argentina.	(. . .) One day I was sitting in front of the computer being bored and thinking internet, internet, my boyfriend says there is everything for anyone, ndeeee† imagine that! and me, what I am going to do? Very well then google: Paraguay, the first thing to appear was cibervalle. com. I entered, registered myself and read the commentaries, occasionally I wrote something [opinaba†] and one day I decided to open up a thread on my own and thought, what can I write to attract attention so that they would read me and know that I exist, because to write that I am new (a newbie) seemed peculiar to me, at any rate I opened one in which I said I was deep into drugs and I got different opinions which I liked very much, hahaha, the Tópico was very good, I managed to shock some of them! But time passed, I left the drugs (in the cupboard), I got to know some [members] from Argentina, I went to an *encuentro* [Span.: meeting] and so I had my first meeting with Paraguayans in Argentina.
Hacía cuatro años que estaba en Argentina y nunca había conocido a un paraguayo acá.	I had been in Argentina for four years and never met a Paraguayan here.
Fué una muy buena experiencia y volví a apreciar mi cultura y mi pais.	It was a really good experience and I learnt to reappreciate my culture and my country.
Iwashita Cantidad de posteos: 644 **IP:** 200.67.33.* 17/01/2005	Iwashita Number of posts: 644 **IP:** 200.67.33.* 17/01/2005

Forum by chance. On her way through the WWW she oriented herself on her 'natio-ethno-cultural' reference of belonging and entered 'Paraguay' in a search engine. The first result was the link to the Paraguayan web portal Cibervalle. Like most Cibervalle members, Iwashita initially observed the activities in the Forum. She read the discussions and familiarized herself with the topics and practices before she actually presented herself as an active member. The first category of audience relevant for communication in Cibervalle can already be identified here: anonymous readers who are potentially interested in membership, but who first want to get an idea of what it entails.

As Iwashita then describes, she subsequently registered for membership and contributed occasional comments in existing Tópicos. However, this level of activity was seemingly insufficient for her to be perceived as an active member by the other members. She herself based her decision to open her own Tópico on her desire to be noticed by the others ("so that they read me and know that I exist"). In this connection she also supplies an explicit reason for not presenting herself as a new member ("because to write that I am new seemed peculiar to me") and thereby points to an implicit rule that she apparently disobeys, which in turn requires an explanation. The analysis of the welcoming pattern shows a normative preference for a form of presentation of new members that adheres to certain rules of communication. If these rules are not followed, the older members tell the new one, at least if he or she is identified as Novato/a (Spanish for 'novice'/'newbie') and not as Clon† of an already known member. So, what exactly are the rules of integration in Cibervalle? And why does Iwashita not adhere to the required course and even take it as a success that she managed to shock the other members with her Tópico?

"HI, I'M A NEWBIE!" FORM AND FUNCTIONS
OF WELCOMING PATTERNS

The normative rules derived from the data are summarized here before being discussed by means of specific examples. In order to get in contact with the Cibervalle community, it is recommended that one open a Tópico in which one introduces oneself as a new member. The title should make it as clear as possible that this particular Tópico is that of a new member. The opening turn should definitely contain some point of contact for other members, most importantly personal details, especially one's geographic path of life taken so far, one's current place of residence and other intermediate stages of migration, so that other members can establish mutual local references with the new member. Alternatively, one should at least present a concrete issue or suggest a theme suitable for beginning a conversation or discussion. The following example (Table 15.4) illustrates the introduction of a new member that is 'successful' in the normative sense, i.e., it meets the expectations of the community.

Table 15.4 Welcoming Tópico "Elroseño"

1	*Un cibervallero nuevo.*	*A new Cibervallero*
2	Es la primera vez que escribo, pero quisiera que alguien que quiera un amigo paraguayo en Buenos Aires que viva tambien acà, o cualquier parte del mundo. Ademas me gustaria unirme a los cibervalleros de argentina. Por hoy es todo, espero respuestas.pedro A.M. **Nick: elroseño** E-mail: p-dr-sm-r-c-@*.com.*r **IP: 200.82.28.*** Respuestas: 15 Última respuesta: 20/04/2004	It is the first time for me to write here, but I would like someone who is looking for a Paraguayan friend in Buenos Aires, who lives here too or in any other place of the world. Also, I would like to join the Cibervallers in Argentina. That is all for now, I am waiting for answers. Pedro A.M. **Nick: elroseño** E-mail: p-dr-sm-r-c-@*.com.*r **IP: 200.82.28.*** Answers: 15 Last answer: 20/04/2004
3	Hola Pedro, mi amistad incondicional para ti, bienvenido a estos lares!!!!!!!!!!!!!!! **Eduga** **IP: 66.356.22*** 17/04/2004	Hello Pedro, [I offer you] my unconditional friendship, welcome to this place!!!!!!!!!! **Eduga** **IP: 66.356.22*** 17/04/2004
4	ahhhhhhhhh hola ches ke te tals mal venido jijijijiji **SHAKIRA** **IP: 200.85.155.*** 18/04/2004	ahhhhhhhhhh hello ches how are you come badly[35] hihihihihihihi **SHAKIRA** **IP: 200.85.155*** 18/04/2004
5	misionero pio?? elroseño **Kamba** **IP: 66.199.40.*** 18/04/2004	misionero pio[36] ?? elroseño **Kamba** **IP: 66.199.40.*** 18/04/2004
6	Hola elroseño! que pases bien por acá! :D **Amanda** **IP: 64.84.166.*** 19/04/2004	Hello elroseño! Have a good time here! :D **Amanda** **IP: 64.84.166.*** 19/04/2004
7	santa rosa misiones yo soy de san juan misiones. **feli** **IP: 200.85.34.*** 19/04/2004	santa rosa misiones I am from san juan misiones. **feli** **IP: 200.85.34.*** 19/04/2004
8	hola! yo vivo en Bs. As. y buena onda†! bienvenido a cibervalle **Iwashita** **IP: 200.67.33.*** 19/04/2004	Hello! I live in Bs.As.[37] and buena onda†! welcome to Cibervalle **Iwashita** **IP: 200.67.33.*** 19/04/2004

(continued)

Table 15.4   (continued)

9	vivo en bs.as.bienvenido!! cesar **IP:** 200.69.125* 19/04/2004	I live in bs.as.welcome!! cesar **IP:** 200.69.125* 19/04/2004
10	elrosenho, bienvenido y que te divi-ertas mucho, ciao amico **Rafael** **IP:** 62.154.79.* 19/04/2004	elrosenho, welcome und enjoy your-self, ciao amico **Rafael** **IP:** 62.154.79.* 19/04/2004
11	Yo soy de misiones . . . quien es de misiones?? vos elroseño de donde sos y bienvenido viejo!! **Sam** **IP:** 64.86.123.* 20/04/2004	I am from misiones . . . who is from misiones?? you elroseño where do you come from and welcome buddy!! **Sam** **IP:** 64.86.123.* 20/04/2004
12	hola feli . . . stas todavia por ahi . . . stas en san-juan o stas por asuncion . . . contesta. .sip. **Sam** **IP:** 64.86.123.* 20/04/2004	hello feli . . . still there, aren't you, are you in sanjuan or are you in asuncion . . . answer, okay . . . **Sam** **IP:** 64.86.123.* 20/04/2004
13	Hola Bienvenido a Cibervalle! **Manuela** **IP:** 216.223.207.* 20/04/2004	Hello Welcome to Cibervalle **Manuela** **IP:** 216.223.207.* 20/04/2004
14	vivo en san ignacio, de ves en cuando voy por asu.saludos Sam y VIVA MISIONES! feli **IP:** 200.85.34.* 20/04/2004	I live in san ignacio, now and then I go to asu.regards to Sam and LONG LIVE MISIONES! feli **IP:** 200.85.34.* 20/04/2004
15	bueno pedro yo el nene te doy la bienvenida a cibervalleros arg, aca con los pibes la vas a pasar re bien hacique vas a conocer chichis -_- yea y a muy buenos amigos p.d. para vos feli y sam yo soy de san ignacio misiones si se quieren contactar con migo pueden agre-garme en su msn *@*.com y para los q me quieran agregar tambien el_nene_py **IP:** 24.250.242.* 20/04/2004	Ok, pedro I el nene welcome you to the cibervalleros arg, it's going to be super-good here for you with the guys you will get to know chi-chis here -_- yeah and really good friends P.S. to you feli and sam I am from san ignacio misiones if you want to get in contact with me you can add me to your msn *@*.com and also all the others who want to add me el_nene_py **IP:** 24.250.242.* 20/04/2004

Identifying

The most striking aspect of this Tópico's opening turn is that the author identifies himself in the title. He does not, however, do so with his own name, but rather with a transitive identity as a *novato*. The title as much as the author's introductory text appear strangely formal—almost like a job application—in contrast to the answers of the older members. Other than in face-to-face encounters, in which identification is communicatively organized as interplay between identification and recognition, the moment of interactivity is missing in forum-based contacting. As a result, the newbie must identify himself, and in doing so anticipate the common categories of the social field in which he presents himself.

By initially emphasizing his novice status, he uses a category that is associated with a number of typical activities that Sacks calls "category-bound-activities" (cf. Wolff 2006). One can, for example, expect novices to be unpracticed and more or less unknowledgeable about the communicative practices and rules. Self-identification as a newbie therefore also entails an anticipated excuse or plea for tolerance concerning any possible mistakes. The author here differentiates his status as a newbie in the very first sentence of his opening text. Even though it is his first contribution, he appears to have been informed by other members about the existence of a local group of Cibervallers. But it is equally possible that he has acquired this knowledge by observing activities in the Forum. Also, he gives a reason for planning to actively participate in the Forum events from now on.

His reasoning contains two requests directed at the Forum community. These requests simultaneously clarify the global reach and the local embeddedness of Cibervalle. On the one hand, he uses the Forum to get in contact with Paraguayans in his vicinity. More precisely, he plans to join a group that he knows exists and is linked to the Forum. In addition, he presumes that it is also possible to get in contact over and above the local context. The identity of a newbie appears to have a somewhat catalytic function that leads to a more biographical identification, which in turn is more interactively organized. In this interplay of identification and recognition, the older members and the newbie establish relations with each other by searching for common interests and points of contact.

Establishing Relations

The most frequent way of establishing relations that can be observed in the Cibervalle Forum is conducted via place-related categories that provide information on geographical and cultural belonging. For example, the nickname "elroseño" presumably points to a certain location in Paraguay with the name *Santa Rosa*, possibly his place of origin, with which he identifies. Accordingly, the other participants first of all relate to elroseño's hint on his regional belonging. In line five, elroseño is asked whether he can be localized in the regional context of Misiones. In lines seven and eleven, two participants identify themselves as belonging to the Misiones region. Sam directly addresses elroseño in line eleven by asking him to clarify his local belonging. In line twelve he then turns—in a conversational sideline—to feli, in order to ascertain her current place of residence. In line fourteen feli does not only answer Sam's question in some detail, but she emphasizes their mutual regional belonging by exclaiming "LONG LIVE MISIONES!" In lines eight and nine common regional links are established, but this time they do not concern their shared place of origin but their current mutual place of residence. Even if Rafael does not in line ten make any reference to localities, his way of writing ("elrosenho") suggests that he uses a computer with a non-Spanish keyboard layout, possibly because he does not reside in Spain, Paraguay or Argentina. His Italian greeting "ciao amico" can also be interpreted as a linguistic indication of his being from or living elsewhere.[38]

Addressing

In line fifteen, a participant who considers himself to be in the position to welcome the newbie in the name of the Argentinean group of Cibervallers raises his voice. On the one hand, el_nene thereby complies with elroseño's wish to join the Argentinean group, but he simultaneously addresses the two other nicks as well who describe themselves as belonging to the Misiones region and he also offers to link up with them via IM. In view of the public communication situation, he then extends this offer in the second half of his sentence to include all those interested ("and also all the others who want to add me"), thereby enclosing the potential global but indistinct circle of recipients of his message. El_nene's contribution thus comprises several levels and relates these with each other: the local level of the current place of residence, the level of virtual-local spaces that are maintained by the buddy lists of the IM and, finally, the virtual-global level of the Cibervalle Forum.

So el_nene's contribution serves to illustrate the practices of relating and addressing with which the phenomena already described are communicatively organized: The simultaneity of two diametrically opposed dynamics that, on the one hand, lead to a permanent differentiation into local subgroups and, on the other hand, conceive of themselves as part of a global overall context that they reproduce again and again. In addition to the current place of residence, the regional (more than the national) origin also appears to be an important category that influences the differentiation of the global social entity into local subcommunities. What we have elaborated in Part C on the basis of ethnographically generated data is now confirmed in the analysis of the communication in Cibervalle: As the larger part of Paraguayan commuting migrants in Argentina is connected to the border regions Misiones and Itapúa, the group of Cibervallers living in

Buenos Aires also describes itself as belonging to these two rural areas.[39] This collective belonging is permanently emphasized in the local conversations as much as in the Forum communications, and it is also reproduced in almost every welcoming of a newbie with whom one shares the same history of origin.

Instructing

We come back now to the most obvious of the categorization options of a welcome Tópico. The self-identification as a newbie is usually followed by effusive welcomes by the older participants. These welcomes indicate recurring patterns. Besides the obligatory "welcome" with which individual Cibervallers greet the new member, spatial metaphors are frequently used, sometimes ironically ("do come in, but clean your feet first"), sometimes highlighting the kind and intensity of the relations between participants ("Welcome to this wonderful family"). Furthermore, the welcoming commentaries provide information for the novice that in a sense reflects members' experience and knowledge of the social order in the Forum, and thereby prepares the new member for what he or she can expect in Cibervalle. But formulations like the one in line six ("have a good time here") or ten ("enjoy yourself here") also insinuate that the new member is expected to share in the preferred interpretive framework and the mutually produced enjoyment. The commentary (Table 15.5) from another welcoming Tópico explicitly warns a new member that, in the Forum, there are some malicious voices that should be ignored because they threaten the social order of the harmonious and joyful togetherness.

With this commentary and ones similar to it that remain uncontested by other members, the participants do not merely emphasize the value of enjoyment in their community, but they also present themselves as experienced members who are competent to legitimately define what is typical in the Forum. Remarks like "If Antonio has already welcomed you, you can feel welcomed by the whole team!!!" reflect and at the same time reproduce the author's knowledge of the group's social hierarchy. Each act of welcoming thus appears to be not merely an act of inclusion for a

Table 15.5 Welcoming Tópico "Mafalda"

Bienvenida seas a este lugar de diversión y locura. No le hagas caso a la gente de mala onda . . . sonríe siempre que acá te vas a divertir a lo grande.	Be welcomed in this place of joy and madness. Do not pay any attention to the nasty people . . . Always smile because here you are going to have a lot of fun.
Carlos	Carlos
IP: 64.135.245*	IP: 64.135.245*
20/03/2004	20/03/2004

newbie, but even more so a communicative act of self-inclusion for the welcoming persons themselves.

The welcoming Tópicos receive an almost ritual character by means of, on the one hand, redundant comments or answers devoid of any content and, on the other hand, by the exaggerated delight with which novices are welcomed. Durkheim ascribes ritual acts as having the function to strengthen the feeling of togetherness and solidarity within a community (cf. Barfield 1997). Soeffner, however, emphasizes that ritual acts provide for certainty of proper action, describing ritual behavior as "formed, expectable, somewhat calculable behavior that maintains the given order" (1995, 108; *own translation*). At this point it should be stressed that Cibervalle is an extremely fragile social entity that must constantly come to terms with communicative risks. The susceptibility of communication to fail, which is higher here than in face-to-face communication, as well as the multicontextual lifeworlds of the participants, geographical distances and—last but not least—the transitory nature of participation due to the global scope and public access to the Forum, are all structural characteristics that provoke uncertainty regarding the question of how to act properly.

The welcoming communication thus appears to have essential functions for the community itself, rather more than for the new member. By preparing the novice for what lies ahead, how he or she should behave and what the hierarchy of the group looks like, the community itself ensures maintenance of the social order. Moreover, the welcoming and the effusive reception of newbies seem to contain aspects of a collective ritual that reproduce the fragile social formation of Cibervalle as a community. The new member, however, who may initially be moved by the effusive reception, will have to realize in due course that integration into the group is a more difficult matter than it first appeared. Sandra, a Forum user living in Paraguay, expresses this dilemma as follows:

> In Cibervalle you have to pay an 'entrance fee' in order to be accepted and perceived by the others. While you must at first endure that you are not even noticed, you still have to show up. You also have to write contributions regularly even if the others ignore them. You have to open Tópicos even if they remain unanswered and quickly disappear from the list of currently discussed Tópicos, and you have to go to the meetings. (Sandra, Asunción, field diary, face-to-face conversation)

The experience of being ignored after the initial hearty reception by the Forum community irritates and angers the participants, as Table 15.6 illustrates.

A communication that introduces and welcomes a novice according to the normative expectations of the community does not automatically lead to integration into this community. Rather, for the new members to reach this goal, they need to have staying power and be prepared to solidify their profile not only by showing up on the Forum level, but also by extending

Table 15.6 Tópico "el Clan Cibervalle"

... El clan este de socios existe desde hace mucho tiempo atras, ellos se cubren las espaldas, opinan† una y otra vez en el topic de cualquiera que sea del clan, y asi llenan los topics a veces hasta mas absur-dos,. . . . .que ignorancia, que capacidad de auto engañarse tienen, no tienen nada de original, son unos falsos, y cuando yo o cualquier otra persona que no sea del clan abre un topico (. . .) no opinan† un carajo, solo dicen boludeces, o simplemente no opinan* . . .	... The clan of members exists for a long time, they support each other, they write [opinan†] contributions again and again regardless of topic, it only matters that the contribution is by one of the clan and so they sometimes even fill their topics with absurd contributions . . . what stupidity, what capacity for self-deception they have, they are not in the least original, they are wrong and whenever I or some other person who does not belong to the clan open up a topico (. . .) they do not write a single damn contribution, either they only talk rubbish or they simply write nothing . . .
Kurupí **IP:** 68.193.245.* 20/03/2004	**Kurupí** **IP:** 68.193.245.* 20/03/2004
... le damos prioridad a la gente que se hace conocer, que participa y se mues-tra, como por ejemplo en reuniones y cosas asi, ya que hay muchos Clones† y muchos se esconden solo tras un Nick, aparece socio en las reuniones y vas a ver que facil es o sea hoy por ej llego una niña nueva a una reunion que tuvimos, (. . .) y a partir de hoy por eso sera considerada, despues vas a ver las fotos de la reunion . . . si estas en el exterior por lo menos participa mas . . .	... we prefer those who allow us to get to know them, who participate and show themselves, for example, in meet-ings and such things, because there are many Clons† and many just hide behind a nick, so show yourself at the meetings and you will see how easy it is, I mean, for example, today a girl came to a meeting we had (. . .) and from today on she will be noticed, later you will see the photos of that meeting . . . If you are abroad (you should) at least participate more . . .
Albertino **IP:** 200.85.34* 20/03/2004	**Albertino** **IP:** 200.85.34* 20/03/2004

their communication to other media as well as copresent encounters, as Albertino's answer to Kurupí's reproach illustrates.

Provocation

Many participants who are disregarded after the first effusive welcome try out an alternative form of integration in the next step. This does not cor-respond to the normative expectations of the community, but it seems to be effective: The novice brings up a topic that attracts attention and makes feel-ings run high, or she or he creates one or more Clons† who stir up trouble and force the remaining members to react. Table 15.7 demonstrates such a breach of rules as well as the members' attempts to settle things down.

Table 15.7   Welcoming Tópico "adan_nyc"

1	*no invertiria en py*	*I would not invest in py [Paraguay]*
2	soy nuevo asi q tratenme bien please **adan_nyc** E-mail: -d-n——@*M**L.COM **IP: 64.47.162.*** Respuestas: 44 Última respuesta: 02/12/2003	I am new here, please treat me well **adan_nyc** E-mail: -d-n——@*M**L.COM **IP: 64.47.162.*** Answers: 44 Last Answer: 02/12/2003
3	Yo te doy la bienvenida, pero de entrada te digo que el título de tu presentación no es el más adecuado para que la gente te trate bien **Carlos** **IP: 64.81.105.*** 11/11/2003	I welcome you but I tell you straight away that the title of your presenta- tion is not the most conducive for people to treat you well **Carlos** **IP: 64.81.105.*** 11/11/2003
4	hola, apoyo a Carlos . . . suerte en cibervalle, la vas a necesitar amigo **Gerardo** **IP: 62.45.111.*** 11/11/2003	Hello, I support Carlos's (position), I wish you luck, you will need it, friend **Gerardo** **IP: 62.45.111.*** 11/11/2003
6	Otro "Clon†" de nuevayork pio? Encima abriendo el paraguas antes de llover. . . . . . **Manu** **IP: 200.58.34*** 12/11/2003	Another "Clon†" of nuevayork pio? And [he is] even opening his umbrella when it is not yet raining. . . . **Manu** **IP: 200.58.34*** 12/11/2003
8	Que lo que es tu titulo, ademas no decis nada para justificar, mba'e la nde porte, aporta algo para que los perros† te respondan **diabolo** **IP: 143.107.26.*** 12/11/2003	What's the title all about, and then you do not even say anything to justify it, mba'e la nde porte, make a contribution so that the perros† will answer you. **diabolo** **IP: 143.107.26.*** 12/11/2003
10	EL TITULO KO ES SOLO ESTRATEGIA PARA QUE LE LEAN, MARKETIN QUE LE DICEN **Enrique** **IP: 200.85.34.*** 12/11/2003	THE TITLE IS JUST STRATEGY, SO THAT HE WILL BE READ, THIS IS CALLED MARKETING **Enrique** **IP: 200.85.34.*** 12/11/2003
11	que mala onda tu presentación! a causa de ese tipo de comentarios el Paraguay no prospera **Manuela** **IP: 210.25.207.*** 12/11/2003	Such a malicious presentation! It is because of commentaries like this that Paraguay does not prosper **Manuela** **IP: 210.25.207.*** 12/11/2003

13	eeee ha reguahe pora mba'ena ja'e nde-ve. . . . y la verdad que espero sea de joda nomas tu titulo. .	That you arrive well we tell you [*Guaraní*: literally, welcome] . . . and I really hope that your title is just (meant as) fun. .
	flor_de_coco IP: 200.85.34* 12/11/2003	flor_de_coco IP: 200.85.34* 12/11/2003
14	(. . .) un beso para adan_nyc, no hagamos leña del arbol caido, yo soy tu amigo	(. . .) a kiss for adan_nyc, let us not pick on him when he is down on the ground already,[40] I am your friend
	Enrique IP: 200.85.34.* 12/11/2003	Enrique IP: 200.85.34.* 12/11/2003
24	GRACIAS A TODOS POR LA BIEN-VENIDA LOS Q LE INTERESE TENGO 25 AñOS NACI, CRECI Y ME MALCRIE EN CONCEPCION, REPUB-LICA DEL PY VIVI EN ASU POR DOS AñOS. VINE A NY CUANDO TENIA 17 Y NO SOY UN MOJADO SOY RECIDENTE LEGAL A PUNTO DE SER CIUDADANO. MAS INFORMA-CION ESCRIBANME -d-n——@*M**L.COM ANY-WAY, LA RAZON POR LA CUAL DIJE ESO: DIGANME , EN Q BANCO PUEDO METER MI PLATA Y Q DESPUES DE DOS MESES NO SE SIERRE Y ME DEJEN PELADO DONDE PUEDO INVERTIR Y CO-FIAR EN MIS TRABAJADORES	THANKS EVERYONE FOR THE WELCOME. FOR THOSE INTER-ESTED I AM 25 YEARS OLD, BORN, RAISED AND SPOILT IN CONCEPCIÓN, REPUBLIC PY [Paraguay], LIVED FOR 2 YEARS IN ASU [ASUNCION], CAME TO NY [NEW YORK] WHEN I WAS 17 AND I AM NOT A MOJADO,[41] I AM A LEGAL INHABITANT WHO WILL SHORTLY GET CITIZENSHIP. FOR MORE INFORMATION WRITE TO ME AT -d-n——@*M**L.COM ANYWAY, THE REASON WHY I SAID THIS, TELL ME WHICH BANK I CAN TAKE MY MONEY TO, WHICH WILL NOT CLOSE TWO MONTHS LATER AND LEAVE ME NOTHING, WHERE CAN I INVEST AND TRUST IN MY WORKERS
	adan_nyc IP: 64.47.162.* 12/11/2003	adan_nyc IP: 64.47.162.* 12/11/2003

For his own introduction to the Cibervalle Forum adan_nyc chooses the title "I would not invest in Paraguay." The Tópicos' titles are indicated on the main page of the Forum in the list of *Recientes*. Due to the format input requirements titles should be short and at the same time raise the interest of the recipients so that they will have a closer look. The titles of the Tópicos in the Cibervalle Forum can be compared to headlines in newspapers, the function of which Wolff summarizes as follows:

Titles make it possible to direct the reader's attention to a particular story; they persuade him to *actually* read the announced report and, finally, they prepare him for a certain *way of reading* the text and instruct him how to understand the following story. (2006, 260; *italics in the original, own translation*)

As the answers to this Tópico indicate, the title tends to be interpreted as a provocation. Because he is new, the author's demand to be treated well is interpreted by his respondents as being in contrast to his provocative opening sequence. In comparison to 'successful' welcoming Tópicos, the answers here are more guarded. Also, the participants repeatedly refer the author to his 'ethnomethodical mistake.' The first answer already points to a grave breaking of the rules by the author. Carlos not only enlightens the author that because of the title he forfeits his entitlement to be treated well, but, moreover, Carlos underlines his opinion in the phrasing of his greeting with an 'account' ("I welcome you" instead of the usual "welcome"). Which function does an 'account' have in this instance?

Accounts, or explanations of what one is doing, do not have a function in interactions, as what one does is self-explanatory. Therefore, the 'account' likely points to something more subtle, namely, to contingent courses of action. The 'account' emphasizes that these options are not chosen. Thus, if Carlos not only welcomes the new member, but explicitly says that he is doing so, he implicitly includes other possible courses of action in his account. He could just as well not have welcomed adan_nyc, or even ignored the Tópico altogether. He also could have disregarded the aspect that the author is a novice, instead reacting only to the argument announced in the title. With his account of the welcoming, the welcoming itself and the subsequent briefing about the author's 'ethnomethodical' mistake, Carlos repairs the mistake of adan_nyc and thus reestablishes the social order essential for all welcoming communication in the Forum. In lines eight and eleven adan_nyc is also being reprimanded by others. But Diabolo in line eight does not merely criticize him. In his command to "make a contribution, so that the other perros†
will answer," he also informs adan_nyc that every Tópico author should provide points of contact with other participants.

Inherent in the simultaneity of approach and repulse, which adan_nyc expresses so clearly in the title and opening sequence of his Tópico, is the paradoxical crux of a provocation. One approaches the other with a communicative act of repudiation, which, because it does not obey the rules, at the same time provokes a reaction from the addressee, thereby commanding his or her attention. In Cibervalle, provocations are important enough to warrant a separate status of participation. As Manu alludes to in line six, provocations are usually ascribed to Clons†. But which rule does adan_nyc actually break with his Tópico? What is so provoking or forbidden about his title? This question leads to another dimension of Cibervalle's social order that Manuela indicates in her contribution in line eleven.

Imagined Representation

In the second sentence of her reply to adan_nyc's Tópico, Manuela explains her criticism of his title with the ramifications of "such commentaries," which, according to her, reach far beyond the Forum context ("it is because of commentaries like this that Paraguay does not prosper"). By associating the lack of progress in Paraguay with a specific type of commentary, she suggests that the Forum has a public representation function in the service of Paraguay. If the issue had been primarily focused on practiced allegiance with one's home country, her criticism would presumably have related more to the stance or conduct mediated by the commentary, so that she would say, for example, that because of this position not to invest in Paraguay, there is no progress in that country. But if she ascribes remarks made in the Forum with such far-reaching effects, she must assume that, firstly, communication in the Forum reaches others—in this case potential investors—and, secondly, influences their course of action.

In lines six and ten the Tópico is then positioned in an alternative frame of interpretation. María questions whether adan_nyc is a novice and instead suspects that the author of the Tópico is a Clon† of a known participant of the Forum. As will be explained later on, this participant with the nickname Nuevayork is known for having "agitated against what is ours, what belongs to Paraguay" (*puteando en contra nuestro, de los paraguayos*). As a result, she had temporarily lost her right to contribute and was repeatedly excluded from active participation in the Forum. But again and again she registered with new nicknames. Most of her Tópicos and Clons† are designed to insult other participants. Whereas Cibervallers usually treat insults directed at individual nicks quite humorously, they cannot take a joke when Paraguay is presented in a bad light.

The way to treat Clons† is a continuing controversy in Cibervalle. Again and again the suggestion is made to ignore participants who are out for a fight or quarrel in order to gain the attention. Even though this strategy seems evident, it is rarely kept up in practice. A provocative opening turn of a Tópico always provokes a multitude of answers, which in turn cause the Tópico to remain in the list of *Recientes*, where it receives even more attention. The dilemma inherent in handling the obnoxious troublemaker Nuevayork or other Clons† in turn points to the public framing of communication. The awareness that such insulting contributions can be read by Forum users who do not belong to the community of active actors forces the other members to issue a statement that explains the self-conception of the community. To leave an offensive utterance uncommented could be misunderstood by the anonymous readers and thus give the Cibervalle community a bad image.

Using the example of Internet usage in the context of Trinidad, Miller and Slater emphasize that there is also a hyperawareness that one is also constantly 'representing Trinidad': one is both a representative of Trinidad, and hence responsible for presenting it well by being personally successful, and one is producing representations of Trinidad, and therefore constructing it as the thing known by both members and outsiders. (2000, 86)

The public framing of communication with potentially global reach, on the one hand, and the doubts as to whether one's own national context "constitutes a recognized place in the world at large" (ibid., 99), on the other hand, seem to lead to "being Trini and representing Trinidad" turning into one of the central patterns of Internet usage. The *motif* to represent one's own nation can thus be explained through the members' experience of meeting up with a lack of knowledge about their own national context of belonging—an experience members make during migration or virtual travels. The *expectation* of representation, however, results especially from the triadic communication structure and the role of the imagined audience.

Earlier, it was explained why it is improbable that Trinidadians' or Cibervallers' Internet activities are perceived by a considerable global public. But in relation to whom do the Cibervallers represent Paraguay when hardly anyone has heard of this country? At this point it already becomes apparent that the anonymous public is an entity that is difficult to appraise: It oscillates between the paradox tension of the potential global scope of the communication, on the one hand, and Paraguay's marginal position in the world and, respectively, Cibervalle's position in the WWW, on the other hand. But let us first return to the reactions to adan_nyc's provocative self-presentation.

Integrating

The answer in line ten presents an alternative reading concerning the motivation of the Tópico author. Whereas the previous answers assume a mistake on the part of the author that calls for correction, Enrique seems to detect a communicative pattern in this Tópico, or to be more precise a strategy on the part of the author to attract attention ("the title is just a strategy, so that he will be read, it is called marketing"). Enrique thus in a sense transports the discussion to a meta level by setting aside the communicative rule of the introduction of novices and focusing on an alternative kind of integration for new members. However, like the other participants, Enrique also takes part in repairing the course of communication. His remark "let us not pick on him when he is down on the ground already" is designed to warn the community to restrain themselves and to de-escalate the situation before everyone becomes aggravated and the communication ends up in a *flame war*†. At the same time, he accentuates the friendly mood in which novices are normally welcomed with "a kiss for adan_nyc" and the remark "I am your friend" (line fourteen).

The subsequent contributions are oriented on the same basic pattern until adan_nyc again raises his voice in line twenty-four. Contrary to his first contribution, he now respects the rules of welcoming communication. He initially thanks everyone for their contributions before supplying some information about his person and the geographic course that his life has taken so far. By publishing his e-mail address and the request "write to me," he extends the communication options to further, nonpublic levels. Finally, he takes up the recommendation from line eight to spell out his initial comment so that the controversial discussion that follows concentrates on the economic system in Paraguay. By means of his provocative opening statement, adan_nyc first commanded attention onto himself. By respecting the rules in his subsequent contribution, he repaired his 'mistake' himself and thereby appeased the other participants. This combination of provocation and withdrawal ensures that the novice receives sufficient attention while also contributing to his integration.

It has been illustrated in this section that welcoming is an institutionalized form of communication in Cibervalle that solves specific communicative problems, but at the same time creates new ones. For older members more so than for new ones, the welcoming communication fulfills the function of self-inclusion as well as of the reproduction of the social hierarchy and the essential qualities of Cibervalle. New members are attuned to the rules and characteristics of the community by means of the welcoming communication. They learn that communication in Cibervalle should mainly be cheerful and that the main purpose is for spending quality time with each other. They are simultaneously being prepared for another rule, namely, that the main mood of harmony and enjoyment—the *buena onda*†—is sometimes threatened and that they are expected to resist these troubles. Finally, the newbies learn that their communicative activities are under constant public surveillance and that they in a sense take a representative role by participating in the Cibervalle Forum.

The introduction of novices in the Forum and their effusive welcoming do not, however, suffice for being integrated into the community—even though it seems so at first. New participants are expected to supply interesting contributions and thereby to take part in maintaining communication in Cibervalle, because the social life in Cibervalle and the existence of its relations are essentially dependent on the continuity of communication. But new participants also learn that the integration process necessitates the successive consolidation of one's own address. Therefore, the introduction of a novice does not merely require this person to present an e-mail address or to immortalize him- or herself within the Cibervalle community by publishing photos in the community's album. Rather, details about one's geographic path of life are also required so as to enable other participants to establish mutual local relations, to extend the relations that have been made virtually into physical lifeworlds and to invite the novice to the next local meeting.

At the same time, the new members become acquainted with an alternative course of integration, which although morally questionable appears to be effective. By making provocative remarks, they command attention and cause the others to read them and make note of their existence. The question raised by Iwashita's contribution cited earlier can now be answered. Iwash-ita was successful with her welcoming Tópico exactly because she deviated from the norm of new introductions by drawing attention to herself with a provocative subject matter. The novices' dilemma, which Sandra so aptly describes as 'entrance fees,' can thus easily turn into the (whole) community's dilemma when the community on the one hand welcomes new participants with effusive enthusiasm and accentuates the value of Ciber-valle's harmonious togetherness, but on the other hand does nothing else to integrate new members and even reacts with heightened attention to their provocations.

"HELLO TO ALL!" MULTIPLE ADDRESSINGS AND IMAGINED AUDIENCES

It has been illustrated repeatedly—such as in Iwashita's contribution and in the analysis of the welcoming communication—how the awareness of the public bears upon the Forum activities. Also, there are indications that the audience in Cibervalle is not imagined as a homogenous entity. In el_nene's welcoming contribution it was possible to decode the potential global audience into its individual dimensions that comprise possible recipients from the local level of the current place of residence to the global level of observers potentially interested in Cibervalle. If one now takes a look at the modes of addressing in Cibervalle, the audience imagined by Cibervallers can be subcategorized into, firstly, anonymous observers presumed to be unknown, and, secondly, known users. The latter, however, are only identified as users if they make active contributions. They remain in the role of observer for the rest of the time. It is, nevertheless, implicitly understood that other users watch one's own communicative acts, so that one can refer to the others and even speak in the name of the others, as Table 15.8 illustrates.

Lisa's contribution is part of a Tópico in which a local meeting in Buenos Aires on the occasion of the Cibervaller Ana's birthday is recounted. The modes of addressing used by Lisa herself clearly demonstrate her awareness that her communicative act takes place in front of a public that cannot be closely identified. Her first sentence starts with an all-embracing general greeting ("Hi there, everyone"). She subsequently employs more concrete addressings that appear in this Tópico (and indeed in all Tópicos concerned with local meetings) and by means of which the different roles of participation can be identified. Lisa uses a statement about the quality of the event to initially identify herself as an active participant of this local meeting. She then addresses the main protagonist of the gathering and assures her how much she likes her. At this point, she does not merely speak for herself, but also plays on the fact that her communicative acts are being observed. Thus, she speaks in the name of everyone ("You know that all of us here

Table 15.8 Tópico "Local Meeting *Megafiesta Ana*"

HOLISSSSSS A TODOS LA VERDAD LA FIESTA DE ANA ESTUVO PADRI-SIMO ES LA PRIMERA VES QUE ME DIVERTI TANTO EN UNA FIESTA DE QUINCE AÑOS . . . JIJIJI Y BUENO ANA VOS YA SABES QUE TODOS NOSOSTROS TE QUER-EMOS UN MONTON Y SIEMPRE TE VAMOS A APOYAR EN TODO NENA O NO CHICOS??? VOS PARA MI SOS Y SERAS COMMO UNA HERMANA MAYOR TE QUIERO MUCHO YA SABES Y TE VUELVO A REPETIR TE QUER-EMOS TODOS NO SOY LA UNICA TODOS Y LOS QUE NO QUE SE JODAN VOS NO PERDES NADA NI LA OTRA PERSONA.PERO ESO SI PIERDEN UNA AMIGA FANTAS-TICA Y RE BUENA ONDA†. SEBAS-TIAN MUY BUENAS TODAS LAS FOTOS GRACIAS NENE	HI THERE EVERYONE TO BE HON-EST ANA'S PARTY WAS BRILLIANT IT WAS THE FIRST TIME FOR ME TO HAVE HAD SUCH A GOOD TIME AT A FIFTEENTH BIRTHDAY[42] PARTY . . . HIHIHI WELL ANA YOU KNOW THAT ALL OF US HERE LIKE YOU VERY MUCH AND THAT WE WILL ALWAYS SUPPORT YOU IN EVERYTHING WON'T WE, GUYS??? YOU KNOW THAT FOR ME YOU WILL ALWAYS BE LIKE AN OLDER SISTER I LIKE YOU VERY MUCH AS YOU KNOW AND I REPEAT WE ALL LIKE YOU I AM NOT THE ONLY ONE EVERYONE AND THOSE WHO DON'T CAN FUCK THEMSELVES NEITHER YOU NOR THAT OTHER PERSON WILL LOSE ANYTHING DOING SO. BUT THEY WILL LOSE A FANTASTIC AND BUENA ONDA† FRIEND. SEBASTIAN THE FOTOS ARE ALL VERY GOOD THANKS BUDDY
lisa Cantidad de posteos: 55 **IP:** 201.252.34.* 01/03/2005 (#583618)	lisa number of posts: 55 **IP:** 201.252.34.* 01/03/2005 (#583618)

like you very much and that we will always support you in everything"). In doing so, she simultaneously excludes certain indistinct members of the group ("And those who don't can fuck themselves"). In other words, the unity of 'everyone' to whom the contribution is addressed and whom Lisa welcomes at first is not identical with the unity in whose name she speaks.

In one contribution Lisa is thus engaged in at least three communicative acts. She speaks for herself and in the name of those of whom she assumes that they feel—like herself—positive and loyal towards Ana. But at the same time she speaks *to* them and requests that they affirm her statement ("or won't we, guys???"). Finally, in an indirect manner Lisa also addresses the participants she presumes not to be loyal towards Ana. Assuming that her contribution will also be read by them, she delivers a message to the 'non-loyals' without directly addressing them or having to start a dialogue with them. Thus, Lisa relates in her contribution primarily to a known audience—one could say a Cibervalle-internal audience. Concerning the local meetings and their subsequent media-based re-creations, this part of the audience acquires special importance, as we shall see in the following section.

CELEBRATING, PHOTOGRAPHING, COMMENTING: *DOING GLOCALIZATION*

Let us return once more to Iwashita's description of her integration in Cibervalle. After she had opened her first Tópico, she got to know several Cibervallers in the Forum and then went to a *meeting*, as she writes. As has been illuminated in the ethnographic illustration, social life in Cibervalle is not restricted to virtual spaces. The members organize regular meetings at their different places of residence and these local events are then shared with the other geographically distant members and, in a sense, are re-created in a media-based form.

The local meetings in their media framing are one of the cornerstones that carry global togetherness within Cibervalle. In this process the geographically separated, physically grounded lifeworlds of the individuals are connected with each other and transformed into a virtual-global level of social reality. Here, too, communicative patterns have emerged over the course of time that recur in the Tópicos of the local meetings. The media-based re-creations of the local events are organized in an almost ritualized form with these same communicative patterns. But the individual subcommunities do not merely organize meetings in Asunción, Buenos Aires, New York and elsewhere in order to share them as new fabrications with the global community. They also observe one another and take an interest in the happenings at their respective places of residence. This level of social reality differs from the physically grounded local levels, especially regarding the aspects of media and audiences, as will be seen in the following. However, the following question must first be answered: For what communicative problems of the Cibervalle community do the Tópicos of local meetings present a solution?

As I had the opportunity to observe Cibervalle for a relatively long period of time, I was able to track the development of specific communicative patterns as they emerged. Especially remarkable in this context is the changing application of irony, which is conducive to demonstrating the particularities of the specific social reality that arises from the linking of physically grounded local and virtual global dimensions. The Tópicos of local meetings were at first a precarious territory in which conflicts flared up quickly; the subgroups abroad in particular tended to be offended by commentaries written by their virtual counterparts. In more recent Tópicos, a tendency toward the standardization of comments and recurring activities can be observed.

Showing and Commenting on Photographs

The undoubtedly most important elements of these Tópicos are the photographs. The title of a Tópico, which is meant to encourage following the link, usually announces that photos are displayed here. Commentaries like "Come on, show the photos" or "and the photos?" can be found in these Tópicos without the simultaneous display of the respective photographs. These commentaries show that Tópicos that are based on local meetings are expected to contain photos and that the written commentaries about the local event are meaningless without the relevant pictures. Table 15.9 explains why photos have obtained such a fundamental importance:

Sandra in Asunción has been keeping track of the activities of the Cibervallers in France for some time. She emphasizes the value of the Cibervalle Forum as a medium that helps her to get to know the persons hidden behind the nicks. By means of the photos she can not only see how the community is growing, but she is also presented with a visual image of the geographically distant members. Thus, photos are media that assist in the visual consolidation of the addresses (profiles) of participants, allowing the nick to turn into a personality.

Moreover, formulations like *por lo visto* (literally "through the seen"), *que placer saber y ver* ("what a pleasure to know and to see"), *se ve* ("one sees") or *veo* ("I see"), with which those Forum users who have not physically attended the meeting start their commentaries, illustrate that the intention is not just to lend the virtual counterparts a physical appearance. In addition, the photos present an opportunity to see with one's own eyes how the others *do what they are*[43] in their physically grounded local lifeworld.

Moreover, Sandra's contribution in the preceding example exhibits another linguistic pattern often found in the commentaries on photos. By choosing the gerund, i.e., the continuous form with statements like *va creciendo* (literally "is growing") and *vamos conociendo* ("we are getting to know") the Cibervallers emphasize the progressive nature of the happenings.

Table 15.9 Tópico "Local Meeting *Encuentro en Francia*"

que lindas las fotos! va creciendo la comunidad en Francia tambien. Felicidades por la organizacion y gracias por compartir las fotos, por este medio vamos conociendo a las personas que estan detras de un nick.	How beautiful the photos are! The community in France is gradually growing too. Congratulations for the organization and thanks for sharing the photos, via this medium we are slowly getting to know the persons behind each nick.
sandra	sandra
Cantidad de posteos: 1161	Number of posts: 1161
IP: 200.85.34*	IP: 200.85.34*
28/05/2005	28/05/2005

With the combination of these two linguistic patterns—i.e., the use of the continuous form in combination with verbs that relate to one's visual perception—the actors express that even if they are not physically present at the meeting, they take part nevertheless in the social processes that are taking place in the physically grounded environments of the others.

The photos and the way in which they are being commented on thereby solve at least two structural problems of the Cibervalle community: Firstly, the photos present a possibility to consolidate participants' profiles, to give a face to anonymous nicks and to back up what would otherwise be purely text-based communicative acts with visual material. Secondly, the specific way of handling photos enables the participants to interconnect their physically grounded lifeworlds, to participate in the local social events and thereby create a kind of proximity and togetherness. It was shown during the analysis of the welcoming communication that the willingness to densify one's own address is an essential criterion for membership in Cibervalle. One's own address can be densified by providing not merely a nickname, but also information about the places of origin and residence, as well as by extending one's communication to other channels and by establishing textual presence. This being said, the local meetings in combination with their media-based re-creations first and foremost contribute to the *synthetization of copresence* in virtual spaces.

Thanking and Congratulating

A central communicative activity in the Tópicos on local meetings consists of the mutual expressions of thanks and congratulations. All participants never tire of thanking and congratulating each other: for the successful organization of the meeting, for providing a room (if the meeting had not taken place in a public arena), for the cooperation and assistance of all concerned parties, for the delicious *asado* (Spanish for 'grilled food') and for all the other dishes prepared by individual members. The Cibervallers abroad are being complimented for meeting with other compatriots and for "being able to share moments with each other like in Paraguay."

But above all participants emphasize the value of photos by praising photographers and thanking the local group for sharing their photos with the global community. Just as was seen in welcoming communication, ritual elements can be found here that not only serve the purpose of collectivization, but also provide for certainty of proper actions and assist in prevention of misunderstandings. Redundancies, comments devoid of any content as well as disproportionately positive commentaries about the meetings and the participants characterize the commentaries, especially from those participants who did not experience the meeting in physical presence. It is thus repeated again and again how nice the participants look, how good the photos are, how well all the participants get on and that it is noticeable how good the atmosphere was at the meeting. This tendency to highlight the celebrative aspects of the meetings and the simultaneous standardization of the communicative course in the respective Tópicos points at structural peculiarities in the relation between local meetings and their media-based re-creations.

As already detailed in the discussion of the characteristics of forum communication, the degree of fleetingness of social reality in Cibervalle differs between the virtual and the physically grounded levels. In contrast to what is happening on the Forum, the moments participants experience together in the physically grounded sites are ephemeral. The attempt to connect the physically grounded local meeting to the global level of the Forum inevitably transforms the event. Manning (1998) observed a similar phenomenon in the relationship between local social activities and their media-based replicas transmitted via Televisión. Manning uses the term "media loop" to describe the characteristic feature of Televisión to separate events and acts from their original context so as to reproduce them in other contexts and to make them in a sense "re-experiencable." Among the different kinds of loops that Manning identified, the "ambiguous loop" describes exactly this mutual dependency of social activity and media (re)production, which is reflected in the relationship between local meetings and the corresponding Tópicos, because in the end result it cannot be detected "what is being looped into what" (1998, 27).

The following example (Table 15.10), in which the participants comment on the strange relationship between their social activities during a local meeting and its media-based reconstruction, illustrates two phenomena. Firstly, the meaning of the meetings is inextricably interwoven with their virtual loops in Cibervalle. Secondly, in the irony of the local meeting's Tópico, the peculiar relationship between private and public in Cibervalle becomes apparent.

The commentaries on this Tópico indicate that this was the first meeting of a group of Forum users who live relatively near to each other in two neighboring states in the US. The intensive but conflicting relationship between two Cibervallers who had quarreled repeatedly is deemed to be the motive for this meeting. On the invitation of a third user, a total of four Forum members met and spent a weekend together. But the Tópico, which was started on the Sunday of the weekend in question, does not merely reflect excerpts from the weekend spent together. Rather, an illustrated narration was constructed—an ironic pictorial story—which turned the private meeting into a public act, or more precisely declared a 'peace treaty' between the two squabbling participants.

The title of the Tópico as well as the unusual manner of speech (unusual both for the communication in the Forum and in local meetings) contribute to the construction of a special frame of interpretation for this meeting. Within the frame of a gathering aimed at reaching a peace agreement, the different protagonists are allocated certain roles. Thus, the host who had invited the other participants to the meeting is turned into a judge, and even a dog that happens to be present is integrated into the proceedings as the 'official clerk.' At this point the irony of the narration cannot be overlooked, an irony

Table 15.10   Tópico "Local Meeting *Tratado de Paz*"

Tratado de Paz entre Enrique y Perro	*peace treaty between Enrique and Perro*
Siendo las 14:00 horas (Eastern Time de EE UU) del día domingo 21 de Marzo de 2004, en el domicilio del cibervallero fede sito en X, Estado de New York, y bajo los auspicios del mismo, se procedió a la firma del Tratado de Paz, Amistad y Convivencia Pacífica entre Enrique y perrito. Fueron testigos de la firma del Tratado el citado fede y corina, quien ha traído las buenas voluntades de los representates de Paraguay.	At 02:00 p.m. (Eastern Time, USA), Sunday, the 21st of March 2004, at the house of the Cibervaller fede in X, State of New York, and under the auspices of said person we proceded to sign the treaty of peace, friendship and peaceful togetherness of Enrique and perrito. Witnesses of the signing of this treaty were the said fede as well as corina, who had brought the good will of the representatives of Paraguay.
pedro	pedro
E-mail: p-dr-sm-r-@*m**l.com	E-mail: p-dr-sm-r-@*m**l.com
IP: 67.123.45.*	IP: 67.123.45.*
Respuestas: 69	Answers: 69
Última respuesta: 24/03/2004	Last Answer: 24/03/2004

Los firmantes del Tratado bajando del ferry, acompañados de corina, quien los acompañó en todo momento, a fin de evitar finales malentendidos antes de tan histórico momento.	The signatories of the treaty as they are disembarking the ferry, accompanied by corina, who accompanied them the whole time in order to prevent last misunderstandings before this historical moment.
pedro	pedro
IP: 67.123.45.*	IP: 67.123.45.*
21/03/2004	21/03/2004

(continuned)

Table 15.10 (continued)

Histórico momento de la firma del Tratado por parte de Perrito, ante la atenta mirada del Juez fede y Enrique.	Historical moment of signature on the part of Perrito, before the watchful eyes of the judge fede and Enrique.
A la izquierda de Perrito, se puede apreciar la presencia del Escribano Público de Cibervalle, quien luego de las firmas, procedería a verificar la autenticidad de las mismas	To the left of Perrito the clerk of Cibervalle, who was to verify the authenticity of the signatures after they had been supplied.
pedro IP: 67.123.45.* 21/03/2004	pedro IP: 67.123.45.* 21/03/2004

Para finalizar la firma del Tratado de Paz, los nuevos aliados de CIBERVALLE se estrechan la mano ante la innegable felicidad de fede y la fotógrafa corina, quien derramó lágrimas de emoción en tan histórico momento.	As to finalize the peace treaty, the new allies from CIBERVALLE shake hands under the clearly delighted eyes of fede and the photographer corina, who in this historical moment was moved to tears.
pedro IP: 67.123.45.* 21/03/2004	pedro IP: 67.123.45.* 21/03/2004

that is—apart from the involvement of the dog—transported by the writing style, which differs from everyday communication in the Forum.

A closer look at the photographs inevitably leads to the question, "what is being looped into what?" because the photos do not simply display incidents from a meeting during which four people, who had hitherto only known each other as virtual counterparts, got to know each other personally and spent a weekend together. The scenes that were conserved with the aid of the photos appear to have been specifically showcased for the retroactive communicative construction of the "Peace Treaty Story." Here, too, the ironic character of the 'staging' is apparent. The formality and seriousness of the linguistic construction of the event is ironically twisted not only by the spatial context (living room), but also by the actors' laughter. The protagonists' posture and viewing direction, which especially in the last photo is turned toward the camera, indicates that the actors and their acts are less focused on each other and the moment than on an imagined audience that assumingly will look at these pictures at a later date.

The Cibervallers play with the characteristic of "media looping," and thus with the given possibility to isolate local events from their context and to reinvent them in any other context. Awareness of both this characteristic and the existence of an (invisible) third person simultaneously and reflexively affects the local situation, which was dramatized for retelling. However, the "ambiguous looping" in Internet-based media differs in one decisive aspect from that of Televisión. The detail of the Tópico discussed so far shows exclusively contributions by a single participant who is trying to construct a coherent story with photos and commentaries. In contrast to Televisión, where producer and recipient are clearly differentiated, these two roles fuse with each other in social media.[44] As a rule, the virtual narrations about the meetings are communally produced by all participants, regardless of whether they are physically present. It is especially this moment of joint production that constitutes the special value of these Tópicos, in the sense of a practice of global collectivization. The individual photos and the activities depicted in the photos are mostly commented on and interpreted by the participants. The contributions relate to past experiences or emphasize typical behavior or visible changes in other participants such as a new haircut. This kind of participation in the collective interpretation of photos and activities happens by recourse to background knowledge that cannot be derived from the Tópico and thus emphasizes members' belonging.

Looking at the course the Tópico takes (Table 15.11), it is noticeable that the interpretation frame offered by the Tópico author is initially repudiated or rejected for its ironic character ("such a lie") by other Forum participants who were not physically present at the meeting. Esther, on the other hand, suggests in her contribution that she associates the Tópico with "real" conflicts in the Forum. She apparently knows of some such events in the Forum and now draws on this knowledge for her interpretation of this thread. In doing so, she emphasizes the progressive nature of social life in Cibervalle and interprets the Tópico in the context of the gradual transformation of an anonymous communication situation into a real community.

Finally, another participant manipulates one of the photos, copies it and places it—together with a suitable commentary—into an alternative interpretation-frame.

MisterDarkness sabotages the group's whole dramatization by placing the photo into a completely different context (Table 15.12). He frames the scene depicted by the photo with "Just married" and "Congratulations" and thus reinterprets the orchestration of a peace treaty into the wedding ceremony of the two participants. Apparently MisterDarkness, too, deploys an ironic interpretation-frame, as both participants are categorized as male and the introductory commentary assumes the wedding of two males to be an unlikely event. By marking his commentary with laughter ("huaasss"), he emphasizes the preferred reading of his commentary and explicates it for the other participants. MisterDarkness thus does not merely corrupt the interpretive frame of the Tópico author, but in a sense he doubles the

Table 15.11 Tópico "Local Meeting *Tradado de Paz*"

que bolaaaaaaaaaaaaaaaaaa soledad **IP:** 43.234.24 21/03/2004	Such a lieeeeeeeeeeeeeeeeee soledad **IP:** 43.234.24 21/03/2004
hoy hace un año que leí una de las peleas más horrendas entre los dos FIRMANTES DEL TRATADO!!, lo que es este ciber mundo, que se vuelve tan REAL de repente . . . ay me emocioné, de verdad!!, Felicidades y ojalá puedan compartir lazos indestructibles de amistad entre los 4 allí e ir agregando a los demás tambien! . . . Besitos******	One year ago today I read one of the most terrible quarrels between two SUBSCRIBERS OF A TREATY!! This cyber world suddenly becomes so real . . . ay I am moved sincerely!! Congratulations and hopefully you can tie up an indestructible friendship and gradually integrate the others too! . . . kisses ******
Esther **IP:** 65.145.230* 21/03/2004	Esther **IP:** 65.145.230* 21/03/2004

ironic frame of the Tópico and thus points to the essential qualities that characterize the relationship between the social activities on site and their media-based re-creation.

In the case of Cibervalle, the practices of "media looping" are ambiguous in a number of ways. Firstly, the physically grounded activities and their virtual (re)constructions are so enmeshed that it cannot be clearly discerned which is the replica. Also, at the very moment in which a Tópico is started and the photos are presented to the public eye, the group, which has experienced the event in embodied copresence, loses the privilege of

Table 15.12 Tópico "Local Meeting *Tratado de Paz*"

FELICIDADES!! No sabia que en New York ya se podia hacer casamientos gay !! . . . >>>>juasssss<<<<< MisterDarkness **IP:** 113.153.156.* 21/03/2004	CONGRATULATIONS!!. . I did not know that gay marriages are possible already in New York!! . . . >>>>huasssss<<<<< MisterDarkness **IP:** 113.153.156.* 21/03/2004

interpretation. The media-based documentation of the event and its publication in an interactive communication space now opens up for all active
members of the Forum the option to actively participate in the construction
of new frames for interpreting the published photos. The extent to which
the structural possibility offered by the Forum is welcomed by the participants now depends primarily on the meaning attached to this local meeting
by those who have experienced a particular event in copresence.

The ethnographic multiperspective description of Cibervalle has illustrated that local meetings in Paraguay tend to gain their social meaning
via their virtual transformation. For members abroad, on the other hand,
meeting each other means, first and foremost, sharing moments with compatriots. The meetings' media-based re-creations attain in some sense a
surplus of meaning, the function of which is the intensification of the translocal relationships between geographically distant members. The purpose
is to let the others participate in what one has already experienced. In this
"replaying of old experience" (Goffman 1974, 538), the roles of actors
and audience are—similar to a stage performance—clearly distinguished.
"What is said onstage is not said to them [the audience; *note H.G.*] but for
them; appreciation, not action, is their proper response" (ibid., 540). Even
in the clearly ironic orchestration of the 'Peace Treaty,' the interpretative
self-empowerment on the part of MisterDarkness and other participants is
not welcomed by the local group. After several back-and-forth homophobic
insults, MisterDarkness finally yields and hands the interpretative might he
had usurped back to the group: "If those affected do not like it they have
the right to ask the moderators to remove the photo from the Tópico . . .
anyway, I will not place it again."

The local meetings in Paraguay, on the other hand, are—as we have
seen—mainly addressed to those who are not physically present and who
can participate only in the subsequent virtual event. The example of the
birthday party that the Cibervallers organized for the absent Nora has
shown that the local meetings in Paraguay exhibit a strong orientation on
the absent members to whom those living in Paraguay in a sense lend their
bodies. The meetings that take place in the Cibervalle community's geographical context of belonging are like "raw materials for scriptings, the
replaying of which provides viewers with an opportunity for vicarious participation" (Goffman 1974, 550). This explains why participants tend to
react more sensitively toward alternative interpretations of the remaining
participants and why they claim the privilege for interpretation, and also
why participants in Paraguay as a rule find it easier to leave their Tópicos at
the disposal of the global community as a kind of 'open source.'

Considering the immaterial quality of virtual space, one could interpret the dynamic of the concatenation of physically grounded and virtual
spheres in terms of the lack of concreteness of the shared social space Cibervalle Forum. In other words, the Tópicos cannot simply be understood as
reconstructions of past experiences. If one associates locality with the
phenomenological features of social life and interprets it as a "complex

Table 15.13   Tópico "Fuera los Clones."

Disculpen . . . por lo visto que yo soy el único habitante de este planeta que toma a Cibervalle en joda. Parece que muchos hacen que sus vidas giren en torno a lo que se haga o diga en este espacio virtual. Estoy loco? **SEBASTIAN** Cantidad de posteos: 4538 **IP:** 193.197.67* 05/05/2005 (#563829)	Excuse me . . . apparently I am the only inhabitant of this planet who does not take Cibervalle seriously. It seems as if the life of many here revolves around what is said or done here in this virtual space. Am I crazy? **SEBASTIAN** Number of posts: 4538 **IP:** 193.197.67* 05/05/2005 (#563829)

phenomenological quality, constituted by a series of links between the sense of social immediacy, the technologies of interactivity, and the relativity of contexts" (Appadurai 1998, 178), the following conclusion seems likely: The Tópicos of the local meetings are so important for social life in Cibervalle because their visual representations (i.e., the photos) in a sense form the phenomenological material with which the Forum users line the virtual space and newly design it as a communal global part of their own life-world. This virtual global space that is communicatively created and visually embellished by means of photographs is therefore more than just the sum of the localities that it connects. An additional level of reality comes into being here, the order structures of which differ from those of the physically grounded localities and at the same time influence and under certain circumstances come into conflict with each other.

The participants emphasize the ambiguity of this reality, of which they cannot say unequivocally whether it is only computer-mediated or brought about only by the medium itself, through the use of irony. "Irony is a means for the perception and articulation of ambivalence, for getting involved in circumstances for which the simultaneity of yes and no is constitutive" (Mecheril 2004, 131–32; *own translation*). To engage in relationships and life in 'cyberspace' is in many ways an ambivalent business. Needs for authenticity meet up with the phenomenological enrichment of social relations in a virtual reality; a "reality, that may become a real one even if it is not yet" (Münker 1997, 109; *own translation*). In this virtual state the meaning of reality is not fixed, there is hardly anything that is self-evident, much is possible and the interpretative authority is constantly being contested. Irony seems to be an adequate means to face this ambivalence. One says something that one does not really mean, thus evading hurried predefinitions with which one could be contradicted or become the object of ridicule by the other participants. But the longer one participates in the construction of this virtual reality, the more it becomes a de facto part of one's own everyday life. And suddenly one poses questions such as that by SEBASTIAN from England.

Thus, the extent to which the ironic framing is adequate for an event depends on the degree of the integration of the virtual and the physically grounded spheres of each participant's lifeworld. But it is quite another question as to whether irony in a primarily text-based medium is understood as such. This conundrum makes the use of irony more difficult. How can one express that one does not mean what one says if one only has the communicative means of saying at one's disposal? In other words, how can one discern whether a commentary contains irony or whether it is meant cynically with the intention to hurt the addressed person? Again and again the use of irony leads to conflicts in Cibervalle. On the one hand, the reality content of the virtual space is on trial in these conflicts. But they also come about when the communication partners slip on the narrow edge between irony and cynicism and drift off into *flame wars*†. I observed that the irony gradually disappears from the Tópicos of local meetings, being replaced by the tendency to ritualize and standardize answers. This may serve to avoid conflicts. But on the other hand, it may be an expression of the virtual reality having become more real.

The activities taking place on the physically grounded level are not only interpreted in a global context, the construction of which all Forum users contribute to. The Cibervalle Forum also facilitates observation between the groups. Thus, Cibervalle members are not merely participants, but also simultaneously the audience of their own performances and those of others. In this process the shape of the local meetings appear to influence each other. To be more precise: There are indications that the media-based transformation leads to a synchronization of local events and even to a competition between the groups. A look at the temporal development of the activities reveals a chain reaction that was sparked off by the first meeting in Asunción and was still going on when the research for this study was completed. Each new Tópico that is opened on the basis of a meeting in one of the physically grounded localities prompts the other groups to organize further meetings and more Tópicos. During this process it seems to be important to match or exceed the success of the previous meeting, its degree of amusement and the number of participants.

The global scope and public accessibility of the Forum not only sets a scene for the local subgroups of reciprocal observation between participants. In addition, nonparticipants from anywhere in the world can also watch. This peculiar characteristic is also ironically treated in Pedro's Tópico. The reinterpretation of a private meeting into a 'Peace Treaty' and the ostentatious dramatization style of the author exhibit certain parallels to interactions in the political system that are dramatized for the public eye and disseminated by the mass media. These ironic references are now taken up by other participants.

With his remark "this is like Arafat and Sharon embracing," Ramón associates the social situation in Cibervalle with the global political situation at the time (Table 15.14). Herewith Ramón augments the Tópicos'

Table 15.14   Tópico "Local Meeting *Tratado de Paz*"

es como si Arafat se abrazara con Sharon!!!	This is like Arafat and Sharon embracing !!!
Ramón	Ramón
IP: 200.215.188.*	**IP**: 200.215.188.*
22/03/2004	22/03/2004

ironic self-referencing to the paradox situation that the Cibervallers' private relations and everyday activities are drawn into a public framing so that they in a sense become global players in their everyday life.

But which audience is interested in the events happening on a Paraguayan Internet forum? Considering on the one hand that Paraguay is relatively unknown and on the other hand that Cibervalle activities are so strongly related to their everyday life, it should be assumed that the Cibervalle Forum attracts little attention other than by its active members and by a few Paraguayan migrants. Considering also the linking structure of the WWW, it is unlikely that the Cibervalle Forum can be found by chance within the depths of the WWW in the first place. The irony of Pedro's Tópico possibly relates exactly to this paradox discrepancy between the potential and the actual globality of the Cibervalle Forum. Are the Cibervallers therefore merely imaginary global players? In the following section an event that brought Paraguay worldwide attention for a short time is examined. A fire in a supermarket in Paraguay's capital city became a global sensation. How this came to be and how the sudden interest in Paraguay affected the social life of Cibervallers are described in the following.

"THE TRAGEDY OF *YCUA BOLAÑOS*"

Table 15.15 shows the opening part of a Tópico that was started in Cibervalle in connection with the fire. The author's IP suggests that this participant lives in Paraguay. The gerund form "what is happening" indicates that the events is still going on. In fact, gato_verde was the first Cibervaller who opened a Tópico on this subject. He did so shortly after the fire started, before the extent of the catastrophe was known.

Whereas the readers find no concrete information in the title of this Tópico, they are being prepared that something terrible has happened. A tragedy is announced, which is likely to affect a large number of people because it is happening at a supermarket, i.e., a place usually frequented by many people. Thus, the title refrains from a factual specification of the event and classifies it instead. The readers are enticed by the negative headline, which contains very little information, to open the Tópico in order to learn what terrible thing has happened. At the same time, the readers are attuned to a certain interpretation and prepared for bad news.

Table 15.15   Tópico "Ycua Bolaños 1 *Tragedia*"

Tragedia en el supermercado Ykua Bolaños	Tragedy in the Supermarkt Ykua Bolaños
A las 13:00 aproximadamente se inició un incendio de proporciones extraordinaria en el supermercado Ykua Bolaños ubicado en el barrio Trinidad de la ciudad capital.	At about 1 p.m. an extraordinarily large fire broke out in the supermarket Ykua Bolaños in the Trinidad quarter of the capital city.
Es lamentable lo que está ocurriendo. Una vez más nos damos cuenta de que el país no está preparado para una tragedia como esta.	What is happening must be deplored. Once again we realize that the country is not prepared for tragedies like this.
gato_verde	gato_verde
IP: 200.85.34.*	IP: 200.85.34.*
Respuestas: 224	Answers: 224
Última respuesta: 01/08/2004	Last Answer: 01/08/2004

Opening the Tópico, one finds meticulously exact matter-of-fact information about the event, such as the time the fire started ("1 p.m." with the explicit hint that this is an approximation). Furthermore, it informs about the character of this event ("an extraordinarily large fire") and the locality ("in the supermarket Ycua Bolaños in the Trinidad quarter of the capital"). The capital, however, is neither assigned to a national context nor is it named. It is not the capital of the country X but *the* capital. In other words, the author takes it as given that the readers know which capital he refers to here. He also presumes that the readers of the Tópico, just like himself, assume that this town is *the* capital, or more precisely, *their* capital. It appears that he can take for granted the shared nature of this knowledge because none of the subsequent contributions asks for the national context of the event. In the first paragraph, the reader learns what happened where and when, and the author restricts himself to the role of an "emitter" of a piece of news who is himself neither "principal" nor does he feature as a "figure" (Goffman 1974) in the event he describes.

The opening contribution is then followed by a chronological and detailed list of what has happened at the scene of the fire so far. Gato_verde had copied this list from the online version of a national newspaper. He cited his source and added it to his Tópico. Gato_verde thus uses the public globally accessible Cibervalle Forum to spread news about an event that is happening in real time in the regional context in which he lives. The rapid and abundant gathering in the Tópico of users who live outside of Paraguay emphasizes the value of the Forum as an information network (table 15.16).

This and other similar remarks that could be read repeatedly in connection with *Ycua Bolaños* mark the situation as exceptional in two ways: The country attracts sudden and extraordinarily unusual amounts of attention, so much so that too many people try to access the available websites of the

Table 15.16 Tópico "Ycua Bolaños 1 *Tragedia*"

Gracias Gato_verde y Anastasia por informar a los que estamos lejos, pues es imposible conectarse a los sitios radiales en estos momentos, todo está saturado, no se afichan las páginas porque quizás hay mucha gente que se conecta	Thanks Gato_verde and Anastasia, that you informed us who are far away, because at the moment it is not possible to receive the Internet radio stations, everything is overloaded, the pages cannot be opened, maybe because many people try to access them at the same time
Lola	Lola
IP: 213.65.346*	**IP:** 213.65.346*
01/08/2004	01/08/2004

national mass media simultaneously. Moreover, many users normally quench their hunger for information about their country of origin via these Internet versions of local or national mass media like newspapers and radio stations. Only when this normal practice was no longer possible did they turn to the Forum looking for detailed information. The interactivity and synchronicity of this medium then led to the situation that the geographically dispersed actors followed the course of the tragedy together and discussed its causes and consequences with recourse to the most varied sources.

The Forum users who had direct access to mass media coverage reacted to the information deficit by replicating news they found in the mass media in the Forum. In doing so they used firstly the 'copy and paste' procedure (i.e., they searched for news, lists of victims' names and photos in the Internet; copied them; and collected them in the Tópicos of the Forum). Secondly, some of the participants reported what they had seen on Televisión and heard on the radio and commented on the course of the ongoing tragedy in their own words. Thirdly, eyewitnesses, volunteer helpers and firefighters came forward at a later point in time to give an account of the course of the tragic events from their own points of view. The geographically distant participants also profited not just from the many different information sources, but they also contributed to the translocal knowledge production by reporting how the event was perceived and commented on by the media outside of Paraguay. Here, too, it can be illustrated that the actors interpret the fact that an event in Paraguay is covered on an international level as an exception. The contribution of a Cibervaller who lives in Buenos Aires (Table 15.17) expounds on the fact that the Televisión station *TN Argentina* had stopped the regular program to present a live report on the fire.

Due to its global public scope, the Cibervalle Forum firstly presents the opportunity to globally disseminate information about a local event. Secondly, its pluri-local structure facilitates the illumination of an event from different local perspectives and evaluation of its meaning using all the available pieces of information.

Table 15.17   Tópico "Ycua Bolaños 29 *Links Importantes*"

. . . tampoco kiero desmeritar la TN Argentina por la gran nota ke nos hizo ver los sucesos al por detalle.	. . . and I also do not want to fail to savor TN Argentina for the extensive reporting that enabled us to watch the events in detail.
frederico	frederico
IP: 134.67.23*	IP: 134.67.23*
01/08/2004	01/08/2004

But how can it be explained in the first place that a fire that breaks out in a supermarket in Paraguay—a country that on the global level is unknown and irrelevant—turns into a global sensation? Further down in gato_verde's Tópico, a new piece of information about the fire can be found. Anastasia in Ciudad del Este, who is following the course of the terrible event on Televisión, writes this:

In order to prevent the customers of the supermarket from leaving without having paid for their merchandise, the owner ordered all doors to be locked when there were still hundreds of people inside the building. Thus, the issue here is not just a tragic accident, the fatal consequences of which can be blamed on the general dilapidated state of the country, as gato_verde had first assumed ("once again it becomes clear to us that the country is not prepared for such a tragedy"). Rather, a calculated decision has led to a human catastrophe. Instead of doing the utmost to save the people in the building from the flames, the supermarket owner ordered the doors to be closed, thus causing the death of hundreds of people in order to save his merchandise. The inconceivability of this act, its 'never-has-beenness,' ultimately constitutes the novelty factor of this piece of news and the global interest in it. Accordingly, this news spread quickly via the global news agencies and finally transformed the local event into a global sensation.

In the Cibervalle Forum, the reaction to Paraguay suddenly being on the daily agenda of international (primarily European) mass media was not merely surprise, but also effort chance to rectify the national image.

Table 15.18   Tópico "Ycua Bolaños 1 *Tragedia*"

Es una vergüenza . . . cuando comenzo el incendio cerraron las puertas del supermercado para que la gente no salga. . . .	It is a shame . . . when the fire broke out they closed the doors so as to hinder people from leaving the building . . .
Anastasia	Anastasia
IP: 66.105.41	IP: 66.105.41
01/08/2004	01/08/2004

Numerous contributions also expressed their disconcertment with *how* Paraguay was perceived in the world. The descriptions of Paraguay that the concrete event of the fire had suddenly made possible prompted a general discussion about the overall situation of Paraguay. Cibervallers living in Europe and the US now reported in the Forum on how Paraguay had become a focal point in the TV news of their respective countries. They also copied excerpts from articles they found in the online versions of their respective local and national newspapers. Paraguay was in this connection repeatedly called one of the poorest countries in Latin America, a classification the Cibervallers found surprising and even scandalous (Table 15.19).

How can the irritation about the descriptions of Paraguay that suddenly appeared in the international mass media be explained? Considering the regular participation in the Forum activities, which includes discussions of current political and social affairs, and remembering that the participants living outside Paraguay also use the online versions of the national newspapers and radio stations, it cannot be a lack of information that surprises the Forum members. And indeed there are a few (such as Lola who lives in France) who share this appraisal of Paraguay, even though they do not live there but derive their impressions from media-based images. The surprising and unexpected thing about the sudden availability of external appraisals of the country to which the Cibervallers feel attached is mainly that these appraisals draw Paraguay into a comparison that is constructed according to the Western, modern model in which Paraguay does not normally feature. On this global level of comparison, such 'details' as, for example, a perforated hosepipe, which are unremarkable everyday matters for Paraguayans, are turned into symbols of extreme poverty and the dismal state of the country's development. The national media cover the social grievances every day and possibly also evaluate them in comparison to other countries, and the condition of country is also critically discussed inside Paraguay. Nevertheless, this external view on Paraguay seems embarrassing precisely because it contains descriptions by others that are not normally available. Thus, the exception proves the rule because Paraguayans normally do not see anything when they look into the global mass media "second order mirror."[45]

We return once more to gato_verde's opening contribution. Whereas he has restricted himself in the first paragraph to the mere transmission of news, he changes to another speaker role in the second paragraph, marking this changeover with a new paragraph. In this second paragraph he comments on the factual information published by him ("it is deplorable what is happening there. Once again we realize that the country is not prepared for tragedies like this"). Thus he takes the role of "the *principal* or *originator*, the party [. . .] who is held responsible for having willfully taken up the position to which the meaning of the utterance attests " (Goffman 1974, 517; *italics in the original*). Similar to the example of the "birthday party" discussed earlier, gato_verde, too, claims to speak in the name of an

Table 15.19   Tópico "Ycua Bolaños 51 *Somos Pobres*"

estoy en españa, no solo pasaron por la tele,sino que ademas nos tildan de ser uno de los paises más pobres de sudamerica. . europeos del orto	I am in Spain, they have not only shown it in the Televisión, they have also called us one of the poorest countries of South America. . arsehole-Europeans
Bossman **IP:** 80.58.50.* 04/08/2004	**Bossman** **IP:** 80.58.50.* 04/08/2004
Bossman, en Inglaterra se dio mucha cobertura a lo sucedido en Paraguay, la noticia todavia esta en los principales diarios y tambien la BBC paso la noticia por varios minutos en sus noticieros. Tambien mencionaron varias veces que el Paraguay es uno de los paises mas pobres de Sudamerica (sera cierto eso?) y mencionaron que, durante el incendio, los bomberos debian pisar las mangueras para que el agua no salga por los agujeritos de las mismas.	Bossman, in England they paid much attention to the events in Paraguay, the news are still in the most important daily newspapers and the BBC has also broadcast these news in their newscast for several minutes. They also mentioned that Paraguay is one of the poorest countries in South America (can this be true?) and they mentioned that during the fire the firefighters had to stand on the hosepipes so that the water would not run out of the holes.
José **IP:** 172.134.84.* 04/08/2004	**José** **IP:** 172.134.84.* 04/08/2004
si. . eso es verdad . . . en esos detalles se fijaron los internacionales. . pero bueno. . es la verdad. .	Yes. . that is true. . . . the internationals payeid attention to such details. . but well . . . it is the truth. .
rosita **IP:** 200.101.154.* 04/08/2004	**rosita** **IP:** 200.101.154.* 04/08/2004
No sé que les sorprende de oir que somos pobres, es verdad basta con ver las imagenes de las calles de como se viste la gente !!Sí no somos los màs pobres estamos entre, y no es una ofensa es la pura verdad!!	I do not know why it surprises you to hear that we are poor, it is the truth, it is enough to see the photos of the streets, how the people dress!!! Maybe we are not the poorest, but we belong to the poorest and that is not an insult but the pure truth!
Lola **IP:** 84.134.62.* 04/08/2004	**Lola** **IP:** 84.134.62.* 04/08/2004

undefined 'we'-group ("once again *we* realize."). But in whose name does he speak? Is it indeed the same 'we'-group in whose name Lisa spoke on the occasion of Ana's birthday (Table 15.8)?

During the virtual reenactment of Ana's birthday party, Lisa expressed her affection for Ana—albeit not as an individual, but rather acting in the name of all the members of the group ("you know that we all like you very much"). Lisa writes her comment knowing that it *can* be read by everyone as soon as she has published it in the Forum. Furthermore, she presumes that her contribution *will* be read at least by the known members. Therefore, she does not merely speak *for* but also *to* the others and asks them to confirm her message ("won't we guys?"). She primarily addresses the known public, namely, the members, who slip into the role of the imagined public as soon as they are not present with their own contributions.

In gato_verde's contribution there are indications that the 'we'-group in whose name he speaks, as well as the audience he addresses, extends beyond the known Cibervallers. As was the case in his first paragraph, he refrains here as well from specifying the national context. He says *the* country, not Paraguay, is unprepared for such a tragedy. By not specifying the national context of which he speaks, but instead by choosing formulations like "the country" or "the capital," he affiliates the 'we'-group with the spatial context in which the event is happening. He speaks thus not only for all the other Cibervallers, but also acts as a representative for the Paraguayans (Table 15.20).

Furthermore, the replies of other participants address possible anonymous spectators. In doing so the communication comprises those who participate directly or indirectly in the event but do not belong to the Cibervalle community. For instance, statements of commiseration are addressed to the relatives of the victims even though there are no indications that any one of the known Cibervalle members is directly affected by the tragedy. Many contributions express indignation about the behavior of the

Table 15.20 Tópico "Ycua Bolaños 12 *Quebrar a Paiva*"

Sepan hermanos y hermanas Paraguayas que desde Uruguay estamos orando por ustedes. Es cierto que le paso lo mas horrible que se pueda imaginar a ese hermoso pueblo de uds., pero ahora el mundo les está mirando, juntense y muestren lo unidos que son, lo buena gente que son, y por favor muestren que en Paraguay se puede hacer justicia, que los responsables sean castigados como merecen. Un gran abrazo y acá támbien hay mucha gente orando por ustedes. AGUANTE PARAGUAY Y LOS PARAGUAYOS **ALBERTOUY** **IP:** 200.125.1.* 03/08/2004 (#419068)	You should know, Paraguayan brothers and sisters, that in Uruguay we pray for you. It is true that the most terrible thing one can imagine has happened to you, this wonderful people, but now the world is watching you, come together and show how unified you are, what good human beings you are and please show that justice is possible in Paraguay and those who are guilty will get the punishment they deserve. A big hug and there are many people here too who pray for you. KEEP IT UP PARAGUAY AND PARAGUAYANS **ALBERTOUY** **IP:** 200.125.1.* 03/08/2004 (#419068)

supermarket owner and voice criticism of the government, which—so the participants say—has neglected to control the adherence to safety precautions. Moreover, the Cibervallers like Anastasia (Table 15.18) also communicate feelings of shame. But why are the Cibervallers embarrassed, and most importantly, in whose eyes?

In his decision to close the doors of the supermarket, not despite the presence of people in the building but because of it (as he feared that these people would harm his business), the owner placed his rights of ownership above the lives of his customers. His behavior prompted worldwide indignation. A statement of disgust and criticism is oriented at least ostensibly[46] on a certain issue or activity of a counterpart and places the speaker into the role of an observer. But in the expression of shame, the orientation of the speaker veers towards the imagined audience. In anticipation of an evaluation on the part of a third person the speaker him- or herself now shifts into the role of an observed person. The Cibervallers are both: observers and observed persons. As observers they express their disgust with the supermarket owner's behavior, criticize the government and set themselves off from both. In this respect they form an audience of the national context. At the same time, as observed actors they are part of the same national context, which is now drawn into the focus of the global audience.

The sudden global interest in Paraguay is now reflected in a stronger interest in Cibervalle. Not only geographically distant compatriots consult the Forum to get detailed information about the event. A multitude of contributions by new members—especially from Latin America—who have registered especially for this purpose, confirm the Cibervallers' assumption that their activities are being observed all over the world. In this situation Cibervalle turns into an interactive audience in which each Spanish-speaking member can address his personal message to Paraguay and all Paraguayans.

Contributions like this do not merely emphasize the aspect of observation. They also insinuate that the world has a normative expectation of how Paraguay should handle this situation. The Cibervallers whose interest in Forum communication is primarily of a private nature suddenly find themselves in the peculiar situation that these expectations are addressed to them. The sole reason for these expectations is that they are active in a Paraguayan public online-forum. When Anastasia and many of her fellow commenters evaluate the owner's behavior to be a disgrace, they are fully aware that his decision does not 'only' endanger the lives of hundreds of people, but that it also puts Paraguay in a very bad light. But when they use the public discussion forum to communicate their stance, they set themselves off from the person of the owner and his behavior and at the same time they accept as Paraguayans the responsibility that the expectations of the world public have to be met.

A multitude of activities can be found in the Tópicos that were started in the course of the fire event, activities that can be interpreted as reparations to the national image. Thus, positive aspects such as the extraordinary helpfulness and unconditional solidarity of the Paraguayan citizens were emphasized in the discussions, and communal praise-hymns were sung for the volunteer helpers and especially the indefatigable commitment of the volunteer firefighters.

Figure 15.1 depicts a fireman saving an injured child. This photo was copied online from a Paraguayan daily newspaper by a Cibervaller and decorated with national symbols and a mourning ribbon. The title stylizes the firefighter as "our anonymous hero" into a symbol of the good altruistic Paraguayan who risks his own life by helping others. The fireman is thus turned into a foil to the selfish Paraguayan supermarket owner who jeopardizes lives to save his property.

The dynamics between a local event and the global interest in it, as well as the anticipated expectations, seem to have transformed the Forum into a platform for the coordination of volunteer help activities. This impression arises when one looks at the numerous calls for and offers of solidarity contributions in the form of money transfers; donations of goods, pharmaceuticals, food and blood; or, last but not least, assistance such as looking after the injured given by people not personally affected. The aid activities represented in these communications seem to have culminated in a local meeting of Cibervallers living in Asunción. As the Tópico following the meeting documents, the meeting was prompted by the national day of friendship during which donations were collected for the victims of the fire of *Ycua Bolaños*. A question by a newly registered member, who had read this Tópico but was not informed about its background, was answered by one of the main organizers of the meeting as shown in Table 15.21.

Apart from the communicative patterns common to these Tópicos, such as the mutual thanking, praising, appreciating and the hyperbolic expressions of delight about the successful gathering and the shared pleasure, in this case the participants especially highlight the solidarity of the members. Already in the title of her Tópico, "Meeting 07 August . . . résummee and collected

Figure 15.1 Ycua Bolaños "bombero": "Gracias a bomberos voluntarios!!" ("Thanks to the volunteer firemen!!").

Table 15.21   Tópico "Local Meeting *Ycua Bolaños*"

Fue un encuentro el 07/08/04, por festejo del dia de la amistad y para recaudar una platita o ayuda a las personas que sufrieron el accidente del 01-A, en el CLUB LEON **Felina** **IP: 200.85.34.*** 10/08/2004	It was a meeting on the 07/08/04, to celebrate the day of friendship and to collect some money or help for the persons affected by the accident on the first of August, in the CLUB LEON **Felina** **IP: 200.85.34.*** 10/08/2004

donations," Felina defines the special character of this meeting. In her opening contribution she thanks the other participants explicitly for their help and participation in this act of solidarity for the 'compatriots.' She also emphasizes the success of the meeting by pinpointing the sum of donations collected by all of them, a sum that "will make many people in the hospitals and also in some houses very happy." The commentaries of other members also emphasize the aspect of solidarity and the group's sense of being a national community: They congratulate and thank each other and constantly highlight the characteristic of sharing and helping as an idiosyncratic feature of the Cibervalle community, and respectively the national community (Table 15.22).

The photos published in this Tópico contributed strongly to presenting the meeting as an act of solidarity with the victims of the fire tragedy *Ycua Bolaños* (Figure 15.2).

However, a slightly different picture emerged in the conversations I had with Cibervallers I got to know during my field research in Paraguay and whom I had interviewed about the activities in relation to *Ycua Bolaños*. It emerged that the meeting had been planned a long time before the tragedy. Originally this gathering had been planned to celebrate the farewell of Tomás, a Cibervaller living in the US who had spent his holidays in Asunción. According to Eduardo, Tomás had given a considerable amount of money to Felina, who was to organize the meeting. In consideration of the fire of *Ycua Bolaños*, Felina then talked the situation over with Eduardo. Even though none of the members of the group were directly affected by the fire, Felina was unsure whether the meeting should take place in light of the national tragedy. Eduardo suggested that the meeting could be announced

Table 15.22   Tópico "Local Meeting *Ycua Bolaños*"

„ESTOY MUY ORGULLOSA DE MI PAIS Y DE MIS PAISANOS. Felicidades gente y que sigamos asi, luchando por construir de nuestro pais un lugar cada dia mejor.	I AM VERY PROUD OF MY COUNTRY AND MY COMPATRIOTS. Congratulations folks and may we carry on like this, fighting each day to make our country a better place.

Figure 15.2 Tópico "Local meeting *Ycua Bolaños*": "Un minuto de silencio en memoria de los compatriotas que fallecieron en la tragedia 1A" ("A minute of silence in memory of the compatriots who died in the 1A tragedy").

in the Forum as a solidarity campaign event, together with a call addressed to the participants to bring goods in aid of the victims as an 'entrance fee.' Eduardo maintained that it would have made a bad impression in such a situation to have a meeting only for fun. However, he acknowledged that it was a party in the end, with the added side effect that a little money and some other donations would be collected that Felina would then direct to the organizations concerned with aiding the victims.

Other members of the group were more critical of this venture. One of them was Sandra. However, her suggestion to donate Tomás's money straightaway and to refrain from the planned meeting met up with strong protests. Sandra decided to boycott the meeting.

> A lot of money was spent that one could have donated. Tomás paid everything. Nothing was collected at all, I mean, more was spent than they had come in. Everything was very expensive, the rent for the Club, the T-shirts and the digital cameras that were raffled. (Sandra, Asunción, field diary, face-to-face conversation)

In the narration of the meeting constructed on the Forum level, the critical voices remained in the background. They even took an active part in the dramatization. Even though Sandra had boycotted the meeting, she appeared in the Tópico praising the beautiful photos and even pretending that she had been at the meeting.

This example again shows that the local meetings and their virtual recreations are two levels of the social reality in Cibervalle, which in structure and appearance differ to a large extent even though they mutually influence each other. Whereas the meeting on the physically grounded local level was planned as a farewell party to Tomás, its character was changed in consideration of the fire event. The content of the meeting was now placed into the context of the fire event, donations were collected and the victims were commemorated. But crucial for this semantic transformation was not so much the fire as such, but the public framing of the local meeting through its linkup to the Forum and the anticipated observation of the Cibervalle activities from outside the group. Nevertheless, the transformation regarding the content of the meeting only comes to full blossom on the virtual stage. For the participants on the physically grounded local level, the event was primarily a farewell party, whereas the solidarity activities related to the fire event were specially highlighted in its media-based re-creation.

STRUCTURES OF A GLOBAL LIFEWORLD

In this chapter we have seen that the everyday life of the Cibervalle inhabitants is decisively molded by the global public framing of the communication. The latent awareness of the possibility that members are anonymously observed increases the self-reflexivity of the participants regarding their communicative acts in the Forum. But this awareness also impinges on their activities in the physically grounded environments. The online-forum serves as a global sphere of observation of the Cibervalle community. The anticipated view from outside and the possibility of reciprocal observation are elements that guide the social activities of the members. Globality, however, is not a clearly definable entity. Rather, the reflexive awareness of the public observation oscillates between different globality references depending on which audience happens to be imagined at the time. Whereas the addressings in the example of the "birthday party" resort primarily to the known public, or perhaps to Cibervalle's internal global public, in the example "Peace Treaty," an overall world public is addressed ironically. This expresses the discrepancy between the potential global accessibility of the communication and the marginality of Paraguay, and respectively Cibervalle, in the media-based world maps. Finally, the analytical example of *Ycua Bolaños* illustrates that the structural possibility of being drawn into the focus of a world public may become reality.

In order to describe the social structure of the Cibervalle audience, a differentiated concept of the audience is necessary. There are *anonymous* and *familiar* spectators in Cibervalle. The anonymous public is in turn separated into *transitory* and *permanent* observers. The transitory anonymous observers are being thought of as people potentially interested in membership who want to get an impression of Cibervalle before they register. The permanent anonymous observers, however, always remain in the dark. This diffusiveness of the anonymous audience that never exposes itself, but whose existence Cibervallers assume, seems to strengthen the imagined relevance of this audience in the minds of the members. One does not know exactly who and how many people observe the Forum activities, from where and how often. But one has a diffuse knowledge that the Forum tends to raise the interest of private persons as well as politicians, journalists and social scientists[47] as a resource. The imagined public interest in their own private activities is continually activated in the communications, when the participants remind one other to behave appropriately. In doing so, they indicate that there are people, including non-Paraguayans, who follow the Forum activities even though they are not registered. Firstly, members tell each other that it is important to keep in mind that other members observe one's own communicative acts and can comment on them later. Secondly, members are told to remember that they have to present the most attractive appearance of the Forum as possible for potentially interested persons. Thirdly, being aware that the Forum is globally accessible, members should present themselves to the world as Paraguayans. The anticipated external view thus becomes a very relevant matter for the evaluation of one's own acts.

Whichever public happens to be addressed at a particular moment apparently also changes the relevant reference of belonging. When the Cibervallers in their everyday life address mainly known members and those members of the audience who are potentially interested in membership, they construct their belonging to the respective local subgroups and the global community Cibervalle by reciprocal observation. The latent possibility that they are also being watched by an extra-Paraguayan world audience always influences the communications and obliges the Cibervallers to foster the national image. In situations like the fire of *Ycua Bolaños*, this comprehensive globality reference occupies the main stage, because as an extra-Paraguayan audience raises its voice in the Forum communication, the image with which one presents oneself to the world is communicatively affirmed. Now the Cibervallers start to relate with the world public as representatives of the "imagined community" of Paraguay. Cibervallers do not become global players only by maintaining private relationships and dealing with everyday life matters. It can also be ascertained that national belonging and the motivation to represent the nation is strengthened by the participation in global public communication spheres.

The social formation Cibervalle is more than a global electronic network based on communication. This social formation is also more than the sum of localities that it connects. Cibervalle has acquired a particular social-spatial quality for its users. Cibervalle occupies a place without geographic coordinates, which nevertheless offers a constant address. One can go there and share experiences with others. One develops common everyday routines and *thinking-as-usual-schemes* (Schütz 1972). These in time become unquestioned and self-evident, even though they may differ from the patterns of interpretation that are valid for the physically grounded social environments, because this part of the everyday lifeworld is bound to a different *temporal and spatial structure* (Schutz and Luckmann 1973) than the virtual-global part. The placeless place thus becomes a sphere of direct social experience one shares with one's fellow men and women, but its meaning is experienced within a challenging field of diverging (and competing) structures of local, global, media-based and copresent layers of its inhabitants' lifeworlds.

Final Remarks

MIGRATIONAL MEDIA USERS—MEDIA-SAVVY MIGRANTS: GLOBALIZATIONS' AVANT-GARDE

Considering their development over time, the practices of media usage have played an essential role in migration contexts since well before the times of satellite Televisión and the Internet. They have always been used in making preparations for changes of residence, in building social networks, in sustaining social relationships across places of origin and migrants' destinations, in applying political influence on the nation-state to which migrants feel they belong and in producing in the first place a collective imagination of the nation. Only the media formats and density of communications have continued to develop and change over time.

The Internet in particular, with its complex technological structure, the possibility for real-time global communication and the potential for integration of various media formats, has greatly accelerated the global media consolidation process. At the same time, the creative practices with which users appropriate the various media formats also further drive the development of communications media. Comparison of the results of the present study with those of the study by Thomas and Znaniecki ([1918–20] 1958) on the exchange of letters in the 1920s between Polish farmers in the US and their families in Poland reads like a socio-technological evolution and shows that migration is associated with media-driven socialization. Just as Polish farmers learned to read and write as in the course of migration to the US, today in Internet cafés Paraguayan grandmothers and their grandchildren become introduced to online chat, e-mail and video calling, and Cibervallers become familiar with HTML. Through written communication, the Polish families were able to substitute the presence of the geographically distant relatives. The communication practices in Cibervalle produce varieties of interaction and presence through which the boundaries between imagined, virtual and physical reality, presence and absence, sociality and technology become increasingly blurred. From the results of the present study, it can be concluded in general that populations in migration, along with their specific use of communications technologies, are predestined to produce new forms of sociality as a means of overcoming geographical distances. In other words, to the question of how globalization processes unfold in the everyday lives of individuals and become promoted and shaped by them, the migrational media users represent, in a way, an avant-garde.

THE POWER OF THE METHOD: THE RELATIONSHIP
BETWEEN THEORY, EMPIRICISM AND METHODOLOGY
IN QUALITATIVE SOCIAL RESEARCH

Briefly summarized, the essential challenges of the present study include, firstly, the investigation of a field that transcends the notions of classical ethnography in the literal sense; secondly, the analysis of data types for which there are few proven analytical techniques; and, finally, the description of a reality for which the social sciences are literally at a loss for words. An introductory theory chapter would be sought in vain by the reader. Instead, the research takes a reflexive methodological approach to the subject matter, meaning that a subject-oriented methodological discussion throughout the entire research process is accompanied by reflection and representation of the methodological genesis. With the development of a methodological approach that encompasses concrete, field-tested possibilities for ethnographic *multi-siting* as well as analysis techniques for Internet-based communication, and moreover combines ethnographic and communications-analytical methods with one another, this study makes an innovative contribution to the study of global microstructures that come about as a result of mobility and media use. The methodological contribution of the present research, however, extends beyond the mere development of concrete methods. The methodology developed gradually during the research process and combines different methodological approaches in an innovative manner designed to inspire similar research. However, for different subject matter, further work would be required, because the methodology inherently recognizes that the research subject and the manner in which it is recorded and collected are connected to one another by a reflexively constituted relationship. The present study shows, furthermore, how reflexivity is used systematically as a resource for the development of a research subject, and to this end motivates a stronger reflection in the research process of the insight-generating power of the method. With regard to the relationship between empiricism, theory and methodology in qualitative social research, this book argues thus for a stronger focus on methodology.

THE GLOBALIZATION OF EVERYDAY LIFEWORLDS:
A SUBJECT FOR WORLD SOCIETY STUDIES?

As Greve and Heintz (2005) assert, the "discovery of the world society" is hitherto restricted as an independent social science research subject by and large to macroscopically observable, institutionalized structural patterns. "The size of the global context invites macroscopic observation and macrosociological explanation, whereas the microsociology is banished to the reserve of the (g)local and—with respect to the theory of world society is considered irrelevant" (2005, 111; *own translation*). According to the authors, the necessity for a microsociological approach comes about because highly institutionalized structural patterns themselves must be locally interpreted, interactively negotiated and practically implemented by the participants. Furthermore, in a strict macrosociological approach to global social research, "global contexts that are less institutionalized and therefore unstable and interaction-dependent would be lost from sight" (ibid.). The present research empirically demonstrates that "world society" is discoverable not only within large, highly institutionalized social contexts such as functional systems and organizations. It validates the criticism of Greve and Heintz, but goes further by suggesting that globality should also be sought in the smaller, more nondescript features of the private everyday lives of individuals. As a microsociological foundation of globalization and world society studies, the present study contains an array of links to potential further research.

On May 16, 2007, an article about the phenomenon of the feminization of migration in Paraguay was published in the online version of the Paraguayan newspaper *Ultima Hora*. The article criticized the lack of social science research on the social outcomes of migration, which, in view of the development of children and family life in Paraguay, "surely brings changes with it, because there is a generation of Paraguayans who are being raised without mothers." Within the same article comes another passage that falls within the context of the present research. To cite a quotation from children in a family where the mother is working Spain:

> We will send her an e-mail. Dad is scanning a card with a heart that I made. I say to her there that I love her and miss her and lots of other things. [. . .] We go as often as possible to the Internet café to go online and talk to her and see her (webcam). She got thinner. (ibid.; *own translation*)

Elsewhere a report is given from a project to strengthen the rights of children, in which the children were asked to draw a picture of the ideal community in which they would like to live. "They mostly drew telephone booths and explained to us that they would like to have one so that they can speak to their mother who is in Spain" (ibid.; *own translation*). In both passages, the implicit nature of media-based communication, telephone and Internet use in the organization of transnational family life comes to light. The fact that the children see not their mother, but rather a telephone booth as a part of their ideal community indicates a development that affirms both the results of the present study and the necessity for deeper research work. For these children, the media-based connection, represented by the telephone booth, takes the place of the mother's physical presence. Her physical absence is accepted without question. The children wish for the communication with their mother. In Paraguay and, undoubtedly, in many other lands, a generation is growing up for whom media-based primary relationships and virtual interactions become commonplace, and through which the understanding of the difference between physical absence and synthesized presence appears decreasingly plausible and the lifeworlds become profoundly mediatized and globalized.

If that is not a subject for globalization and world society studies: *¡Nos seguimos leyendo!* (We keep reading!)

Notes

NOTES TO PART A

1. In agreement with the subjects of my research, I have anonymized the name of the Internet discussion forum as well as the names of individuals and their IP-addresses. This was necessary, because my informants frequently offered more insights into their private lives and thoughts than they would have done in a public discussion forum, even within the Cibervalle community itself. I sincerely thank all participants involved for putting so much trust in me.
2. Cibervalle (èieberbaëe)—composed of the hispanicized form of the English prefix "cyber" and the word "valle" (Guar.: at home)—is a pseudonym for the electronic bulletin board that carries the same name as the website to which it is attached. The participants use this name also for their community as well as for themselves (Cibervallers).
3. Throughout this study, the general composite term "discussion forum" will be discerned from the unique discussion Forum that belongs to Cibervalle. The latter will always be spelled with an uppercase *F*.
4. For better readability, the discussion thread used for the *docu-fiction* is here presented in English translation only. The Spanish original data, however, were interpreted in as literal a way as possible, including the Forum's often slipshod use of punctuation marks, capital letters, etc. Quotations from conversations I had in the field are also presented in English translation throughout the book. In the communication analysis part of the book, original data are presented in the Spanish original as well as in the English translation, so as to render the analysis as transparent as possible for the reader.
5. Software that enables computer-mediated real-time communication with others who also have this software at their disposal. There are several instant messaging clients that normally can be downloaded from the Internet free of charge. The general form of communication is the written word (instant chatting), which can be done by two or more persons. Most IM clients also provide other services, such as data exchanges, games and video conferences.
6. Instead of speaking about national *or* ethnic *or* cultural belonging, the concept of natio-ethno-cultural belonging expresses the diffusivity as well as the interlocking quality of the categories of social belonging—namely, nation, ethnic group and culture. This concept emphasizes "that the categories of social belonging, which are significant in the context of migration, are structured by an indistinct and multivalent 'we'-entity" (Mecheril 2004, 22; *own translation*).

NOTES TO PART B

1. Glick-Schiller and Levitt introduce the analytical distinction between *ways of being* and *ways of belonging* in the context of transnational migration

research: "*Ways of being* refers to the actual social relations and practices that individuals engage in. [. . .] In contrast, *ways of belonging* refers to practices that signal or enact an identity which demonstrates a conscious connection to a particular group" (2004, 606; *italics in the original*).

2. After Malinowski's death, his wife published the diaries he wrote during his stay on the Tobriand Islands. These private records paint a picture of a kind of cohabitation with the islanders that differs from the scientifically objectified representations of his official research report. Contrary to the 'objective' observation protocols written for scientific purposes, they demonstrate Malinowski's highly subjective attitude towards the field: In his private accounts he vents some rather derogatory views about the cultural characteristics of the Trobriand Islanders and describes his personal entanglements and problems of cooperation with them (Malinowski 1967).

3. In this edition only Knoblauch's essay, an ethnographic study of the transvestite scene, briefly mentions the problem of field construction. Knoblauch implicitly refers to the translocal character of this scene when he stresses that it is maintained by organizations as well as by mass media (dominated) contexts/environments. In this connection he briefly talks about the problem of field localization: "In contrast to the usual ethnographic field research a period of permanent residence in the field was not possible, because transvestism only appears in specific locations at specific times. [. . .] Finding the relevant events, scenes and organizations proved to be a very difficult task indeed" (1997, 91; *own translation*). Refraining from a methodological reflection of the field concept, Knoblauch saves himself by using the term 'scene' to describe the 'extremely situative character' of transvestism. He collects his data in different settings, including individual persons and organizations in Germany, the US and England. But his criteria for selection or for the localization and delimitation of the transvestite scene are not—at least in that chapter—methodologically reflected.

4. While on field research, I met a Cibervalle user who was on holiday in Paraguay, but actually lived in a village near my hometown in Germany.

5. A kind of digital journal or Internet diary that can be used individually or together with others in order to air one's personal thoughts, opinions, adventures, etc., online.

6. Short for 'multi-user-dungeon,' meaning (primarily text-based) interactive role games on the Internet.

7. In addition to persistence, searchability and replicability.

8. In the appendix to his famous study *Street Corner Society* (the ethnography of an Italian quarter in Boston), Whyte ([1943] 1981) describes the difficulties involved in the attempt to gain access to the field as well as the importance of informants in this process. Whyte recounts how his relationship with Doc, a resident of the area, changed in the course of the research. "At first, he was simply a key informant—and also my sponsor. As we spent more time together, I ceased to treat him as a passive informant. I discussed with him quite frankly what I was trying to do, what problems were puzzling me, and so on. Much of our time was spent in this discussion of ideas, so that Doc became, in a very real sense, a collaborator in the research" (ibid., 301). During my research, the difference between 'informant' and 'coresearcher' often seemed rather artificial, as I was frequently offered helpful hints and stimuli by my dialogue partners. The Cibervallers often helped me to sharpen my focus and I had the impression that my research interested them insofar as it was close to their own lifeworld experiences and questions. Perhaps the inhabitants of Cibervalle were so interested in exploring this virtual social world because it was still relatively young. In any case, the numerous

discussions about the importance of Cibervalle, which were held not only on my initiative, tend to support this supposition.

NOTES TO PART C

1. Many thanks to Paula and Jimena for their trust and hospitality in Buenos Aires and in their hometown in Paraguay. I thank them also for the kind way in which they helped me to orient myself in their daily lifeworlds and for sharing their stories with me.
2. The household as opposed to the family is not necessarily based on blood relations, but on coresidence and reciprocal help (Han 2003).
3. Habitat or living space (German: *Lebensraum*) denotes a geographic space, which is available as a living space for a population (Klima 1994). As will be explained later, the agroindustrial appropriation of the soil in Paraguay destroys the basic living conditions of a growing part of the population. The transnational agricultural industry reduces the habitat of the rural population not merely in the quantitative sense, but also in its meaning. For the agricultural industry the Paraguayan territory in a sense exists only as agricultural production space for world market products. The terms *habitat* or *living space* as opposed to agricultural production space illustrate this contrast. (The terms are used here for this reason and in explicit demarcation from German Nazi connotations.)
4. Khagram and Levitt (2008) present a review of this discourse. Glick-Schiller and Caglar question the usual theory development in classical as well as transnational migration research (in the US-American context). According to the authors, both approaches fail to reflect adequately on spatial concepts, as the result locally generated data on migratory populations in individual cities are used "to build general theories of migrant incorporation. These theories are then applied to migration processes in an entire country or even worldwide" (2008, 4). They propose a reflexive theorizing of spatial relations, which focuses primarily on "the synergy between the global processes that are restructuring cities and the incorporative processes linking migrants to localities" (ibid., 6).
5. The *Encomienda* was a common principle established in Paraguay and other Latin American countries by the Spanish crown. According to Potthast-Juttkeit (1994), both sides were officially obliged to be mutually committed, but in actual fact the *Encomienda* proved to be a one-sided exploitation of local people's labor power by the immigrants from Europe.
6. In 1767 the Jesuits were extradited from Paraguay, because the settlers wanted to draw on the labor power of the *Guaraní* from the reductions. Thus, the missionary aims of the Jesuits ran contrary to the economic interests of the settlers. Last but not least, the Spanish colonial authorities saw their supremacy threatened by the willfulness of the Jesuits.
7. Lustig (1995) argues that the preservation of the indigenous language as a colloquial and official language meant that the Spanish and Portuguese settlers, who did not speak *Guaraní*, would find it harder to subjugate and abuse the indigenous people as laborers.
8. There was a coup d'état in Uruguay, aided by Brazilian troops. Uruguay's new government allied itself with Argentina and Brazil, and together they waged war against Paraguay.
9. Potthast-Juttkeit (1994) identifies four different explanations, which, on the one hand, relate this war to the continuing geopolitical negotiations in the region and, on the other hand, to the establishment of a world trade system. Paraguay

is accused of deClaríng war on Brazil in order to gain access to the sea. But the Paraguayan perspective insists on the necessity to lend military support to Uruguay, which was being threatened by Brazil. The Paraguayan view was that "a Brazilian invasion of Uruguay would have destroyed the political balance of the region and sooner or later would have endangered Paraguay's very existence" (Potthast-Juttkeit 1994, 260n3; *own translation*). Another interpretation (which, as the author assumes, originates in the context of dependency and imperialism theories) puts the blame on Great Britain, which intended to "align Paraguay, which was neither indebted nor open to the market economy and free enterprise, to its own system and unlock the local market for British capital" (ibid.; *own translation*). The fourth interpretation of the *Triple Allianza War* starts from the premise that Argentina was the main warmonger, as the political and economic success of the new Paraguay had proved to be a source of envy and unrest within Argentina and was therefore to be destroyed.

10. The figures presented in the relevant sources differ considerably. According to Orué Pozzo (1999, 40), the population shrank in the period from 1864 to 1870 from between 420,000 and 450,000 to between 141,351 and 166,351. Fischer, Palau and Pérez (1997) estimate 1.3 million inhabitants before the war and only three hundred thousand survivors.

11. In 2008, after sixty-one years of Colorado rule, the presidential election was won by Fernando Lugo of the Patriotic Alliance for Change (Alianza Patriótica para el Cambio) consisting of eight opposition parties and several social movements.

12. In actual fact, it is rather deceptive to speak of the *Chaco* as a sparsely populated region: This ignores the seminomadic life of those indigenous population groups, who—due to their forms of living and working—draw on larger living spaces than sedentary groups. From the native people's perspective, the *Chaco* is therefore far from sparsely populated.

13. Figures from the year 2007 (CIA 2008).

14. At the time of my field research, there were hardly any reliable data available on the exact number of Paraguayans living in Argentina. The census conducted by the Argentinian Office of Statistics (INDEC) in 2001 concluded that of all migrants, Paraguayans made up the largest group with 21.3 percent (322,962), whereas migrants altogether constituted 4.2 percent of the total population (http//www.indec.gov.ar, accessed August 19, 2008). A report on the situation of Paraguayans in Argentina, which was written by the Regional Office of the International Organization for Migration (OIM), given to me as a working paper during my field research period in Buenos Aires, expresses some skepticism about the INDEC data. The OIM criticizes particularly the lack of differentiation regarding the definition of 'migrants': INDEC did not discern documented and undocumented migration, and did not account for different migration practices. As the *ius soli* is valid in Argentina, all children born in this country are automatically granted Argentinian citizenship. Thus, the generations born to migrants are not incorporated in the figures. Finally, the OIM criticizes that the usual practice of commuting migration led to statistical distortions, as the persons who regularly enter and leave the country are not perceived as migrants. Bruno (2007b), who examined the geographic and socioeconomic mobility of Paraguayan migrants starting from the premise that the INDEC data were correct, however, concluded that the falsifications arising from commuting migration are not statistically significant.

15. The autonomy of the Mennonite communities was politically restricted during the last administrative reform. Since 2007, Filadelfia is a community presided over by a mayor who is elected by *all* citizens (Weber 2008, 28).

16. As the Mennonite religious communities adhere to the practice of adult baptism, the number of their offspring who are not baptized is rising. But these people are still privileged in relation to members of indigenous groups who converted to the Mennonite faith. "An ethnic Mennonite, who is a nonbeliever, is more accepted than a believing Latin Paraguayan" (Klassen 2003, 5; *own translation*).

17. The term 'Latin Paraguayan' seems an interesting word coinage. I only came across this concept in the Mennonite discourse. It seems interesting, because it indicates that the Mennonites in Paraguay have created their own ethnic distinctions of the Paraguayan population. They define themselves as Paraguayans, but at the same time distinguish themselves from 'native' Paraguayans, which explains why they needed to coin a new term.

18. A group discussion with members of a Mennonite community in North Rhine-Westphalia, who had migrated from Paraguay between 1963 and 1973, revealed how close relations are between communities. Letters and money transfers from Germany to Paraguay were a regular feature, and one participant of the discussion said that before the Internet he had installed a ham radio on his roof for communication with his community of origin in Paraguay. Others had local community newspapers sent over to catch up with the developments over there. Today, the Internet is used, primarily for e-mails and for receiving the communities' own radio station. The participants also talked of close relations between the different communities, which were manifested in the shared organization of charity projects in Paraguay.

19. According to Fogel (2005), the transnational agroindustry is in this context composed of several actors: large Brazilian landowners and transnational companies like *Monsanto*, who produce not only genetically modified seeds, but also associated fertilizers and pesticides.

20. Collective term for chemical substances like fertilizers, pesticides and insecticides.

21. This representation is taken from image cultivation material published on the website of the Japanese embassy in Paraguay (http://www.py.emb-japan.go.jp/japon-py-immigracion.htm, accessed August 13, 2006).

22. The assumption of Fischer, Palau and Pérez (1997) that it had primarily been Paraguayan men who initially migrated to the border regions of the neighboring country (mainly to *Misiones, Formosa* and the *Chaco*) in order to work on the Yerba Mate plantations is improbable for two reasons: Firstly, the male population was drastically reduced by the *Triple Allianza War*. In some areas, the gender ratio was 1:4, in others even 1:20 (Potthast 2006). Secondly, there is a tendency towards matrifocality in Paraguay. This means, that quite frequently a type of social organization can be found "in which the woman is the focal point [. . .] including a relatively (in comparison to the neighboring countries) high proportion of female heads of household and an institutionalized lack of fathers taking on responsibility" (Luna Nueva 2005, 39; *own translation*). The Paraguayan family structure is indeed indicative of an "early feminization of migration" (Gregorio Gil 1998): Women are burdened not just with the education of children, but also with the responsibility for the economic upkeep of the family (Luna Nueva 2005, 39). Fischer's limited focus on male migrants yet again demonstrates the consequences of gender-biased migration research, which—due to implicit gender role stereotypes—cannot perceive women as individuals who migrate independently from men.

23. The effects of this unequal development are still visible, for example, on the banks of the river *Paraná*: On the Argentinian side, the major city of Posadas and on the Paraguayan side a rough-and-tumble bankside, roads of red sand and houses more or less in ruins.

24. Hoag   (2000);   http://latinamericanstudies.org/paraguay/greener.htm, accessed November 24, 2005.
25. The administrator kindly agreed to a spontaneous conversation with me.
26. According to the administrator, *Radio Evolución* is used by Paraguayans abroad to listen to Paraguayan music and local news. In addition, it broadcasts greetings sent from family members to those abroad and vice versa. It is even possible to buy broadcasting time and dedicate it to a friend or relative. In addition, local cultural events are transmitted live so that people who live abroad can feel "as if they were here."
27. The chapel in which the *Fiesta de San Juan* is celebrated does not belong to the Paraguayan community. It is only used by the community on special occasions.
28. According to Halpern, §120 was included in the course of the constitutional reform of 1992 with an explanatory statement that the citizens of Paraguay who live outside the country were so numerous that they would otherwise have too large an influence on the results of elections in Paraguay. The voting right, particularly §120, however, has currently been under debate in Paraguay (Rodríguez 2011).
29. www.paraguayglobal.com, accessed May 14, 2006.
30. The Inter-American Development Bank estimates the remittances in 2007 to amount to US$700 million (http//www.iadb.org/mif/remesas_map. cfm?language=English&parid=5, accessed November 21, 2008). The World Bank assumes a much lower total of US$341 million, although it emphasizes the significance of the remittances as the most important income source from abroad. The report also states that the relative poverty rate had by 2007 sunk to 35.6 percent, whereas the part of the population that lives in absolute poverty had risen to 19.4 percent (http//go.worldbank.org/DSVOJMHDC0, accessed November 21, 2008). Relative poverty motivates for migration. But people living in absolute poverty as a rule do not have the resources needed to migrate, as they are engaged in the daily fight for survival (Faist 2000). Therefore, the shifting poverty rates insinuate a connection with the remittances.
31. This information was published by a Cibervalle Forum participant, who cited the Paraguayan magazine *Enfoque Económico* as his source. However, I was not able to verify this information.
32. http//www.internetworldstats.com/sa/py.htm, accessed April 23, 2010.
33. At the beginning of the 1990s a free market for mobile (radio) communications arose in addition to the state monopoly on the landline telephone system. At first, this mobile communication system served primarily the communication needs of the rural areas of Paraguay, which had previously been neglected (Orué Pozzo 1999, 35). But also for a great number of households in the urban centers this system proved to be a good alternative. As a result, the number of households with a landline sank continuously. In 2004 a mere 16.1 percent of private households had a landline (Lachi 2004, 6). Accordingly, the number of households with Internet access was at the same time even lower (1.8 percent).
34. Peru in comparison had 271,745 Internet hosts in the same year; Bolivia 68,428; and Uruguay 480,593 (CIA 2008).
35. In 2005, the minimum wage in Paraguay was 972,413 Guaranís (Gs), which corresponds to about €136, whereas Internet usage in a cybercafé cost between 2,500 and 5,000 Gs (€0.35–€0.70) per hour depending on the quality of access.
36. This is also reflected in the categories used by INDEC: Here, migrants from neighboring countries (*migrantes limítrofes y del Peru*) are distinguished from those not coming from neighboring countries (*migrantes no-limítrofes*).

Significantly, Peruvians are classified under the first category, even though Peru is not a neighboring country.

37. The *Virgin of Caacupé*, the patron saint of Paraguay, is carried through Caacupé in a procession each year on the eighth of December. These religious festivities, which last for several days, attract numerous pilgrims from all over the country.

38. Puns that play on the similarity between 'Paraguayan' and 'Paragua' (Spanish for 'umbrella') or 'Bolivian' and 'Bolita' (Spanish for 'pellet').

39. Here the practices are, in a sense, practices of *self-othering*, which react to a revaluation to the disesteem of migrant culture that is inherent in the *othering* of the majority society.

40. This quotation derives from the numerous conversations I had with Iwashita during my field research, while she and her family allowed me to accompany them in their private living spaces in Buenos Aires, Paraguay and in between. I would like to thank Iwashita and her family very much for tolerating my curious glances and questions with so much openness and patience.

41. Clorinda is a Paraguayan town bordering on Argentina.

42. "Zur Sozialwelt des Internet" ("About the Social World of the Internet"), http//www.socio5.ch/ii/virt_d.html, accessed June 2, 2007.

43. *Chipa guazu* and *sopa paraguaya* are typical Paraguayan dishes.

44. This conversation took place while I stayed in Esther's house for several days. She invited me to stay with her after she heard that I was in her town. I would like to thank Esther and all her relatives and colleagues, who not only looked after my well-being, but also told me about their intention to migrate, their wishes and worries and allowed me to participate in their way of life.

NOTES TO PART D

1. Beisswenger (2002) uses the term "typed conversations" (*own translation*) for the communicative form of the chat. Thus, he points to the hybrid character of computer-mediated chatting, a kind of crossover of the conceptual characteristics of speech (phonic) and writing (graphic).

2. One can be well practiced in the reading of transcripts, but reading alone is never the same as simultaneously hearing the audio material as well.

3. Goodwin nevertheless began already in the 1970s to examine video data by means of conversation analysis. For a survey of the history and fields of application of video analysis, see Knoblauch et al. (2006).

4. This also applies to electronic bulletin boards, as will be shown below.

5. A blog or weblog is a kind of online diary, in which the so-called blogger talks about her everyday life and/or publishes her opinion on current affairs/topics.

6. Several observations suggest that socio-structural differences that have to do with education are communicatively marked. Thus spelling mistakes or the—in the lexical sense—incorrect use of foreign words are repeatedly deplored and corrected by other participants. The correction of supposed mistakes has been institutionalized by the members by way of creating a particular nick named "diccionario" (Spanish for 'dictionary' or 'encyclopedia'), whose only function is to correct other users' contributions. Moreover, as shown by participant observation, the local groups' writing and reading practices are clearly different. Unlike their counterparts in Paraguay, the participants in Buenos Aires tend to consult online dictionaries while preparing their own contributions as well as while they read the commentaries/contributions of others when they are not sure of the meaning or correct spelling of a word.

7. This is not to say that communication here is limited to these three tools. The actors communicate via telephone, SMS and e-mail. In the present analysis these forms of communication can, however, only be considered in passing.

8. By now a commercial service similar to online dating services, albeit with a focus on mutual national or regional belonging. Customers can ask for place of origin (alongside age and gender), which facilitates their getting in contact with acquaintances they have lost touch with in the course of migration and hope to find near their current place of residence.

9. One of the auto transcriptions carried out in the Forum communication is that participants often mark the end of a turn with a line break.

10. The meaning of the audience for communication in Cibervalle will be discussed in more detail later. Apart from the audience, which does not reveal its identity to the active members but directly watches their activities, another role is identifiable in Cibervalle: persons from the circle of friends and acquaintances of Cibervallers who do not have Internet access or cannot follow the online activities regularly but are kept up by active members with the goings-on in Cibervalle.

11. Yerba [Span.: herb] here refers to yerba mate, the basis of the Paraguayan national drink.

12. Typical Paraguayan food.

13. As a result of some renovations on the Forum, the signature of a Tópico author now also contains visual information about his whereabouts or provider location in the form of a symbol in the respective national colors and the number of total contributions that a nick has accumulated during his participation so far. The meaning of this information will be discussed later.

14. The example also demonstrates—besides the similarity with the communication form chat—the irony with which the participants treat the nonmaterial character of virtual spaces. The meaning of irony in dealing with virtuality will be discussed later, in connection with local meetings and their virtual (re)construction.

15. Technically it is also possible to save chat conversations and read them back later in chronological order. Contrary to the chat, the Forum format however, is designed specifically for this purpose.

16. After the last renovations on the Cibervalle Forum, which were carried out after the data collection for this study, the exact time of each contribution is now also indicated.

17. See http://www.archive.org/web/web.php, accessed July 20, 2006.

18. The logo was blackened for anonymization purposes in all figures, and the size of the pages were reduced, so that users' names cannot be read.

19. The distinction between replies and visits is quite revealing, as it reflects and at the same time intensifies active members' orientation towards an imagined audience. Because of this renovation, an anonymous reader now leaves a trace merely by opening a Tópico, as the displayed number of visits increases. The audience is thus in a sense lifted out of the dark. It is assigned with a more active role within the structure of communication and thereby becomes more visible and more predictable.

20. The last renovation made toward the end of my active participation in the field started to integrate this practice into the system infrastructure. Since then, each registered member can choose an avatar that is then integrated into his or her signature.

21. http://www.albion.com/netiquette/corerules.html, accessed June 25, 2011.

22. The format of the signature presumably changed in the course of copy-pasting Terry's contribution, so that nick, IP-address and date are displayed in a single line, whereas normally these kinds of data are displayed in three lines.

23. The distance to the company Cibervalle was also apparent in my conversations with Cibervallers. Without having been asked, users emphasized that they were not interested in the other services offered by the web portal. Either they had installed the Forum page as the homepage of their browser or they told me that they usually head from the Cibervalle main page straight for the Forum page without taking any interest in the remaining services, information or otherwise.

24. Admittedly, it is possible to save log files of IM conversations and to forward parts of these to other contacts. They can even be published in the Forum. Also, an IM conversation between two users does not preclude that there are other people in front of the screen following and possibly influencing the two-way conversation without being noticed by the virtual counterpart. Simmel had once stated for letter writing: "written expressivity is in essence diametrically opposed to secrecy" (1908, 287; *own translation*). The inherent paradox of a letter that, on the one hand, addresses a certain person, but, on the other hand, simultaneously includes an unlimited public, potentially increases in IM communication because the system facilitates replicating a confidential utterance by a mere movement of the hand. It can thus be sent to others or even be presented in a public and globally accessible communication space. So it is a delicate business to conduct a conversation in the IM client, which is why it can often be heard or read in conversations with participants that they prefer to discuss tenuous subjects on the phone or face-to-face.

25. This differentiation also reappears on the local level, as we shall see in the following. And it continues on the Forum level, so that in the meantime some subgroups have opened their own forums that they now settle in without leaving the Cibervalle Forum. The process of differentiation over and beyond the Forum can only receive limited attention in this study because its consequences for Cibervalle's overall entity were not predictable at the time.

26. The methodological implications of this multidimensionality have been discussed already.

27. Goffman defines a social situation "as an environment of mutual monitoring possibilities, anywhere within which an individual will find himself accessible to the naked senses of all others who are 'present,' and similarly find them accessible to him" (1964, 135).

28. This also applies for most other established IM client programs (cf. Schneider et al. 2005).

29. According to Goffman these are situations in which participants have "the right but not the obligation to initiate a little flurry of talk, then relapse back into silence, all this with no apparent ritual marking" (1981, 135).

30. Tipp (2008) speaks of "temporally bound physicality" (*own translation*).

31. As Hirschauer (1999) has shown, bodily presence can be minimized by communicating nonperception. Thus it is true of both forms of interaction that the desired degree of presence has to be communicated.

32. This report is based on a conversation that was held during a visit of several days in the house of Irén's family. She had heard about my research in the Cibervalle Forum and had contacted me via IM, because she assumed that her relationship with Tomás could be interesting for my study. She invited me to her house and declared that she would like to take part in my research. I am so grateful for the trust, openness and friendliness with which she granted me access to the house of her family, her room and the virtual rooms in which she lives.

33. According to Stichweh (2005) "global public" implies a conception of the audience, which is always based on general accessibility for everyone,

including strangers. In other words, potential globality and general anonymity are the elements that turn a public into a global public.

34. Quoted in http://www.lonelyplanet.com/worldguide/destinations/south-american/paraguay, accessed February 16, 2007.

35. Pun made up of "bienvenido," Spanish for "welcome," literally "come well" versus "mal venido," literally "come badly."

36. Pio = question particle of *Guaraní.*

37. Abbreviation for Buenos Aires.

38. Rafael is one of the few Cibervalle members who does not originate from Paraguay. He writes that he has spent some time there and now lives in France with his Paraguayan wife.

39. The migration practices of Cibervallers are also expressed in the Forum conversations. For example, the Tópicos of local meetings often give as the reason that a member of the local group has been missing from a local meeting that he or she is currently in Paraguay. Similarly, the description of who attended a local meeting refers to the past or future journey of a particular member to Paraguay. The circular movement between two places of living is thus turned into a common everyday feature of this partial community's form of living.

40. "Hacer leña del arbol caido" is a Spanish figure of speech that literally translated means roughly "make firewood from a fallen tree."

41. *Mojado* [Spanish: wet] is a term for undocumented immigrants in the US. It was originally used for those who had averted the legal authorities by crossing a border river between Mexico and the US.

42. This was not really a fifteenth, as the protagonist is a grown woman. It is interesting to note that regardless of the age of female participants birthdays in Cibervalle are often connected with the fifteenth birthday. In Paraguay, the fifteenth birthday is of special importance, as it symbolizes the beginning of a new phase of life (transition from child to woman). As a rule a big festivity is held to which all relatives, neighbors and friends are invited. The girl wears a white dress similar to a wedding dress. So this framing marks an activity as gender specific. Moreover, the analogy could also be a metaphoric kind of exaggeration, which can often be found in the description of local meetings, emphasizing the positive, valuable and beautiful nature of local events.

43. The formulation "do what they are" refers to ethnomethodology's central concept of "doing being" (cf. Sacks 1984). "Doing being" means that attributions of meaning within a social situation or attributions of certain characteristics are not simply given, but recognizable for others only through the participant's practical accomplishment. "To feel good," for example, is not recognizable for the counterpart as a mental condition and remains socially irrelevant as long as one's mental state is not communicated by means of the respective "ethno-methods."

44. However, media research within Cultural Studies has shown that in Televisión, too, the clear demarcation between production and reception is questionable. In Hall's ([1974] 1997) communication model the interpretational effort of recipients is emphasized in contrast to the classical model of transmitter and receiver. According to Hall, the recipients play a major role in the interpretation of media production. The different kinds of interpretation are strongly dependent on the lifeworld context of each recipient.

45. Stichweh calls the public sphere that is constructed by mass media a "second order mirror" because "the self-observation of a system which is made possible via its public sphere is made possible by the system observing others in observing the system and from these observations of others the system

takes information regarding itself. Second order mirror then means a mirror in which one can never see oneself, but incessantly sees others who observe oneself" (2002, 3).

46. In the awareness that communication is happening in front of an audience, a statement or utterance of indignation or disgust always has a dramatizing character.

47. Thus, this book too contributes to bolstering up Cibervallers' imagination that their private lives are of public interest.

Glossary

buena onda
[Spanish:
good wave]

Onda is a colloquial term for the charisma of a person, the atmosphere or the mood in a situation or group. In Cibervalle the term *buena onda* is frequently used. It denotes a positive basic mood in the community and emphasizes the good intentions of its members.

Clericó

Clericó is a kind of wine cooler, which consists of very thin slices of fruit and added lemonade as well as sparkling wine. At Christmas neighbors customarily visit each other to wish everyone a happy Christmas and to taste their *Clericó*.

clon, clonarse
[Spanish: clone,
to clone]

The practice common to the Cibervalle Forum of registering with several nicks, so that one person can participate in the Forum communication with several personae. The individual nick can be furnished with different characteristic traits. In that case it is seen as a field for experimentation with one's identity. But often the new registration is also a possibility for avoiding the sanction of temporary exclusion from participation in the Forum. As a rule, an original nick is distinguished from the clones that are attributed to it. The original nick is the name with which Cibervallers introduce themselves personally, when they meet, for example, at a local meeting. The legitimacy of cloning is a much-debated controversy in the Forum communication. In Cibervalle the clone is a synonym for any kind of undesirable behavior. The Cibervallers presume that clones are at work as soon as a quarrel starts in a Tópico, provocative positions are voiced, individual participants are insulted, Paraguay is given a bad name or the Cibervalle community is collectively abused.

compadre, comadre
[Spanish: literally
co-father, co-mother] The term for godfather and godmother in Paraguay. As the word suggests, 'co-parents' usually play an important supportive role in the upbringing of and care for the godchild.

flame war, to flame   Internet jargon terms that denote the outbreak of highly aggressive verbal fights. A flame war usually develops from an initially factual discussion, which then deteriorates into an exchange of impertinent and insulting comments.

lurker, to lurk   Internet jargon for the position of anonymous readers in discussion forums, newsgroups, chat rooms or mailing lists.

nde, ndera   *Nde* or *ndera* is a particle of *Jopará* that is used very often to express disbelief, surprise or doubt. But *ndera* can also indicate that one agrees with what the other person has said.

opinar, opinión
[Spanish: opinion]   The term used in Cibervalle for the writing and publication of contributions in an existing Tópico.

perros
[Spanish: dogs]   Colloquial term used in Paraguay to denote a group of friends.

tags   Abbreviations enclosed in angle brackets that serve to format textual elements for websites in markup languages (e.g., HTML).

tereré
[Guaraní:
mate, cold]   A cold drink based on yerba mate to which more herbs (so-called *yuyos*) are added. In Paraguay, *tereré* is served at any occasion during the warm season. As a hot infusion, it is known in wintertime as mate. *Tereré* or mate are drunk from a special mug (*guampa*) with a straw (*bombilla*). As a cultural practice, *tereré*- or mate-drinking have a communal function, meaning that *tereré* and mate are usually

consumed in the company of others. One person takes up the task of serving the *tereré* and filling up the empty mug again with water and passing it on to the next person. If one chances upon a group of *tereré*- or mate-drinking people, politeness demands that the drink is shared with the newcomer.

video calling   A kind of messenger-communication combining several media with each other. In addition to instant chatting (i.e., written communication), synchronous video and audio transmission techniques are also used.

yuyos   A *Guaraní* term that denotes the aromatic herbs used for preparing tea or that are added to the *tereré*.

Bibliography

Abu-Lughod, Lila. 1991. "Writing against Culture." In *Recapturing Anthropology*, edited by Richard G. Fox, 137–62. Santa Fe: School of American Research.

Adams Parham, Angel. 2004. "Diaspora, Community and Communication: Internet Use in Transnational Haiti." *Global Networks* 4 (2): 199–217.

Ahrens, Daniela. 2001. *Grenzen der Enträumlichung: Weltstädte, Cyberspace und transnationale Räume in der globalisierten Moderne.* Opladen: Leske and Budrich.

Alvaréz-Fleitas, Ramona. 2002. "Presentation Manuscript." In *Documentación del IV. Encuentro Nacional Metropolis Argentina. La ciudad como nexo entre la política migratoria y la integración de los migrantes,* 36–39. Buenos Aires.

Amann, Klaus, and Stefan Hirschauer. 1997. "Die Befremdung der eigenen Kultur. Ein Programm." In *Die Befremdung der eigenen Kultur: Zur ethnographischen Herausforderung soziologischer Empirie,* edited by Stefan Hirschauer and Klaus Amann, 7–52. Frankfurt a.M.: Suhrkamp.

Anderson, Benedict. 1985. *Imagined Communities. Reflections on the Origin and Spread of Nationalism.* London: Verso.

Androutsopoulos, Jannis. 2003. "Online Gemeinschaften und Sprachvariation. Soziolinguistische Perspektiven auf Sprache im Internet." *Zeitschrift für Germanistische Linguistik* 31 (2): 173–98.

———. 2005. "Virtuelle Öffentlichkeiten von Migranten." In *Jahrbuch für Kulturpolitik,* vol. 5, edited by Institut für Kulturpolitik der Kulturpolitischen Gesellschaft e.V., 299–308. Bonn: Institut für Kulturpolitik der Kulturpolitischen Gesellschaft e.V.

Appadurai, Arjun. 1998. *Modernity at Large. Cultural Dimensions of Globalization.* Minneapolis: University of Minnesota Press.

Atkinson, Paul, Amanda Coffey, Sara Delmont, John Lofland and Lyn Lofland. [2001] 2007. "Editorial Introduction." In *Handbook of Ethnography,* edited by Paul Atkinson, Amanda Coffey, Sara Delmont, John Lofland and Lyn Lofland: 1–7. London: Sage.

Ayaß, Ruth. 1997. *Das Wort zum Sonntag: Fallstudie einer kirchlichen Sendereihe.* Stuttgart: Kohlhammer.

———. 2006. "Zur Geschichte der qualitativen Methoden in der Medienforschung: Spuren und Klassiker." In *Qualitative Methoden der Medienforschung,* edited by Ruth Ayaß and Jörg R. Bergmann, 42–71. Reinbek: Rowohlt.

Bakardjieva, María, and Simon Fraser. 2001. "The Internet in Everyday Life. Computer Networking from the Standpoint of the Domestic User." *New Media and Society* 3 (1): 67–83.

Bareiro, Line. 2004. "Paraguay empobrecido. Análisis de coyuntura política 2004." In *Derechos Humanos en Paraguay 2004,* edited by CODEHUPY, 13–28. Asunción: Editora Litocolor.

Barfield, Thomas, ed. 1997. *The Dictionary of Anthropology.* Oxford: Blackwell.

Basch, Linda, Nina Glick-Schiller and Cristina Szanton Blanc. 1994. *Nations Unbound: Transnational Projects, Postcolonial Predicaments, and Deterritorialized Nation-States.* Amsterdam: Gordon and Breach.

Bauman, Zygmunt. 2000. *Society under Siege.* Cambridge: Polity Press.

Baym, Nancy. 1995. "The Emergence of Community in Computer Mediated Communication." In *CyberSociety—Computer Mediated Communication and Community*, edited by Steve Jones, 138–63. London: Sage.

Beaulieu, Anne. 2004. "Mediating Ethnography: Objectivity and the Making of Ethnographies of the Internet." *Social Epistemology* 18 (2–3): 139–63.

Beisswenger, Michael. 2002. "Getippte Gespräche und ihre trägermediale Bedingtheit." In *Moderne Oralität*, edited by Ingo W. Schröder and Stephane Voell, 265–99. Marburg: Reihe Curupira.

Berg, Eberhard, and Martin Fuchs, eds. 1993. *Kultur, soziale Praxis, Text. Die Krise der ethnographischen Repräsentation.* Frankfurt a.M.: Suhrkamp.

Berger, Peter A. 1995. "Anwesenheit und Abwesenheit. Raumbezüge sozialen Handelns." *Berliner Journal für Soziologie* 5: 99–111.

Bergmann, Jörg R. 1985. "Flüchtigkeit und methodische Fixierung sozialer Wirklichkeit. Aufzeichnungen als Daten der interpretativen Soziologie." In *Entzauberte Wissenschaft: Zur Relativität und Geltung soziologischer Forschung*, edited by Wolfgang Bonß and Heinz Hartmann, 299–320. Göttingen: Schwartz.

———. 1988. *Ethnomethodologie und Konversationsanalyse*, course books (1–2). Hagen: Open University.

———. 1993. "Alarmiertes Verstehen: Kommunikation in Feuerwehrnotrufen." In *Wirklichkeit im Deutungsprozeß. Verstehen und Methoden in den Kultur- und Sozialwissenschaften*, edited by Thomas Jung and Stefan Müller-Doohm, 283–328. Frankfurt a.M.: Suhrkamp.

———. 1995. "Anwesenheit und Abwesenheit. Raumbezüge sozialen Handelns." *Berliner Journal für Soziologie* 5:99–111.

———. 2003a. "Ethnomethodologie." In *Qualitative Forschung. Ein Handbuch*, edited by Uwe Flick, Ernst von Kardoff and Ines Steinke, 118–35. Reinbek: Rowohlt.

———. 2003b. "Konversationsanalyse." In *Qualitative Forschung. Ein Handbuch*, edited by Uwe Flick, Ernst von Kardoff and Ines Steinke, 524–37. Reinbek: Rowohlt.

———. 2006. "Qualitative Methoden der Medienforschung—Einleitung und Rahmung." In *Qualitative Methoden der Medienforschung*, edited by Ruth Ayaß and Jörg R. Bergmann, 13–41. Reinbek: Rowohlt.

Bergmann, Jörg R., and Thomas Luckmann. 1995. "Reconstructive Genres of Everyday Communication." In *Aspects of Oral Communication*, edited by Uta M. Quasthoff, 289–304. Berlin: de Gruyter.

Bergmann, Jörg R., and Christoph Meier. 2003. "Elektronische Prozessdaten und ihre Analyse." In *Qualitative Forschung. Ein Handbuch*, edited by Uwe Flick, Ernst von Kardoff and Ines Steinke, 429–37. Reinbek: Rowohlt.

Berié, Eva, and Heide Kabert. 2006. Der Fischer Weltalmanach 2007, 384. Frankfurt a.M.: Fischer, Online Version: http://weltalmanach.de.staat/staat_details.php?fwa_id=paraguay.

Betrisey, Débora. 2000. "Retóticas de exclusión. La construcción social de la migración limítrofe como 'problema.'" *Revista de Antropología Avá* 1:141–58.

Boase, Jeffrey, Wenhong Chen, Barry Wellman and Monica Prijatelj. 2002. *Is There a Place in Cyberspace: The Uses and Users of Public Internet Terminals.* Toronto: NetLab, Centre for Urban und Community Studies, University of Toronto. http://www.chass.utoronto.ca/~wellman/publications/index.html (accessed July 27, 2004).

Boden, Deirdre, and Harvey L. Molotch. 1994. "The Compulsion of Proximity." In *NowHere: Space, Time and Modernity*, edited by Roger Friedland and Deidre Boden: 257–86. Berkeley: University of California Press.

Bommes, Michael. 2002. "Migration, Raum und Netzwerke." In *Migrationsforschung und Interkulturelle Studien—IMIS-Schriften*, edited by Jochen Oltmer, 91–105. Osnabrück: Institut für Migrationsforschung und Interkulturelle Studien (IMIS).

———. 2004. "Migration, Belonging, and the Shrinking Inclusive Capacity of the Nation-State." In *Worlds on the Move. Globalization, Migration and Cultural Security*, edited by Jonathan Friedman and Shalini Randeria, 209–27. London: I.B. Tauris.

Boyd, Danah. 2009. "Response to Christine Hine." In *Internet Inquiry. Conversations about Method*, edited by Annette N. Markham and Nancy K. Baym, 26–32. Los Angeles: Sage.

Büscher, Monika, and John Urry. 2009. "Mobile Methods and the Empirical." *European Journal of Social Theory* 12 (1): 99–116.

Braune, Ines. 2008. *Aneignungen des Globalen: Internet-Alltag in der arabischen Welt. Eine Fallstudie in Marokko*. Bielefeld: Transcript.

Bruno, Sebastián F. 2007a. "Cifras imaginarias de la inmigracion limitrofe en la Argentina." Paper presented at VII Jornadas de Sociología, Buenos Aires University, November 5–9.

———. 2007b. "Movilidad territorial y laboral de los migrantes paraguayos en el Gran Buenos Aires." Paper presented at the IX Jornadas Argentinas de Estudios de Población, AEPA, Huerta Grande, Argentina, October 31–November 2.

Burawoy, Michael, Joseph A. Blum, Sheba George, Zsuzsa Gille, Teresa Gowan, Lynne Haney, Maren Klawiter, Steven H. Lopez, Seán ó Riain and Milli Thayer. 2000. *Global Ethnography. Forces, Connections and Imaginations in a Postmodern World*. Berkeley: University of California Press.

Candea, Matei. 2009. "Arbitrary Locations: In Defence of the Bounded Field-Site." In *Multi-Sited Ethnography: Theory, Praxis and Locality in Contemporary Research*, edited by Marc-Anthony Falzon, 24–46. Farnham: Ashgate.

Cerruti, Marcela, and Emilio A. Parrado. 2007. "Remesas enviadas por inmigrantes paraguayos en Argentina: prevalencia, montos y usos." *Integración & comercio* 27:21–46. http://dialnet.unirioja.es/servlet/oaiart?codigo=2538958 (accessed September 7, 2010).

Chen, Wenhong, Jeffrey Boase and Barry Wellman. 2002. "The Global Villages, Comparing Internet Users and Uses around the World." In *The Internet in Everyday Life*, edited by Barry Wellman and Caroline Haythornthwaite, 74–113. Oxford: Blackwell.

CIA, ed. 2008. "Paraguay." In *World Factbook*. https://www.cia.gov/library/publications/the-world-factbook/geos/pa.html (accessed January 9, 2009).

Clementi, Hebe. 1987. *La frontera en America. Una clave interpretativa de la historia americana*, vol. 1. Buenos Aires: Leviatan.

Clifford, James, and George E. Marcus, eds. 1986. *Writing Culture. The Poetics and Politics of Ethnography*. Berkeley: University of California Press.

DGEEC. 2002. *Atlas Censal del Paraguay*. http://www.dgeec.gov.py/Publicaciones/Biblioteca/Atlas%20Censal%20del%20Paraguay/atlas_censal_paraguay.html (accessed August 11, 2006).

Dillon, Andrew, and Barbara A. Gushrowski. 2000. "Genres and the Web: Is the Personal Home Page the First Uniquely Digital Genre?" *Journal of the American Society for Information Science* 51:202–5.

Dittmer, Dörte, and Ulrike Fullriede. 1996. *Como agua y aceite: zum Verhältnis von Mennoniten und Indígenas in der multiethnischen Gesellschaft im paraguayischen Chaco*. Berlin: Wiss. Verlag Berlin.

Drori, Gili S. 2010. "Globalization and Technology Divides: Bifurcation of Policy Between the 'Digital Divide' and the 'Innovation Divide.'" *Sociological Inquiry* 80 (1): 63–91.

Faist, Thomas. 2000. *The Volume and Dynamics of International Migration and Transnational Social Spaces.* Oxford: Oxford University Press.

Falzon, Marc-Anthony, ed. 2009. *Multi-Sited Ethnography: Theory, Praxis and Locality in Contemporary Research.* Farnham: Ashgate.

Fariña, Gladys. 2004. "Otro año más marcado por la lucha por la tierra." In *Derechos Humanos en Paraguay 2004*, edited by CODEHUPY, 265–84. Asunción: CODEHUPY.

Fischer, Sara, Tomás Palau and Noemia Pérez. 1997. *Inmigración y Emigración en el Paraguay 1870–1960.* Asuncion: BASE Investigaciones sociales. http://www.clacso.org (accessed September 7, 2005).

Fischer World Almanac. 2011. http://www.weltalmanach.de/staat/staat_detail.php?fwa_id=paraguay (accessed March 2, 2011).

Fogel, Ramón. 2005. "Efectos socioambientales del enclave sojero." In *Enclave Sojero: Merma de Soberanía y Pobreza*, edited by Ramón Fogel and Marcial Riquelme, 35–112. Asunción: CERI.

Garfinkel, Harold, and Larry D. Wieder. 1992. "Two Incommensurable Asymmetrically Alternate Technologies of Social Analysis." In *Text in Context*, edited by Graham Watson and Robert M. Seiler, 175–206. London and New Delhi: Sage.

Global Commission on International Migration. 2005. *Migration in an Interconnected World: New Directions for Action. Report of the Global Commission on International Migration.* http://www.gcim.org/attachements/gcim-complete-report-2005.pdf (accessed July 7, 2011).

Georg, Sheba. 2000. "'Dirty Nurses' and 'Men Who Play.' Gender and Class in Transnational Migration." In *Global Ethnography*, edited by Michael Burawoy, Joseph A. Blum, Sheba George, Zsuzsa Gille, Teresa Gowan, Lynne Haney, Maren Klawiter, Steven H. Lopez, Seán Ó Riain and Millie Thayer: 144–74. Berkeley: University of California Press.

Gille, Zsuzsa, and Sean O Riain. 2002. "Global Ethnography." *Annual Review of Sociology* 28:271–95.

Gillespie, Marie. 1995. *Televisión, Ethnicity and Cultural Change.* London: Routledge.

Glaser, Barney G., and Anselm Strauss. 1967. *The Discovery of Grounded Theory. Strategies for Qualitative Research.* Chicago: Aldine.

Glick-Schiller, Nina. 2003. "The Centrality of Ethnography in the Study of Transnational Migration: Seeing the Wetlands Instead of the Swamp." In *American Arrivals: Anthropology Engages the New Immigration*, edited by Nancy Foner, 99–128. Santa Fe: School of American Research Press.

Glick-Schiller, Nina, and Ayse Çaglar. 2008. "Migrant Incorporation and City Scale: Towards a Theory of Locality in Migration Studies." *Willy-Brandt-Series of Working Papers in International Migration and Ethnic Relations* 2(07). http://hdl.handle.net/2043/5935 (accessed January 18, 2009).

Glick-Schiller, Nina, and Georges Fouron. 2001. *Goerges Woke Up Laughing: Long-Distance Nationalism and the Apparent State.* Durham, NC: Duke University Press.

Glick-Schiller, Nina, and Peggy Levitt. 2004. "Conceptualizing Simultaneity: A Transnational Social Field Perspective on Society." *International Migration Review* 38 (145): 595–629. http://www.peggylevitt.org/pdfs/Levitt-Glick.conceptsimult.pdf (accessed May 30, 2010).

Goffman, Erving. 1964. "The Neglected Situation." *American Anthropologist* 66 (2): 133–36.

———. 1974. *Frame Analysis. An Essay on the Organization of Experience.* Cambridge, MA: Harvard University Press.

———. 1981. *Forms of Talk.* Philadelphia: University of Pennsylvania Press.

Goll, Michaela. 2002. *Arbeiten im Netz: Kommunikationsstrukturen, Arbeitsabläufe, Wissensmanagement.* Wiesbaden: Westdeutscher Verlag.

González de Bosio, Beatriz. 2000. "Ocupación de espacios en el Paraguay colonial." In *Mercosur. Una historia común para la integración,* edited by Gregorio Recondo, 181–92. Asunción and Buenos Aires: Multibanco.

Gregorio Gil, Carmen. 1998. *Migración femenina. Su impacto en las relaciones de género.* Madrid: Narcea Ediciones.

Greve, Jens, and Bettina Heintz. 2005. "Die 'Entdeckung' der Weltgesellschaft. Entstehung und Grenzen der Weltgesellschaftstheorie." In *Weltgesellschaft. Theoretische Zugänge und empirische Problemlagen* (Special Issue of *Zeitschrift für Soziologie*), edited by Bettina Heintz, Richard Münch and Hartmann Tyrell, 89–119. Stuttgart: Lucius and Lucius.

Grimson, Alejandro. 2002. *El otro lado del río. Periodistas, Nación y Mercosur en la frontera.* Buenos Aires: Editorial Universitaria de Buenos Aires.

Guarnizo, Luis E. 2003. "The Economics of Transnational Living." *International Migration Review* 37 (3): 666–99.

Guber, Rosana. 2001. *La etnografía. Método, campo y reflexividad.* Bogota: Grupo Editorial Norma.

Guillén, Mauro F. 2001. "Is Globalization Civilizing, Destructive or Feeble? A Critique of Five Key Debates in the Social Science Literature." *Annual Review of Sociology* 27:235–60.

Günthner, Susanne, and Hubert Knoblauch. 1995. "Culturally Patterned Speaking Practices—The Analysis of Communicative Genres." *Pragmatics* 5 (1): 1–32.

———. 1997. "Gattungsanalyse." In *Sozialwissenschaftliche Hermeneutik: Eine Einführung,* edited by Ronald Hitzler, 281–307. Opladen: Leske und Budrich.

Hack, Hans. 1960. *Die Kolonisation der Mennoniten im paraguayischen Chaco.* Amsterdam: Medeling/Koninklijk Instituut vor de Tropen.

Hall, Stuart. [1974] 1997. "The Televisión Discourse—Encoding and Decoding." In *Studies in Culture: An Introductory Reader,* edited by Ann Gray and Jim McGuigan, 28–34. London: Arnold.

Halpern, Gerardo. 2001. "Convenios (migratorios) sin inmigrantes." Paper presented at the II Encuentro de Facultades de Comunicación Social del Cono, Santiago de Chile, November 7–9. http://www.periodismo.uchile.cl/encuentroconosur/ponencias/2/2a_gerardohalpern.html (accessed December 15, 2004).

———. 2002. "Presentation Manuscript." In *Documentación del IV Encuentro Nacional Metropolis Argentina. La ciudad como nexo entre la política migratoria y la integración de los migrantes,* 39–42. Buenos Aires.

———. 2009. *Etnicidad, inmigración y política. Representationes y cultura política de exiliados paraguayos en Argentina.* Buenos Aires: Prometeo Libros.

Han, Petrus. 2003. *Frauen und Migration.* Stuttgart: Lucius and Lucius.

Hannerz, Ulf. 2003. "Being There . . . and There . . . and There! Reflections on Multi-Site-Ethnography." *Ethnography* 4 (2): 201–16.

Hanratty, Dennis, and Sandra W. Meditz, eds. [1988] 2005. *A Country Study: Paraguay.* Federal Research Division, Library of Congress. http://lcweb2.loc.gov/frd/cs/pytoc.html (accessed May 23, 2006).

Heft, Kathleen, and Urmila Goel. 2005. "Räume der zweiten Generation." Proceedings of the workshop at Europa University Viadrina, Frankfurt/Oder, November 10–12.

Heintz, Bettina. 2000. "Gemeinschaft ohne Nähe? Virtuelle Gruppen und reale Netze." In *Virtuelle Gruppen. Charakteristika und Problemdimensionen,* edited by Udo Thiedeke, 188–218. Wiesbaden: Westdeutscher Verlag.

Heritage, John. 1984. *Garfinkel and Ethnomethodology*. Cambridge and Oxford: Polity Press.

Herzog, Roman, Vert Hoffmann and Markus Schulz. 2002. *Internet und Politik in Lateinamerika: Regulierung und Nutzung der Neuen Informations- und Kommunikationstechnologien im Kontext der politischen und wirtschaftlichen Transformationen, Band 1 Einleitung und Vergleich*. Frankfurt a.M.: Vervuert.

Hine, Christine. 1998. Virtual Ethnography. Paper presented at IRISS International Conference, Bristol UK, March 25–27. http://www.sosig.ac.uk/iriss/papers/paper16.html (accessed April 23, 2006).

———. 2009. "Question One: How Can Qualitative Internet Researchers Define the Boundaries of Their Projects?" In *Internet Inquiry. Conversations about Method*, edited by Annette N. Markham and Nancy K. Baym, 1–20. Los Angeles: Sage.

Hirschauer, Stefan. 1999. „Die Praxis des Fahrstuhlfahrens und die Minimierung von Anwesenheit. Eine Fahrstuhlfahrt." *Soziale Welt* 50: 221–245.

Hirschauer, Stefan, and Klaus Amann, eds. 1997. *Die Befremdung der eigenen Kultur: Zur ethnographischen Herausforderung soziologischer Empirie*. Frankfurt a.M.: Suhrkamp.

Hoag, Christina. 2000. *Paraguayan townspeople find the grass is greener in U.S.* Miami: The Miami Herald. http://latinamericanstudies.org/paraguay/greener.htm (accessed November 24, 2005).

Holly, Werner, and Heike Baldauf. 2001. "Grundlagen des fernsehbegleitenden Sprechens." In *Der sprechende Zuschauer. Wie wir uns Fernsehen kommunikativ aneignen*, edited by Werner Holly, Ulrich Püschel and Jörg R. Bergmann, 41–60. Opladen: Westdeutscher Verlag.

Honer, Anne. 2003. "Lebensweltanalyse in der Ethnographie." In *Qualitative Forschung. Ein Handbuch*, edited by Uwe Flick, Ernst von Kardoff and Ines Steinke, 194–204. Reinbek: Rowohlt.

Johnstone, Patrick. 1994. *Handbuch für die Weltmission: Gebet für die Welt*. Neuhausen-Stuttgart: Hänssler.

Jones, Steven G. 1995. *Cybersociety: Computer-Mediated Communication and Community*. London: Sage.

Karim, Karim H. 2001. "From Ethnic Media to Global Media—Transnational Communication Networks among Diasporic Communities." *Nord-Süd aktuell* 4:645–54.

———. 2003a. "Mapping Diasporic Mediascapes." In *The Media of Diaspora. Mapping the Globe*, ed. Karim H. Karim, 2–17. Oxford: Routledge.

———, ed. 2003b. *The Media of Diaspora. Mapping the Globe*. Oxford: Routledge.

Kendall, Lori. 1999. "Recontextualizing Cyberspace—Methodological Considerations for Online Research." In *Doing Internet Research: Critical Issues and Methods for Examining the Net*, edited by Steven G. Jones, 57–75. Thousand Oaks, CA: Sage.

Khagram, Sanjeev, and Peggy Levitt, eds. 2008. *The Transnational Studies Reader. Intersections an Innovations*. New York: Routledge.

Kieserling, André. 1999. *Kommunikation unter Anwesenden: Studien über Interaktionssysteme*. Frankfurt a.M.: Suhrkamp.

Klassen, Peter P. 2003. *Was ist aus uns geworden? Die Mennoniten Lateinamerikas im Vergleich*. http://www.jungegemeinde.de/jgakt600.htm (accessed November 24, 2003).

Klemm, Michael, and Lutz Graner. 2000. "Chatten vor dem Bildschirm: Nutzerkommunikation als Fenster zur alltäglichen Computerkultur." In *Soziales im Netz. Sprache, Beziehungen und Kommunikationskulturen im Internet*, edited by Caja Thimm, 156–79. Opladen: Westdeutscher Verlag.

Klima, Rolf. 1994. "Lebensraum." In *Lexikon der Soziologie*, edited by Werner Fuchs-Heinritz, 394. Opladen: Westdeutscher Verlag.

Knoblauch, Hubert A. 1997. "Zwischen den Geschlechtern? Zur In-Szenierung, Organisation und Identität des Transvestismus." In *Die Befremdung der eigenen Kultur. Zur ethnographischen Herausforderung soziologischer Empirie*, edited by Klaus Amann and Stefan Hirschauer, 84–114. Frankfurt a.M.: Suhrkamp.

Knoblauch, Hubert, Bernt Schnettler, Jürgen Raab and Hans G. Soeffner. 2006. *Video Analysis: Methodology and Methods. Qualitative Audiovisual Data Analysis in Sociology.* Frankfurt a.M.: Peter Lang.

Knoblauch, Hubert A., and Thomas Luckmann. 2003. "Gattungsanalyse." In *Qualitative Forschung. Ein Handbuch*, edited by Uwe Flick, Ernst von Kardoff and Ines Steinke, 538–46. Reinbek: Rowohlt.

Knorr-Cetina, Karin, and Urs Bruegger. 2002. "Global Microstructures, the Virtual Societies of Financial Markets." *American Journal of Sociology* 107 (4): 905–50.

Krotz, Friedrich. 2007. *Mediatisierung: Fallstudien zum Wandel von Kommunikation.* Wiesbaden: VS.

———. 2009. "Mediatization: A Concept to Grasp Media and Societal Change." In *Mediatization: Concept, Changes, Conflicts*, edited by Knut Lundby, 21–40. New York: Lang.

Krummheuer, Antonia. 2010. *Interaktion mit virtuellen Agenten? Zur Aneignung eines ungewohnten Artefakts.* Stuttgart: Lucius and Lucius.

Krüger, Hildegard. 1979. *Der Cabildo von Asunción. Stadtverwaltung und städtische Oberschicht in der ersten Hälfte des 18. Jahrhunderts (1690–1730).* Frankfurt a.M.: Peter D. Lang.

Lachi, Marcello. 2004. "Pobreza . . . la única realidad económica paraguaya en crecimiento sostenido." *Acción. Revista paraguaya de reflexión y diálogo* 250:6–9.

Lindner, Rolf. 1981. "Die Angst des Forschers vor dem Feld. Überlegungen zur teilnehmenden Beobachtung als Interaktionsprozess." *Zeitschrift für Volkskunde* 77:51–66.

Livingstone, Sonia. 2009. "On the Mediation of Everything: ICA Presidential Address 2008." *Journal of Communication* 59 (1). http://www3.interscience.wiley.com/cgi-bin/fulltext/122283075/PDFSTART (accessed January 5, 2010).

Luna Nueva. 2005. *La Trata de Personas en el Paraguay. Diagnóstico exploratorio sobre el tráfico y/o trata de personas con fines de explotación sexual.* http://www.oimconosur.org/documentos/buscador.php?tipo=unico&documento=340&categoria=1 (accessed October 11, 2005).

Lustig, Wolf. 1995. "Mba'éichapa oiko la guarani? Ein Portrait des guarani paraguayo." *Hispanorama* 69:19–27.

Lutz, Helma. 2003. "Leben in der Twilightzone. Migration, Transnationalität und Geschlecht im Privathaushalt." In *Entstaatlichung und Soziale Sicherheit. Verhandlungen des 31. Kongresses der Deutschen Gesellschaft für Soziologie. Teil 1*, edited by Jutta Allmendinger, 254–66. Opladen: Leske und Budrich.

MacCormack, C., and Marilyn Strathern, eds. 1980. *Nature, Culture and Gender.* Cambridge: Cambridge University Press.

Macdonald, Sharon. 2007. "British Social Anthropology." In *Handbook of Ethnography*, edited by Paul Atkinson, Amanda Coffey, Sara Delmont, John Lofland and Lyn Lofland, 60–79. London: Sage.

Maffia, Marta, ed. 2002. *¿Dónde están los inmigrantes? Mapeo sociocultural de grupos de inmigrantes y sus descientes en la provincia de Buenos Aires.* La Plata: Al Margen.

Malinowski, Bronislaw. 1967. *A Diary in the Strict Sense of the Term.* London: Routledge and Kegan Paul.

Mann, Chris, and Fiona Stewart. 2000. *Internet Communication and Qualitative Research. A Handbook for Researching Online.* London: Sage.

Manning, Peter K. 1998. "Media Loops." In *Popular Culture, Crime and Justice,* edited by Frankie Y. Bailey and Donna C. Hale, 25–39. Belmont: West/Wadsworth Company.

Marcus, George E. 1995. "Ethnography in/of the World System: The Emergence of Multi-Sited Ethnography." *Annual Review of Anthropology* 24:95–117.

Markham, Annette N. 1998. *Life online: Researching Real Experience in Virtual Space.* Walnut Creek, CA: Alta Mira Press.

Mecheril, Paul. 2003. *Prekäre Verhältnisse: Über natio-ethno-kulturelle (Mehrfach-) Zugehörigkeit.* Münster: Waxmann.

———. 2004. *Einführung in die Migrationspädagogik.* Weinheim: Beltz.

Mecheril, Paul, and Britta Hoffarth. 2004. "Adoleszenz und Migration. Zur Bedeutung von Zugehörigkeitsordnungen." In *Adoleszenz—Migration—Bildung. Bildungsprozesse Jugendlicher und junger Erwachsener mit Migrationshintergrund,* edited by Vera King und Hans-Christoph Koller, 221–40. Wiesbaden: Verlag für Sozialwissenschaften.

Miller, Carolyn, and Dawn Shepherd. 2004. "Blogging as Social Action: A Genre Analysis of the Weblog." Paper presented at AoIR Conference 2004, Sussex University, September 19–22. http://blog.lib.umn.edu/blogosphere/introduction.html (accessed October 4, 2004).

Miller, Daniel, and Don Slater. 2000. *The Internet—An Ethnographic Approach.* Oxford: Berg.

Moes, Johannes. 2000. "Von der Text- zur Hypertextanalyse: Konsequenzen für die qualitative Forschung." *Forum Qualitative Sozialforschung* 1 (1). http://www.qualitative-research.net/fqs-texte/1–00/1–00moes-d.htm (accessed August 15, 2004).

Molinier, Lila. 2004. "Análisis economico. De un modelo de desarrollo insostenible a otro sostenible." In *Derechos humanos en el Paraguay 2004,* edited by CODEHUPY, 29–39. Asunción: Editora Litocolor.

Morley, D., and K. Robins. 1995. *Spaces of Identity—Global Media, Electronic Landscapes and Cultural Boundaries.* New York: Routledge.

Morokvasic, Mirjana. 1994. "Pendeln statt Auswandern. Das Beispiel der Polen." In *Wanderungsraum Europa. Menschen und Grenzen in Bewegung,* edited by Mirjana Morokvasic and Hedwig Rudolph, 166–87. Berlin: Ed. Sigma.

Münker, Stefan. 1997. "Was heißt eigentlich 'virtuelle Realität'? Ein philosophischer Kommentar zum neuesten Versuch der Verdopplung der Welt." In *Mythos Internet,* edited by Stefan Münker and Alexander Roesler, 108–30. Frankfurt a.M.: Suhrkamp.

Orthmann, Claudia. 2004. "Strukturen der Chat-Kommunikation: konversationsanalytische Untersuchung eines Kinder- und Jugendchats." PhD diss., Freie Universität Berlin. http://www.diss.fu-berlin.de/2004/78/ (accessed April 10, 2006).

Orué Pozzo, Anibal. 1999. "Comunicación y Estado en Paraguay." In *La responsabilidad social y la vision del futuro: Paraguay en el Siglo XXI,* edited by Ramón Fogel and James Diego Hay, 35–52. Asunción: CERI.

Palau Viladesau, Tomás. 2004. "La situación migratoria en el país. Para las autoridades, la migración es un problema de seguridad." In *Derechos humanos en el Paraguay 2004,* edited by CODEHUPY, 157–65. Asunción: Editora Litocolor.

Palau, Tomás, Daniel Cabello, An Maeyens, Javiera Rulli and Diego Segovia. 2007. *Los refugiados del modelo agroexportador. Impactos del monocultivo de soja en las comunidades campesinas paraguayas.* Asunción: BASE IS.

Panagakos, Anastasia N. 2003. "Downloading New Identities: Ethnicity, Technology, and Media in the Global Greek Village." *Identities: Global Studies in Culture and Power* 10:201–19.

Panagakos, Anastasia N., and Heather A. Horst, eds. 2006. "Return to Cyberia: Technology and the Social Worlds of Transnational Migrants." *Global Networks* 6 (2): 109–124.

Park, Robert E. [1922] 1970. *The Immigrant Press And Its Control.* Westport, CT: Greenwood Press.

Pertierra, Raúl. 2006. *Transforming Technologies: Altered Selves—Mobile Phone and Internet Use in the Philippines.* Manila, Philippines: De la Salle University Press.

Phizacklea, A., ed. 1983. *One Way Ticket: Migration and Female Labour.* London: Oxford University Press.

Poster, Mark. 1997. "Elektronische Identitäten und Demokratie." In *Mythos Internet*, edited by Stefan Münker and Alexander Roesler, 147–70. Frankfurt a.M.: Suhrkamp.

Potthast, Barbara. 2006. "Algo más que heroínas—roles y memorias femeninas de la Guerra de la Triple Alianza." Paper presented at the IV. International Symposium "De patrias y matrias: Género y nación en las Américas," Zentrum für interdisziplinäre Forschung (ZIF) Bielefeld, November 29–December 1.

Potthast-Juttkeit, Barbara. 1994. *"Paradies Mohammeds" oder "Land der Frauen"? Zur Rolle von Frau und Familie in Paraguay im 19. Jahrhundert.* Cologne: Böhlau.

Prasad, Pushkala. 1997. "Systems of Meaning: Ethnography as a Methodology for the Study of Information Technologies." In *Information Systems and Qualitative Research. Proceedings of the IFIP TC8 WG 8.2*, edited by Allan S. Lee, Jonathan Liebenau and Janice I. DeGross, 101–18. London: Chapman and Hall.

Pries, Ludger. 1998. "Transnationale Soziale Räume—Theoretisch-empirische Skizze am Beispiel der Arbeitswanderungen in Mexiko-USA." In *Perspektiven der Weltgesellschaft*, edited by Ulrich Beck, 55–86. Frankfurt a.M.: Suhrkamp.

———. 2006. "Zwischen methodologischem Nationalismus und Weltgesellschafts-Deduktion—Transnationalisierung und relationales Raumkonzept." Paper presented at the Institut für Weltgesellschaft, Bielefeld University, December 5.

Rammert, Werner. 2000. *Technik aus soziologischer Perspektive 2. Kultur, Innovation, Virtualität.* Wiesbaden: Westdeutscher Verlag.

Rawls, Anne, Warfield. 2002. "Editor's Introduction." In *Ethnomethodology's Program: Working out Durkheim's Aphorism*, edited by Harold Garfinkel, 1–64. Lanham, MD: Rowman and Littlefield.

Reichert, Ramón. 2008. *Amateure im Netz. Selbstmanagement und Wissenstechnik im Web 2.0.* Bielefeld: Transcript.

Rheingold, Howard. 1993. *The Virtual Community. Homesteading on the Electronic Frontier.* München: Addison-Wesley.

Riquelme, Marcial Antonio. 2004. "Los desafíos de la inmigración brasileña." *Acción. Revista paraguaya de reflexión y diálogo* 250:31–36.

Robertson, Roland. 1995. "Glocalization: Time-Space and Homogeneity-Heterogeneity." In *Global Modernities*, edited by Mike Featherstone, 25–44. London: Sage.

Robison, Kristopher K., and Edward M. Crenshaw. 2010. "Reevaluating the Global Digital Divide: Socio-Demographic and Conflict Barriers to the Internet Revolution." *Sociological Inquiry* 80 (1): 34–62.

Rodriguez, Fátima. 2011. "El estado paraguayo que excluye a los de afuera." *Revista Acción* 311: 12–15.

Sacks, Harvey. 1984. "On Doing 'Being Ordinary.'" In *Structures of Social Action. Studies in Conversation Analysis*, edited by John M. Atkinson and John Heritage, 413–29. Cambridge: Cambridge University Press.

Sacks, Harvey, Emmanuel Schegloff and Gail Jefferson. 1974. "A Simplest Systematic for the Organisation of Turn-Taking for Conversation." *Language* 50:696–735.

Salim, Celso. 2006. *Migración brasiguayos y MERCOSUR. Fuerza de trabajo rural en el centro-oeste brasilero.* Asunción: BASE Investigaciones sociales. http://www.clacso.org (accessed August 15, 2006).

Schmidt, Gurly. 2000. "Chat-Kommunikation im Internet—eine kommunikative Gattung?" In *Soziales im Netz*, edited by Caja Thimm, 112–30. Opladen: Westdeutscher Verlag.

Schmidt, Henrike, and Katy Teubener. 2007. *Abschlussbericht zum Projekt "Virtuelle (Wieder)Vereinigung? Mechanismen kultureller Identitätsbildung im russischsprachigen Internet."* Russian-cyberspace.org. http://www.ruhr-uni-bochum.de/russ-cyb/news/de/aktuell.htm (accessed May 1, 2007).

Schneider, Daniel, Sebastian Sperling, Geraldine Schell, Katharina Hemmer, Ramiro Glauer and Daniel Silberhorn. 2005. *Instant Messaging—Neue Räume im Cyberspace. Nutzertypen, Gebrauchsweisen, Motive, Regeln.* Munich: Reinhard Fischer.

Schutz, Alfred. 1964. *Studies in Social Theory. Collected Papers II.* Edited and introduced by Arvid Brodersen. The Hague: Martinus Nijhoff.

———. [1953] 1967. "The Problem of Social Reality: Common-Sense and Scientific Interpretation of Human Action." In *Collected Papers*, edited by Maurice Natanson, 3–47. The Hague: Martinus Nijhoff.

———. 1972. *Der Fremde. Gesammelte Aufsätze Band II—Studien zur soziologischen Theorie.* Den Haag: Nijhoff.

Schutz, Alfred and Thomas Luckmann. 1973. *The Structures of the Life-World, Vol. 1.* Evanston, Illinois: Northwestern University Press.

Silverman, David. 2007. *Interpreting Qualitative Data.* London: Sage.

Simmel, Georg. 1908. "Exkurs über den schriftlichen Verkehr." In *Soziologie. Untersuchungen über die Formen der Vergesellschaftung*, edited by Georg Simmel, 287–88. Leipzig: Duncker and Humblot.

Smith, Anthony D. 2004. *The Antiquity of Nations.* Cambridge: Polity Press.

Smith, Michael P., and Luis E. Guarnizo. 1998. *Transnationalism from Below.* New Brunswick, NJ: Transaction Publishers.

Smith, Robert C. 1998. "Transnational Localities: Community, Technology and the Politics of Membership within the Context of Mexico and US Migration." In *Transnationalism from Below*, edited by Michael P. Smith and Luis E. Guarnizo, 196–240. New Brunswick, NJ: Transaction Publishers.

Soeffner, Hans-Georg. 1995. *Die Ordnung der Rituale.* Frankfurt a.M.: Suhrkamp.

Spiegel, Anna. 2005. *Alltagswelten in translokalen Räumen: bolivianische Migrantinnen in Buenos Aires.* Frankfurt a.M.: IKO.

Stegbauer, Christian. 2000. "Begrenzungen und Strukturen internetbasierter Kommunikationsgruppen." In *Soziales im Netz. Sprache, Beziehungen und Kommunikationskulturen im Internet*, edited by Caja Thimm, 18–38. Opladen: Westdeutscher Verlag.

Stegbauer, Christian, and Michael Jäckel. 2008. *Social Software. Formen der Kooperation in computerbasierten Netzwerken.* Wiesbaden: VS.

Stichweh, Rudolf. 2002. "The Genesis of a Global Public Sphere." Working Paper (Institut für Weltgesellschaft). http://www.uni-bielefeld.de/(de)/soz/iw/pdf/stichweh_5.pdf (accessed June 10, 2005).

———. 2004. *Kulturelle Produktion in der Weltgesellschaft.* http://www.unilu.ch/files/30stwkultur.pdf (accessed July 5, 2011).

———. 2005. *Inklusion und Exklusion. Studien zur Gesellschaftstheorie.* Bielefeld: Transcript.

Suchman, Lucy. 1987. *Plans and Situated Actions: The Problem of Human–Machine Communication.* Cambridge: Cambridge University Press.

Thiedecke, Udo. 2000. "Virtuelle Gruppen: Begriff und Charakteristik." In *Virtuelle Gruppen*, edited by Udo Thiedecke, 23–73. Wiesbaden: Westdeutscher Verlag.

Thomas, William I., and Florian Znaniecki. [1918–20] 1958. *The Polish Peasant in Europe and America*. New York: Dover.

Tini, Natalia. 2004. "Argentina-Paraguay, una relación especial." Paper presented at I. Encuentro internacional de Investigadores de la Red Latinoamericana de Cooperación Universitaria. América Latina: Dilemas y desafíos de cara al siglo XXI, Belgrano University, Buenos Aires, March 11–12. www.rlcu.org.ar/destacados/clea/ponencias/I%20Encuentro%20RLCU-Tini.pdf (accessed September 16, 2006).

Tipp, Anika. 2008. "Doing Being Present. Instant messaging aus interaktionssoziologischer Perspektive." In *Social Software. Formen der Kooperation in computerbasierten Netzwerken*, edited by Christian Stegbauer and Michael Jäckel, 175–93. Wiesbaden: VS.

Turkle, Sherry. 1995. *Life on the Screen: Identity in the Age of the Internet*. New York: Simon and Schuster.

Uimonen, Paula. 2003. "Mediated Management of Meaning. Online-Nationbuilding in Malaysia." *Global Networks* 3 (3): 299–314.

Urry, John. 2000. "Mobile Sociology." *British Journal of Sociology* 51 (1): 185–203.

———. 2002. "Mobility and Proximity." *Sociology* 36 (2): 255–74.

Vertovec, Steven. 1999. "Conceiving and Researching Transnationalism." *Ethnic and Racial Studies* 22 (2): 447–62.

Warkentin, Jakob. 2003. "Probleme und Chancen des interethnischen Zusammenlebens im Chaco." In *Jahrbuch 2003 des Vereins für Geschichte und Kultur der Mennoniten in Paraguay*. http://www.menonitica.org (accessed December 13, 2006).

Warschauer, Mark. 2004. *Technology and Social Inclusion: Rethinking the Digital Divide*. Cambridge and London: MIT Press.

Weber, Gaby. 2008. "Das Ende der Abgeschiedenheit. Deutsche Mennoniten im paraguayischen Chaco." *Ila—Zeitschrift der Informationsstelle Lateinamerikas* 312:28–30.

Weidmann, Angelika. 1975. "Die Feldbeobachtung." In *Techniken der empirischen Sozialforschung*, vol. 3, edited by Jürgen Koolwijk and María Wieken-Mayser, 9–26. Munich: Oldenbourg.

Wellmann, Barry. 2000. "Die elektronische Gruppe als soziales Netzwerk." In *Virtuelle Gruppen*, edited by Udo Thiedecke, 134–167. Wiesbaden: Westdeutscher Verlag.

Wellman, Barry, and Caroline Haythornthwaite, eds. 2002. *The Internet in Everyday Life*. Oxford: Blackwell.

Wellman, Barry, and Bernie Hogan. 2004. "The Immanent Internet." In *Netting Citizens: Exploring Citizenship in a Digital Age*, edited by Johnston McKay, 54–80. Edinburgh: University of St. Andrews Press.

Werlen, Benno. 1996. "Geographie globalisierter Lebenswelten." *Österreichische Zeitschrift für Soziologie* 21 (2): 97–128.

Wimmer, Andreas, and Nina Glick-Schiller. 2002. "Methodological Nationalism and Beyond: Nation-State Building, Migration and the Social Sciences." *Global Networks* 2 (4): 301–34.

Wittel, Andreas. 2000. "Ethnography on the Move: From Field to Net to Internet." *Forum: Qualitative Research* 1 (1). http://qualitative-research.net/fqs/fqs-eng.htm (accessed August 15, 2004).

Whyte, William, F. [1943] 1981. *Street Corner Society. The Social Structure of an Italian Slum*. Chicago and London: University of Chicago Press.

Wobbe, Theresa. 2000. *Weltgesellschaft*. Bielefeld: Transcript.

Wolff, Stephan. 2003. "Wege ins Feld und ihre Varianten." In *Qualitative Forschung. Ein Handbuch*, edited by Uwe Flick, Ernst von Kardoff and Ines Steinke, 334–49. Reinbek: Rowohlt.

———. 2006. "Textanalyse." In *Qualitative Methoden der Medienforschung*, edited by Ruth Ayaß and Jörg R. Bergmann, 245–73. Reinbek: Rowohlt.

Zarza, Olga. 1996. *Género y Participación Económica en Paraguay*. Asunción: Universidad Nacional.

Index